Olives & Oranges

Olives & Oranges

RECIPES AND FLAVOR SECRETS FROM ITALY, SPAIN, CYPRUS, AND BEYOND

SARA JENKINS & MINDY FOX

PHOTOGRAPHS BY ALAN RICHARDSON

HOUGHTON MIFFLIN COMPANY
BOSTON • NEW YORK
2008

For information about permission to reproduce selections from
this book, write to Permissions, Houghton Mifflin Company,
215 Park Avenue South, New York, New York 10003.

www.houghtonmifflinbooks.com

Library of Congress Cataloging-in-Publication Data
Jenkins, Sara.
   Olives and oranges : recipes and flavor secrets from Italy, Spain, Cy-
prus, and beyond / Sara Jenkins and Mindy Fox ; photographs by Alan
Richardson.
     p. cm.
Includes index.
ISBN-13: 978-0-618-67764-1
ISBN-10: 0-618-67764-X
1. Cookery, Mediterranean. 2. Flavor. I. Fox, Mindy. II. Title.
TX725.M35J47 2008
641.59822—dc22

                                        2008013753

Book design by Kris Tobiassen
Food styling by Anne Disrude
Prop styling by Denise Canter

Printed in the United States of America

QWV   10 9 8 7 6 5 4 3 2 1

FOR MY HUSBAND, TOUFIQ,
AND OUR SON, NADIR LEANDER

ACKNOWLEDGMENTS

I would like to thank the two women who have taught me the most about food and cooking: my mother, Nancy Harmon Jenkins, and my adoptive Italian grandmother, Mita Antolini. My father, Loren Jenkins, with his passion for fine and rare food and his generous sharing of his knowledge, also helped train my palate and exposed me to many flavors I might not have otherwise tried.

I owe thanks to chefs Barbara Lynch and Todd English of Boston, since I wouldn't have become a restaurant chef without their help and encouragement. I would also like to thank the many cooks I have cooked with and learned from, including Renee Becker, Paola Bottero, Vincent Chirico, David Cruces, Amanda Freitag, Alberta Innocenti, Deepak Kaul, Mark Ladner, Biggie Lemke, Robert Lopez, Dania Luccherini, Benito Molina, Marc Orfaly, Zac Pelaccio, Lindsey Schechter, Zach Shapiro, Joe Simone, Seth Trafford, and Adam Weisel.

Thank you to Rolando Ruiz Beramendi, who brought me back to Italy as a young chef; Alberto Avalle and Donna Lennard, who opened my mind to so many food possibilities and helped me grow as the chef of their New York restaurant, Il Buco; and Roberto Paris of Il Buco, and Jason Bolger too. My thanks to Nancy White Anderson, who cooks for me out of her garden; Faith Heller Willinger, who got me two jobs cooking in Florence; and my brother, Nico, my cousin Matt Lindemulder, and my adopted "sister," Gaia Anderson—my most beloved guests and respected critics.

Thanks, too, to my favorite farmers who grow and raise the food that makes it so easy for me: Rick Bishop of Mountain Sweet Berry Farm, Paul Dench-Layton of Violet Hill Farm, Dave Harris of Max Creek Hatchery, Tim Stark of Eckerton Hill Farms, Franca Tantillo of Berried Treasures Farm, and Dave Size and Ken Ryan, who both introduced me to incredible varieties of tomatoes and inspired me when I was a young chef. To my neighbor Stephanie Sugawara, who is always there with a pot, a lemon, an onion, or a suggestion, and to my friend and former roommate Micah Shapiro, who was always willing to run to the store for a needed ingredient or two in exchange for a meal.

Thank you to Alan Richardson, Anne Disrude, and Denise Canter, who created the gorgeous images in these pages.

I'd also like to thank my agent, David Black, who spent a great deal of time helping me figure out what it was I wanted to say and how to say it, and my editor, Rux Martin, who was enthusiastic about this book before I even knew I would write it.

A big thank-you to my husband, Toufiq, who is fantastically supportive and the most amazing prep cook ever.

And last, but far from least, thank you to my coauthor, Mindy Fox, without whom this book would never have seen the light of day.

—Sara Jenkins

I'd like to thank my parents, Neil and Phyllis Fox, who taught me that food and cooking are among life's greatest pleasures; helped me build my palate at home and as far away as Mexico, France, and Turkey; and inspired my understanding of the farm-to-table connection with our kitchen garden and small but sweet flock of sheep. And my brother, Jason Fox, a beloved sidekick who teaches me so much about wine and food through his own many talents in the field.

Thank you to the many people who gave me important first chances and who will always inspire me: chefs and cooks Bill Pinnone, Jim Stringer, Stan Frankenthaler, James Scoon, Frank Van Overbeeke, Victor Tiernan, and Jack Stevens, who shared their kitchen know-how and food enthusiasm with me at Cambridge's Casablanca and Salamander; Dorothy Kalins and Colman Andrews, who took me under their immeasurably talented wings and gave me my first shot in publishing at *Saveur;* and Carolyn Mandarano and Margot Schupf, who entrusted me with projects that helped me build my book knowledge.

Thank you to *Food & Wine*'s Tina Ujlaki, who has always been so generous and thoughtful, personally and professionally; Nancy Harmon Jenkins, who taught me how to spell "prosciutto" and generously offered ideas, connections, and sage career advice, even when she hardly knew me; and to cohorts and dear friends always willing to read (or drink) a draft, Meeghan Truelove, Gail Simmons, Robin Insley, Jocelyn Morse-Farmerie, and Cameron Kane among them.

Deepest thanks to Sara Jenkins, who trusted me to help her communicate her recipes and food knowledge through the pages of this book and became a valued friend in the process; to our editor, Rux Martin, whose guidance is priceless and her dedication beyond words; and to David Black, my sparky yet serious and very supportive agent.

And, finally, thanks to my canine muse, Guinness, and my loving husband and best friend, Stephen Hoffman, for believing in and sharing every bite.

—*Mindy Fox*

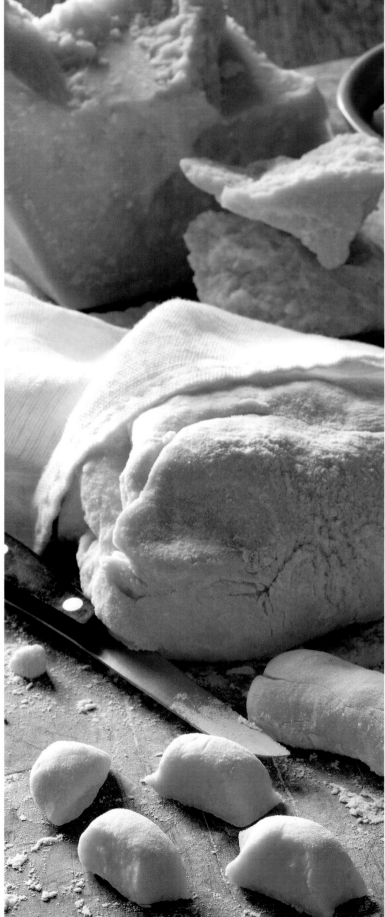

CONTENTS

Introduction | 1

My Flavor Pantry | 5

Small Plates | 21

Salad | 69

Soup | 100

Pasta, Risotto,
and Polenta | 132

Fish | 201

Chicken and Other
Backyard Livestock | 241

Beef, Veal, Pork,
Lamb, and Venison | 277

Sweets and Cordials | 324

Sources | 357

Index | 361

INTRODUCTION

I was lucky enough to be raised gypsy-style. My father was a foreign correspondent, and by the time I was ten, we had lived all over the Mediterranean, from Italy to Spain to Lebanon, with France, Cyprus, and even a spell in Hong Kong squeezed in on the side. We lived in some cosmopolitan cities—London, Paris, Madrid, and Rome—but also in rural hamlets, where people led agrarian existences, much as their ancestors had for centuries before. There we ate vegetables from our gardens and those of our neighbors, subsistence farmers with a deep connection to their land. They raised goats and sheep and grew potatoes, fava beans, plums, and more.

At an early age, my brother, Nico, and I learned the joys of a ripe sun-kissed fig eaten just off the tree and the value of spending an afternoon fighting off wasps and thorns to fill a basket of blackberries that our mother would transform into fresh-cooked jam for breakfast toast. The rabbits that ran around the yard and were raised on a diet of wild grasses and the chickens that scratched for their food in time found their way to our plates. The fish we ate was often just a few hours out of the water, freshly gutted and grilled. With just a drizzle of olive oil, a sprinkle of sea salt, and a squeeze of lemon, it was exquisite in its simplicity.

In Rome I loved to watch the chef-proprietors shopping at the morning markets. If eggplant was in season, you could be sure that night's menu would include it cooked in myriad ways. The sardines in the market would be passed over for mussels or mackerel, depending on what was freshest. Often an old woman would come into the neighborhood trattoria carrying an armload of wild greens just picked from the countryside, and these would appear later in a simple salad.

OPPOSITE: BRAISED RABBIT RAGÙ (PAGE 174)

We eventually put down roots in a tumbledown farmhouse in an impoverished Tuscan village. There our neighbors the Antolinis adopted us as family. Growing up, I stood for countless hours beside Mita Antolini, my Italian "grandmother," in her rustic kitchen while she stirred a pot of ragù, made pasta by hand, or dressed sliced fresh-picked tomatoes with verdant olive oil and sea salt.

It wasn't until we returned to the United States and I was sent off to boarding school in the woods of western Maine that I began to think consciously about food. In an attempt to render the cafeteria food there more palatable, I took cooked rice and added my own pantry staples to it: fresh lemon juice, dried chilies, a drizzle of good olive oil. Looking back, I now realize I was using logical building blocks based on a language of flavor that I had learned in the Mediterranean.

The intent of this book is to show you how flavors work independently and together, so you can follow your own instincts and appetites, make the most out of the ingredients you have, cook without a recipe if you like, or change one to suit your needs, and be a better, more confident cook. Students in my classes often say, "I always wanted to be the kind of person who could just go to the market, see what was there, bring it home, and make a great meal." You can be "that kind of person" once you understand a few basic flavor principles.

So how do you do it? What techniques allow you to get the same integrity from a simple fifteen-minute tomato sauce that you do from a five-hour meat ragù? How do you learn to see a mound of just-picked string beans and a bunch of aromatic fresh mint and decide that supper will consist of a blanched bean, mint, and yogurt salad alongside a grilled lamb chop?

As you start cooking from this book, you'll begin to recognize patterns in basic flavor combinations and technique. For example, you'll see how salt and lemon juice in Carrot Salad with Lemon, Sea Salt, Parsley, and Olive Oil can wilt freshly grated carrots and bring out their natural sugars, or how lime, salt, and the North African condiment called harissa can be used in Tunisian Raw Turnip Salad for a completely different effect. Make these two recipes a few times, and you'll find yourself at the market eagerly reaching for celery root, turnips, or even black radishes, and maybe tossing a tangy apple or two into your basket, then going home to grate them all up and mix with your best olive oil and whatever citrus or vinegar strikes your fancy.

The recipes in this book, rooted in the Mediterranean tradition, include Classic Tuscan Eggplant Parmesan and Southern Italian Pork Ragù as well as dishes with a modern sensibility, such as Salmon with Sugar Snap Peas and Bacon and Spicy Lemon–

Chocolate Ganache Tart. A dish like Pasta with Sweet Corn is one you would never find in Italy, where most home cooks and chefs stick to traditional combinations with only slight changes here and there. Yet to me it's Italian in spirit, because it is based on seasonal ingredients. In less than an hour, you wind up with an extraordinary dish. Some of my recipes are complex feast-day undertakings, but most are the stuff of simple everyday eating. I've cooked many of them in the restaurants I've worked in, and I make all of them often at home. A few are favorites from my childhood, dating back to my days spent in the humble kitchen of my Tuscan grandmother.

So that you can choose the recipes that fit best into your schedule, I've identified them by their general cooking time, as either Quick-Cook (recipes that require anywhere from 10 to 15 minutes to 50 minutes or so) or Slow-Cook. I suggest you read through any recipe that may seem long, since some of these require just an occasional stir or baste over several hours, allowing you to do other things while you cook; others require more involvement.

Throughout the book, you'll find Flavor Tips, optional steps you can take to build additional flavor into a dish, as well as advice on purchasing, storage, and techniques. You'll also find lessons here and there on how and why a particular ingredient is used and how you can make easy substitutions so that you can use the best of what's available at any time.

You'll find that I tend to rely on many of the same ingredients throughout the recipes, most of them common, a few less so. In My Flavor Pantry (page 5), I describe each one in detail. And in Sources (page 357), I list websites and shops that carry them.

Two old-fashioned cooking philosophies have guided these recipes. First, the best meals are made by combining seasonal ingredients with what you have on hand. Second, the greatest honor you can pay a fine ingredient—a fat vine-ripened tomato or a rosy free-range veal chop—is to prepare it with restraint, maybe with nothing more than a good pinch of sea salt, some extra-virgin olive oil, and some fresh-picked herbs.

Not everyone can regularly shop at the farmers' market or live on only what's in season. But once you understand the flexibility of most recipes, you can pass on the cod and take the fresher hake instead, or forgo the weary-looking asparagus for the more peppy green beans. By modifying a recipe to fit what's freshest and most available to you, you will eat well at every meal.

MY FLAVOR PANTRY

The key to a delicious simple meal is a well-stocked pantry. With basics like good pasta, a can or two of San Marzano tomatoes, an onion, a couple garlic cloves, olive oil, and sea salt, you can make fantastic pasta with Slow-Cooked Tomato Sauce (page 140). A batch or two of homemade chicken broth in the freezer will help you make risottos, soups, or stews. Boil up the Mediterranean grain farro and toss it with beets, parsley leaves, Pecorino cheese, and olive oil, and you have a lovely salad. Sprinkle the Lebanese spice za'atar onto toasts spread with thickened yogurt, drizzle with olive oil, and season with sea salt, and you have a tasty party snack.

Some might consider my pantry rather sparse. I don't overload it with exotics that I may use once or twice and then quickly forget. Instead, I keep a small battalion of staples that to me are indispensable, which you'll see used repeatedly throughout this book. Most are fairly common; some are less so. But even those that seem less familiar can be used very simply to turn an ordinary dish into one worth making again and again. The more you cook at home, the more extensive your pantry might be. If you don't cook much at home, you can simplify this list. *See Sources (page 357) for purchasing information.*

EXTRA-VIRGIN OLIVE OIL

More than just a cooking ingredient, olive oil plays a role in nearly every aspect of life in the Mediterranean. Since ancient times, it's been used as a base for cleansers and cosmetics and as fuel for lamps and burners. Olive oil still makes an appearance in important rites of passage from cradle to grave. Newborn babies are bathed in it, teething children gnaw on crusts of bread dipped in it, and it is used to perform the last rites. Whether used in salads and other cold dishes or for sautéing or roasting, it is the essential building block of my cuisine.

Like wine, the quality of olive oil depends on many factors, including *terroir*—which refers to nature's variables, such as soil and weather conditions, that affect each harvest—timing and method of harvesting, the pressing of the olives, and storage.

To be called extra-virgin, the oil must have been extracted from the first pressing of the olives, by mechanical (not chemical) means, and it must contain less than 0.8 percent free oleic fatty acid, which is a measure of rancidity. Extra-virgin oils come mostly from olives that are picked fairly early in the season, when the oil is rich, aromatic, and flavorful.

Mediterraneans generally prefer the olive oil of their own region. Tuscans claim that Tuscan oil is the best, Spaniards argue for Spanish oil, and so on. I like high-quality oils from all over the Mediterranean, though I have a preference for Tuscan and Umbrian oils because they reflect the flavors that I grew up with and that I enjoy. Among my favorite brands are Capezzana, Laudemio, L'Olio di Montevertine, Olio Verde, and Volpaia. But you don't need to keep a multitude of bottles on hand. A high-quality oil that tastes good to you will work with any cuisine. The important thing to do is to frequently taste new oils so that you can identify which you like best.

I do recommend that you have two grades on hand: a less expensive extra-virgin oil for cooking and a fine estate-bottled oil for salads and for finishing—for drizzling over fresh spring vegetables, toasted bread, cooked greens, or roasted fish.

Though it's true that heating extra-virgin olive oil alters its flavor, that flavor is not lost or ruined in the cooking process as some chefs assert. Instead, it is transmitted into whatever is being cooked—a piece of fish or meat, a handful of leeks. Food cooked in vegetable oil never tastes as good to me as food cooked in olive oil. People all over the Mediterranean have been sautéing, frying, and roasting with olive oil for over twenty-five hundred years.

WHAT TO LOOK FOR: For finishing oils, seek out estate-grown and -bottled products from small producers. Some are marked with a vintage and/or a "best by" date (the dates can be small and inconspicuous, often stamped on the bottle or neck). These oils should be used within the first year or two after pressing. "New" Tuscan and Umbrian oils that have just been pressed or are less than one year old are often green to green-gold in color and can be quite piquant in flavor. As oils age, their flavor slowly mellows. When my family is in Tuscany, we use the new oil for "raw" applications (salads and other such dishes) and for finishing dishes, and the previous year's oil for frying, sautéing, and roasting.

If you want 100 percent Italian oil for finishing dishes, seek out an estate-grown and -bottled product. Sometimes the term "made from 100 percent Italian olives" appears on the label. A "DOC" (*denominazione di origine controllata*) mark on the label of an

Italian oil indicates that the oil was pressed from olives from a specific region in Italy and given a seal of authenticity by a panel of experts. These local oils are among the finest you can buy. They have a significantly better and more complex flavor than oils blended from olives from multiple regions or countries.

The words "imported from Italy" on a bottle of olive oil do not necessarily mean that the oil is 100 percent Italian or high in quality. In fact, most exported Italian oils are made with surplus olives from Spain, Greece, Turkey, and Tunisia (you may find this information on the bottle in the fine print), countries Italy relies on to keep its mass-market olive oil industry strong. These oils are fine to cook with, but they don't have much character.

For sautéing, frying, and roasting, I use a commercially produced, higher-production extra-virgin olive oil, such as the Greek Iliada.

Light, air, and heat are harmful to olive and other oils. Store them in a cool, dark place.

VINEGARS AND OTHER ACIDS

Vinegar, citrus juices, and wine are acids. Acids play a huge role in both giving flavor to and drawing flavor from other ingredients. They also help proteins coagulate: for example, vinegar helps eggs come together while poaching; mustards and citrus juices help vinaigrettes emulsify. And acids are used in marinating because they act as tenderizers.

In addition to using vinegar and other acids in salad dressings, I like to add a small amount to soups, stews, and braises both during cooking and for finishing them. Acids used in cooking add depth without overpowering the dish, becoming invisible flavor agents, mellowing into the background as their acidic properties humbly go to work. When drizzled over a finished dish or used in uncooked dishes like salads, acids add a sparkle.

The choice of acid separates the western (Italy, Spain, and France) and Middle Eastern Mediterranean (Turkey, Lebanon, and northern Africa). Because of the Islamic prohibition against alcohol, vinegar, which is commonly made from wine, is not often found in the varied cuisines of the Muslim world. Lemon juice, and a lot of it, is used instead.

There is almost as much variety among vinegars as there is among wines. Champagne, red and white wine vinegar, sherry vinegar, and Vin Santo vinegar are just a few. Different vinegars work better for different applications. Strong cooking greens and rich meats demand a bold red wine vinegar, such as Cabernet Sauvignon. My favorite is an unfiltered vinegar called Forum, produced in El Vendrell in Catalonia, Spain (see Sources, page 357). Delicate greens, salads, and fish do best with wine vinegars, red or white, that are lighter in flavor and acidity, or with aged sherry vinegars. My favorite red wine vinegar in this category comes from Volpaia, a Chianti Classico estate famed for its olive oil and wine. Volpaia produces red and white wine vinegars, plus an herb version of the red that is infused with fennel, juniper berries, and rosemary. All are great.

I am never without Vin Santo vinegar. This very special product is made from an amber-colored wine, primarily from Tuscany and Umbria, that is at once dry and sweet. The sugar-acid balance in the vinegar gives it a rich yet delicate, mild floral flavor. Vin Santo vinegar is not easy to come by, and it is more expensive than many other vinegars, but it is well worth seeking out. Though there's really nothing quite like it, a good aged sherry vinegar—also from a sweet wine, which makes a soft and not too acidic vinegar—comes closest.

What you won't find in this book is balsamic vinegar. Balsamic vinegar is a regional ingredient that was not found outside the region of Modena until relatively recently. Unfortunately, most balsamic vinegar that we find in the United States is of very low quality, with sugar or caramel mixed in; the word "sugar" or "caramel" in the ingredients list indicates that the vinegar is not a true balsamic. True traditional balsamic, *aceto balsamico tradizionale*, whose production is tightly controlled by a consortium of producers, is aged in a series of wood casks—juniper, cherry, oak, and chestnut—for at least twelve years, and often many more. Each bottle is affixed with a numbered seal and packaged in a distinct orange and white box; prices range from about $110 to $300 for 3.5 ounces. It is a condiment designed for drizzling on strawberries or a chunk of aged Parmesan cheese. In such simple combinations, I like it very much, but the flavor of *aceto balsamico* is too complex for salads and cooking.

I keep half a dozen different vinegars in my pantry, but you don't have to. A high-quality mild red wine vinegar and the same in a white are the bare necessities. Choose the ones you like best.

WHAT TO LOOK FOR: When splurging on special vinegars, select those with a stamped lot number and/or a "best by" date (sometimes in fine print on the back label or the neck of the bottle). These are generally high quality and made in small-batch production.

LEMONS AND OTHER CITRUS FRUITS

Lemons and other citrus fruits, especially blood oranges and limes, are staples in my kitchen. Citrus juices, as well as the zest and peel, give vibrancy to food, brightening everything.

Adding a little extra citrus can often help pull up other lagging ingredients. Citrus juice is best freshly squeezed, and zest is best when zested right over the dish you are

adding it to, though it's a little harder to gauge the quantity that way. But once you get a feel for the general yields of zest and juice from each fruit (a large lemon yields 2 to 3 teaspoons zest and about 2½ tablespoons juice; a large lime will give you 1 to 2 teaspoons zest and about 1½ tablespoons juice), you can rely less on measuring spoons and more on taste. If using both juice and zest in a dish, remember to zest the fruit first. Citrus zest and juice are fairly forgiving ingredients, and it's better to learn to use them by taste (as you likely often do with salt and pepper) than by meticulously following a recipe. You can always feel free to add a little more or less citrus juice or zest than a recipe calls for, to suit your palate.

Citrus fruits will release the most juice when they are at room temperature. Pull the fruit from the refrigerator about an hour before using to get the most juice.

WHAT TO LOOK FOR: Select plump fruits, heavy for their size, with a glossy skin and deep color. Avoid those with excessively thick skins, which will have less flesh and juice than fruits with thinner skins.

SALT AND OTHER SALTY FLAVOR AGENTS

SALT

Salt draws out and highlights the flavors of both savory and sweet dishes, simultaneously marrying the ingredients.

A good-quality sea salt (salt obtained naturally from seawater) is an essential pantry item. Sea salt tastes worlds better than kosher and table salt. And medium-coarse and coarse sea salts add a wonderful crunch to food when used as a finishing touch.

From France's sel gris (gray salt) and fleur de sel to pink salts from Jordan, Hawaii, and Australia, sea salts from Wales and Bali, flaky salts like Maldon from England, and beyond, there are a multitude of premium sea salts to choose from. Try them to see how they differ in flavor and texture and which ones you like best. You may want to keep several different salts on hand.

I am partial to untreated Mediterranean sea salts, and within this category, I favor the deeply flavorful salt from Trapani, along the western coast of Sicily, where it has been extracted from the extensive salt flats at least since Phoenician times. It has a high mineral count and great texture, whether coarse or fine, and I love the way it melts into warm food. The Roland brand, available at specialty markets and in many large supermarkets, packages salt from one of the premier salt flats in Trapani.

I often add coarse sea salt to pasta water or to stews, and I use a medium-coarse or fine salt for most everything else.

WHAT TO LOOK FOR: Choose unrefined sea salt. The refined versions are lacking in minerals and can be harsh and unpleasant in flavor.

OLIVES

Olives pack a powerful punch. Chopped and sprinkled into a salad, they add a salty counterpoint to the other ingredients. Their salty, earthy flavor goes perfectly with meats. My favorites are the tiny intense arbequina olives from Spain and the slightly larger Gaetas

from Italy. Both have a piquant, slightly acid flavor that lends a great lift to dishes, raw or cooked; they have soft flesh, which makes for easy pitting. I find Cerignola olives bland, and cured Moroccan olives can be overpowering.

Because the oil used to marinate olives tends to be of low quality, detracting from rather than giving flavor, I buy olives in brine. You can rinse brined olives and bathe them in your own good oil if you like.

WHAT TO LOOK FOR: Seek out plump, shiny olives, completely submerged in their brine.

ANCHOVIES

Anchovies add a unique depth, complexity, and touch of salt to many dishes, yet most of the time, their own distinctive flavor goes unnoticed because they blend so well with other ingredients. For this reason, I think of them as an invisible flavor agent. Wonderful in dressings for crisp bitter greens or in a compound butter for drizzling over roasted vegetables, anchovies also add a fantastic flavor note to meaty stews and sauces like salsa verde.

WHAT TO LOOK FOR: The highest-quality anchovies come still on the bone, not filleted. They're packed in salt and need to be soaked, rinsed, and pulled from the bones before using. However, if this requires more care than you may want to devote, you can do very well with high-quality oil-packed anchovy fillets. Look for anchovies from Italy and Spain; I like Roland brand flat fillets and the more expensive Ortiz brand.

BOTTARGA

A wonderful regional ingredient of the Mediterranean, bottarga is the salted dried roe sac of tuna (*bottarga di tonno*) or gray mullet (*bottarga di muggine*). Salty, iodiney, and lightly fermented, it is, like anchovies and salt, a flavor agent that plays off other ingredients. Italian bottarga comes primarily from Sicily and Sardinia. I like to keep a piece on hand to jazz up pasta with garlic and oil or to grate over white beans. Bottarga also makes a delicious salad with celery heart, cherry tomatoes, and olive oil (page 79), and it pairs well with crisp, slightly bitter vegetables, such as fennel. Tuna bottarga can be sliced thin and eaten on its own, drizzled with olive oil and lemon.

WHAT TO LOOK FOR: When purchasing tuna bottarga, look for compact blocks. Mullet bottarga is smaller and is usually sold as whole roe sacs. Both should appear moist and range in color from bright pink to amber. A darker color indicates aging, and these should be avoided. Before using bottarga, peel away any wax covering and then remove the thin outer skin just from the portion you are using. Avoid powdered bottarga.

Well-sealed bottarga will keep in the refrigerator for several weeks after opening.

CAPERS

Capers add a nice salty element as well as their own briny flavor and aroma to dishes. I use salted capers rather than capers packed in vinegar. I find the brine robs the little buds of both flavor and texture, giving them a tinny, acidic taste unlike the lively, sharp, pure flavor you get from the salted type. Rinse salted capers in several changes of water before using.

WHAT TO LOOK FOR: Generally salted capers from Italy and Spain are best, but Les Moulins Mahjoub also offers especially good ones. The Mahjoubs, a farming family who lives in the Mejerda Valley of Tunisia, make many other wonderful condiments, marmalade, and olive oil, as well as my favorite harissa (see page 16).

CURED PORK PRODUCTS

In Italy and Spain, the various parts of the pig that are not eaten fresh are cured and eaten on their own or used to bring richness, flavor, and salt to a dish. The two best-known products are prosciutto di Parma and jamón serrano, the salted and air-dried hind leg of the pig, cured for 18 to 24 months and then sliced paper-thin to serve. Prosciutto is much sweeter and more delicate in flavor than serrano, which is drier, meatier-tasting, and more intense.

In Umbria, a fatty piece of prosciutto rind is often thrown into a *battuto*, the chopped vegetable mixture that is the beginning of almost every Italian sauce or ragù. Pancetta, cured unsmoked Italian bacon made from the belly meat, is either delicately spiced and rolled up into a cylinder or heavily spiced and left flat, like slab bacon, to cure. The rolled version is sliced thin and eaten on its own or used in various dishes; its flat counterpart is used in soups, sauces, and bean dishes. Guanciale, the cured fatty jowl of the pig, is also used as a flavor enhancer in many dishes.

Because of federal regulations, pancetta and guanciale from Italy cannot be imported into the United States, but high-quality artisan domestic products are available. Salumi Artisan Cured Meats in Seattle offers guanciale, pancetta, salami, and more. La Quercia in Iowa makes a variety of delicious *salumi* (salted cured meat, and sausages, primarily from the pig) from the meat of humanely raised animals. And the California chef Paul Bertolli is making tasty *salumi* under the brand Fra'Mani. All can be mail-ordered.

More readily available is great thick-cut bacon, which I purchase from a local artisan producer at my farmers' market or at the grocery store, where I can find the widely distributed California-based Niman Ranch. Good thick-cut bacon is a fine substitute for guanciale or pancetta in almost any dish.

WHAT TO LOOK FOR: For prosciutto, look for prosciutto di Parma or di San Daniele, another very good prosciutto from Friuli. Jamón serrano, the Spanish version, is tightly controlled by a consortium of producers and has individual stamps marking its authenticity. The meat of prosciutto and jamón should be moist, not dry, and have a good balance of sweet to salt. It should be bright pink to red in color, and the fat should be white, not at all yellowed. The longer the cure, the firmer and drier the meat and the more complex the flavor.

HOMEMADE CHICKEN BROTH

The superior flavor of a good homemade chicken broth compared with its store-bought counterpart can't be overemphasized. Store-bought canned stock tastes tinny and thin, no matter how you doctor it, while homemade is rich and sweet and full of flavor that echoes through any dish.

I make sure to keep a small stash of chicken broth (page 108) in my freezer at all times. Take the time on a rainy Sunday afternoon to make broth and freeze it in 2- or 4-cup containers.

GRAINS AND LEGUMES

Dried beans, lentils, and grains are an integral part of the Mediterranean diet. These are easy items to keep on hand, and with a few vegetables, a little garlic, and some olive oil, any of them can be turned into a satisfying stew, soup, or salad.

Dried beans and lentils age as they sit on the shelf, and older legumes require longer cooking times. Older beans can also affect the overall flavor of a dish, since the other ingredients will need to cook longer as well.

My favorite lentils are the tiny Castelluccio and Colfiorito; both are from Umbria. They have a delicate yet full flavor, with nutty, earthy tones. They cook up deliciously tender while holding their shape, in contrast to the common brown lentils, which become mushy. Spanish pardina lentils (also known as Spanish brown lentils) and French lentils du Puy (which are green), more commonly available than these Umbrian varieties, are excellent as well.

For risottos, you'll need one of several *superfino* rices (highest-quality rices that are especially grown for risotto-making). Carnaroli rice is considered the best variety for risotto, and it makes the creamiest risotto. Arborio rice is good too and more common; Baldo is another *superfino* suitable for risotto. My favorite brand is Principato di Lucedio, which offers both Carnaroli and Baldo varieties. Experiment and use what you like best.

Farro is a hearty, nutty-tasting whole wheat grain about the size of a wheat berry. It can be boiled until al dente, cooked risotto-style, or added to soups. You can find it in gourmet stores and some health food stores.

WHAT TO LOOK FOR: Purchase grains and legumes from a market with a good turnover. Look for packages that have a "best by" date on them.

PASTA

Dried and fresh pastas are equally delicious and good; one is not better than the other. Fresh is a celebration food, mainly because it is labor-intensive when made properly by hand. Dried pasta is everyday fare; it should be cooked just until al dente, when it still has some "bite." Artisanal brands of dried pasta have the best texture and taste. These are extruded through bronze dies, rather than the smooth ones used by large commercial companies. They are dried slowly, so the flavor of the grain has time to develop. (Pasta is discussed in more detail on page 132.)

WHAT TO LOOK FOR: My favorite artisanal brands of dried pasta include Latini, from Le Marche (try the Senatore Cappelli); Pasta Setaro, from just outside of Naples; Benedetto Cavalieri, from Puglia; and Rustichella d'Abruzzo, from Abruzzo.

Buy fresh pasta from a specialty shop that makes and sells its own, rather than packaged "fresh" pastas in supermarkets (these have preservatives that extend shelf life). Or make your own.

ESSENTIAL HERBS AND SPICES

BLACK PEPPERCORNS

Malabar and Tellicherry are among the best of the many varieties of black pepper, but more important than type is freshness. Buy only what you will use in the course of three months. I always grind pepper fresh from a mill, and I set the grinder to a coarse setting.

BAY LEAVES

In the Mediterranean, fresh bay leaves are used more often than dried ones. Fresh leaves have a delightfully strong flavor. If you can find (or grow) fresh bay leaves, by all means use them. You can freeze them in ziplock bags or dry them yourself for longer keeping simply by leaving them out on the counter for a few days. Do not confuse the leaves of the California bay tree with those of the Mediterranean bay laurel. While they are somewhat similar, California bay leaves are more resinous and not as flavorful.

ZA'ATAR

This delicious Lebanese spice mix is said to awaken the mind and strengthen the body. It is traditionally comprised of thyme, sesame seeds, sumac, and salt, but there are many regional variations. Za'atar (also spelled zaatar, zatar, and zahatar) should be predominantly green, with lots of sesame seeds. Try it on warm bread with olive oil or sprinkle it over yogurt or hummus, also drizzled with oil, and serve with bread to dip. Za'atar is a fantastic poultry and fish seasoning too, either as a dry rub or as part of a marinade.

WILD FENNEL POLLEN

Wild fennel grows all over the Mediterranean, where the plant is often used as a culinary herb. In Tuscany and Umbria, the pollen and flowers are dried to make an intensely flavorful spice that is classically paired with pork but is also excellent with rabbit, fish, and chicken. Wild fennel pollen can turn a basic dish into something truly spectacular.

DRIED WILD OREGANO

The dried wild oregano from Greece, France, and Southern Italy is completely unlike the oregano in the supermarket. With a pungent aroma and taste, it adds delicious flavor to soups, stews, and more. Crush it between your palms to release its oils and flavor before adding it to a dish.

    WHAT TO LOOK FOR: Purchase dried oregano and other spices, like all dry goods, from a reliable shop. You'll find dried wild oregano on the stem packaged in cellophane bags, not in jars. As you use it, crumble just what you need.

SUMAC

Sumac is a wild plant that grows throughout the Middle East and southern Africa. Its deep red berries are dried, and most often sold ground, to make a spice that adds a delicious astringent flavor to salads and also meats and fish.

CHILI PEPPERS AND OTHER SPICY NECESSITIES

Chili peppers add more than just heat to a dish; they are complex and extremely varied in flavor. Chilies can be dried by smoke, sun, a low oven, or a combination of methods. These factors, along with type and *terroir*, all contribute to their flavors. The chilies listed below taste worlds better to me than store-bought crushed dried red chili pepper and cayenne pepper, neither of which possesses depth or complexity of flavor.

DRIED ÁRBOL CHILIES

The chile de árbol is a good all-purpose pepper, bright red in color and easy to find in most markets.

DRIED PEQUIN CHILIES

Smaller and spicier than the árbol, the pequin is a hot and smoky chili, also known as "bird pepper."

PIMENT D'ESPELETTE

Piment d'Espelette is a chili pepper from France's Basque region, with a full, round flavor. I use it in its ground dried state; it is also sold as a jarred puree.

ALEPPO PEPPER

A slightly sweet red pepper, Aleppo is grown in Syria and Turkey; it is usually sun-dried and then ground. Aleppo is a touch sweeter and is ground much coarser than piment d'Espelette, although I often use the two interchangeably.

HARISSA

Harissa, a spicy pepper paste from North Africa, is delicious on a melted cheese sandwich, mixed with

lemon and garlic to season a chicken, stirred into a pasta sauce in place of crushed red chili pepper, added to grated turnips or white beans, or rubbed onto beef or lamb before grilling.

The harissa you'll find most often is a rather generic version sold in a can, but the one I like best is a sun-dried-pepper product made by Les Moulins Mahjoub. Sold in a jar, it is significantly more complex in flavor than the canned versions.

WHAT TO LOOK FOR: As with other spices, buy chilies and chili products from good markets and use within 6 months. Keeping dried chilies in the freezer and chili powders, like piment d'Espelette, in the refrigerator preserves their flavor for a longer time. (Once it has been opened, harissa should be refrigerated.)

MY THREE BASIC CHEESES

PARMIGIANO-REGGIANO

Production of this world-famous handmade Italian cow's-milk cheese, with its granular texture and rich, fruity, buttery taste, is strictly controlled. The name is a *denominazione di origine protteta*, meaning it must come from a particular region and be made in accordance with agreed-upon standards. The production area includes the provinces of Parma, Emilia, and Modena, as well as part of Bologna and part of Lombardy. Cheeses from outside of these zones, even when made in a similar manner, cannot be called Parmigiano-Reggiano. Many of the cheeses called Parmesan, such as those in the supermarket, are made outside of Italy and are of low quality. Parmigiano-Reggiano is also a wonderful eating cheese, perfect served at the start of a meal to pique the palate, chunked into salads, or enjoyed in a cheese course before or instead of dessert.

GRANA PADANA

Grana Padana is similar to Parmigiano-Reggiano, in both taste and production with its own consortium, but it does not have the true highs of flavor of a great aged Parmigiano-Reggiano. However, it is a perfectly decent grating cheese for pasta or soup, and it is less expensive than Parmigiano-Reggiano.

WHAT TO LOOK FOR: Both Parmigiano-Reggiano and Grana Padana are made according to the strict regulations of their respective consortiums. Both are made in large cylindrical forms, and chunks are sold with their caramel-colored rind attached. The rind will have the name stamped into it. The date of manufacture and the farm or producer number will also be visible on a whole wheel of Parmigiano-Reggiano, stamped on the side in one place. If you are purchasing a chunk of Parmigiano-Reggiano or another cheese that is packaged, make sure it looks fresh.

PECORINO

Pecorino is a family of Italian cheeses made from sheep's milk. The most commonly known are Pecorino Romano and Pecorino Toscano, both DOP cheeses, but made in a wider variety of styles.

Pecorino Romano Genuino

Best for cooking, Pecorino Romano is a crucial ingredient in many Roman dishes, such as pasta carbonara. It is not as good as an eating cheese, because it is so sharp. *Genuino* refers to the Pecorino Romano made under strict DOP guidelines in Lazio, Sardinia, and the Grosseto region of Tuscany.

   WHAT TO LOOK FOR: Genuine Pecorino Romano, which is made in 65-pound wheels, will have the words "Pecorino Romano" stamped into the rind. The texture is firm and slightly crumbly and the flavor sharp and salty.

Pecorino Toscano

Pecorino Toscano, also a DOP cheese, has a rounder, sweeter flavor than Pecorino Romano. Made in Tuscany in smaller (1½- to 6-pound) wheels, it is a true farmhouse cheese  (most people who have a few sheep make it at home). Pecorino Toscano is enjoyed as both an eating and a cooking cheese at various stages of aging. Very young (about one month old) cheeses have a creamy, almost buttery flavor; one-year-old cheeses are firm and pungent, best sliced and eaten with a little honey and pears. Some boutique versions are wrapped in chestnut, fig, or grape leaves or rubbed with tomato paste before aging. Buy younger, softer cheese for shaving over warm vegetables or for eating, and older Pecorino for grating or eating in a cheese course.

   WHAT TO LOOK FOR: The DOP or consortium sticker on the label ensures that it is a sheep's-milk cheese made in Tuscany.

   When buying any cheese, avoid the pre-grated kind; grate it yourself as needed. After each use, rewrap the cheese tightly. Never freeze cheese. Purchase it in small amounts that you will use within a couple of weeks.

TOMATO PRODUCTS

SAN MARZANO CANNED TOMATOES

San Marzano tomatoes are grown in the volcanic soil around Mount Vesuvius. The hot sun and the soil contribute to their low acidity and extremely sweet flavor. Cultivated for cooking, not eating raw, San Marzano tomatoes have a great deal of pulpy flesh, perfect for sauce-making. They are grown under DOP control, picked at the peak of their ripeness, canned, and shipped all over the world. Fairly widely available, they are the best canned tomatoes you can buy.

WHAT TO LOOK FOR: Make sure "San Marzano" tomatoes actually come from Italy, not elsewhere.

TOMATO PASTE

"Double-concentrate" tomato paste is exactly that: double the concentration; it's both more intense and sweeter than regular tomato paste.

WHAT TO LOOK FOR: Buy tomato paste in tubes rather than cans, for longer storing. Mutti brand is one I use frequently, but as long as the paste is made in Italy and says *doppio concentrato* on the label, any brand will do.

NUTS

I keep a variety of nuts in my larder, including walnuts, pine nuts, and hazelnuts. Nuts are delicate because of their high fat content and must be properly stored. Keep nuts away from heat and light. The best place is in sealed freezer bags in the freezer (the nuts don't need to be defrosted before toasting or cooking).

WHAT TO LOOK FOR: Purchase nuts from a reliable grocer with a good turnover.

If just-purchased nuts smell or taste musty or rancid, take them back and complain: a rancid nut will ruin an entire dish.

WINE

The rule of thumb in choosing wine for cooking is, as with selecting wine for drinking, to buy what you like. You should never use a wine for cooking that you wouldn't enjoy drinking, which is not to say that it needs to be expensive. You can always cook with a good drinking wine that has been opened and then recorked for a few days.

For drinking, I love the red wines of central Italy, Tuscany and Umbria, made by traditional methods: Brunello, Rosso di Montalcino, Vino Nobile di Montelpulciano, and good Chianti Classico, as well as some Rosso di Montefalco and Sagrantino di Montefalco wines.

When it comes to white, I am partial to both Italian and French wine, especially Verdicchio, Gavi, Chablis, Puligny-Montrachet, and Champagne.

SWEET INGREDIENTS

SUGAR
I use organic pure cane sugar, which is fine-grained and light brown, with a subtle molasses taste. It's easy to find in supermarkets.

CHESTNUT HONEY
Used throughout Italy in all sorts of dishes, chestnut honey is dark amber with a robust, earthy flavor. It is not cloyingly sweet, as many honeys can be; in fact, it is a touch bitter in a wonderful way, which makes it ideal for both savory dishes and desserts. I especially like it drizzled over buttered semolina toast or aged Parmigiano-Reggiano.

CHOCOLATE
Chocolate varies hugely in quality, and, of course, the better chocolate you buy, the better the dessert. I use bittersweet chocolate, and some of my favorites are Scharffen Berger, Valrhona, and El Rey.

Store chocolate, tightly wrapped, in a dry, temperature-stable environment (60° to 70°F). Use dark chocolate within a year or so, milk chocolate within 6 months.

POMEGRANATE MOLASSES
A staple pantry item in the eastern Mediterranean, pomegranate molasses is the reduced juices of pomegranates. It adds a concentrated sweet-tart fruit flavor to salads and is great for marinades and in braises. A brand I love for its pureness and complexity of flavor is Mymouné. Another good—and more widely available—brand is Al Wadi Al Akhdar, which can be found in most Middle Eastern grocery stores.

SMALL PLATES

All over the Mediterranean, exquisite meals begin with or are made entirely of a variety of small plates. These tasty morsels—be they *mezze* in Lebanon, Turkey, Bulgaria, and beyond, *tapas* in Spain, or *antipasti* in Italy—are served in a multitude of contexts. In some cases, they exist just to tickle the taste buds, help the anise-flavored arak go down, or encourage friends and neighbors to continue a spirited conversation long into the night. In others they bookend a rich main course or become a modest lunch or dinner. In the hands of a good cook, they always excel at showing off seasonal ingredients, simply prepared.

Small plates are put together, in part, to make easy work of feeding diners in cafés, bars, and restaurants, or friends and family at home. I grew up eating this way, first at the Tree of Idleness Café in Bellapais, Cyprus, where, in the late afternoon, the grown-ups would retreat to calm their nerves with glasses of ouzo and (nasty) retsina. We children, semi-wild from country living, scrambled about the square playing, while a profusion of small dishes came out to accompany the liquor: marinated olives, stuffed grape leaves, fried cheese, pickled green walnuts. We'd stop long enough for a taste before returning to rabble-rousing.

When my family first arrived in Italy, we found that our neighbors the Antolinis often ate the same way. On the hot summer days of the harvest, as the men sweated and worked in the heat to thresh the wheat, plate after plate of Chicken Liver Crostini, pickled vegetables, slices of salty home-cured ham, and wedges of sweet melon from the garden would come out in waves from the cool, dark kitchens where the women worked. And even when I was a broke college student in Rome in the eighties, my friends and I feasted on *antipasto misto* at the local trattorias, where huge tables at the entrance of each restaurant beckoned prospective diners with big bowls of marinated vegetables, steamed clams, thick slices of fresh mozzarella, and steamed spinach drizzled with good olive oil. We would load up our plates, order some wine, and enjoy plenty of the bread, leaving hours later happy and full.

To this day, my family still gathers around the picnic table at our house in the Tuscan hamlet of Teverina for meals made up of small plates. Shaded by the hundred-year-old chestnut tree whose branches hang down like a canopy, with a cool breeze blowing and cicadas chirping, we share with friends the traditions we have learned from a variety of Mediterranean cultures, sometimes putting our own twists on them, depending on our whim. These dishes—even just one or two and a glass of wine—remain my favorite way to eat.

The recipes in this chapter are versatile. Many of them work well on their own, as palate teasers, appetizers, or salads. Any of them can be grouped together as mixed *mezze*—all uncooked, all warm, or a little of both. Two or three together, with a hunk of bread, some sliced *salumi*, and a bottle of wine, supply you with a fine lunch or dinner; five or six can make a meal on their own. Most can be enjoyed as sides to a simple piece of grilled fish or roasted meat.

You could open a meal with a plate of Roasted Cauliflower with Tahini Sauce or Fried Eggplant Balls. Or serve Asparagus with Olive Oil and Queso Iberico, either in place of a green salad or as part of a *mezze* alongside plates of Lamb and Bulgur Tartare, Roasted Red Peppers with Garlic and Celery Leaves, and Fresh Summer Beans Simmered in Tomato Sauce. The slight bite and heat of crisp Tunisian Raw Turnip Salad is great with cocktails. Or pile it atop thick slices of medium-rare rib eye or a whole roasted mackerel.

SMALL PLATES

Carrot Salad with Lemon,
Sea Salt, Parsley, and Olive Oil | 25

Tunisian Raw Turnip Salad | 27

Red and Yellow Tomatoes with Feta
and Fresh Coriander Seeds | 28

Scallop Carpaccio with Lime Juice,
Sea Salt, and Chives | 29

Kibbeh Naye
(Lamb and Bulgur Tartare) | 30

Pan-Roasted Asparagus
with Bacon | 34

Asparagus with Olive Oil
and Queso Iberico | 36

Wilted Cooking Greens | 37

Baked Spinach and Eggs | 39

Teverina Tiny-Potato Salad | 40

Slow-Cooked Cannellini Beans | 42

continued

Fresh Summer Beans
Simmered in Tomato Sauce | 43

Ricotta-Stuffed Squash Blossoms
in Fresh Summer Tomato Sauce | 44

Tabouli with Many Grains | 46

Red Onions Cooked in
Orange Juice | 48

Mechuia (Tunisian
Grilled Caponata) | 50

Roasted Red Peppers with
Garlic and Celery Leaves | 52

Roasted Cauliflower
with Tahini Sauce | 55

Sweet Corn Sformato | 56

Roasted Corn and Brioche Pudding | 58

Fried Eggplant Balls | 60

Pan-Roasted Brussels Sprouts,
Turnips, and Beets with Warm Farro | 61

Maine Shrimp Panfried
in Olive Oil | 63

Grilled Sardines with
Accompaniments | 64

    Pickled Pearl Onions | 65

    Shaved Fennel Salad | 65

    Moroccan Salad | 66

Chicken Liver Crostini | 67

CARROT SALAD WITH LEMON, SEA SALT, PARSLEY, AND OLIVE OIL

QUICK-COOK RECIPE / MAKES 4 SERVINGS

This easy dish illustrates a very basic flavor combination—sweet, sour, and salty—that is the foundation for all of my root vegetable salads. The salt draws the natural juices from the shredded raw carrots and begins a wilting process. The acid from the lemon juice both softens and flavors the carrots. And in the end, the blending of the salty-sweet carrot juices and tart lemon juice, along with good olive oil, makes a simple yet outstanding dressing.

This particular salad is one that I've loved since I was a little girl in France, when my mother would buy it at our local charcuterie to take on picnics in the park. Enjoy it as is, or toss with arugula and tart apple slices and shave a hard cheese over the top for a more substantial dish.

4 large carrots, grated or julienned

¼ cup plus 1½ teaspoons fresh lemon juice, or more to taste

1½ teaspoons fine sea salt, or to taste

¼ cup extra-virgin olive oil

¼ cup chopped fresh flat-leaf parsley

Combine carrots, lemon juice, and salt in a medium bowl. Allow to sit at room temperature for 5 minutes. Stir in oil and parsley. Adjust seasoning if necessary. Serve, or let sit, covered, at room temperature for up to 6 hours, until ready to serve.

SHREDDED ROOT SALADS

Whether served as a light appetizer, part of a *mezze,* or a stand-alone salad, or used as a topping for char-grilled fish or meat, grated root vegetable salads are a mainstay for me. By using different vegetables, acids, and flavorings, you can make a multitude of salads. Grated raw turnip tossed with lime and harissa, for example, is distinctly Tunisian in flavor: snappy, tangy, salty, and fiery. Grated carrot with lemon and olive oil is a softer, sweeter version.

The tool you choose for grating—a box grater, with its large holes, or the narrower blades of a Japanese mandoline—will result in textural variation in your final dish. Use whichever one you prefer.

Try these salads first as is, then add one or more other root vegetables, such as celery root, parsley root, and radishes. You can also add crumbled cheese, nuts, and/or fruit, such as sliced crisp apple or pear, or even blood orange or grapefruit segments. Let what looks good at the market be your inspiration.

TUNISIAN RAW TURNIP SALAD

QUICK-COOK RECIPE / MAKES 4 SERVINGS

This classic Tunisian dish is usually served at the beginning of a meal. Turnip and harissa, a spicy pepper paste, make the salad complex, with a flavor that is at once hot, salty, sharp, and clean. Try it as part of a *mezze,* or spoon it over rich hearty proteins, like grilled steak, pork chops, mackerel, or wild salmon.

- 1 pound turnips, peeled and grated or julienned
- 2 teaspoons fine sea salt
- 3 tablespoons fresh lime juice
- 1 tablespoon harissa (see page 16)

Combine turnips and salt in a medium bowl and let sit for 5 minutes. Add lime juice and harissa; toss to combine. Serve, or let sit, covered, at room temperature for up to 6 hours, until ready to serve.

RED AND YELLOW TOMATOES
WITH FETA AND FRESH CORIANDER SEEDS

QUICK-COOK RECIPE / MAKES 4 TO 6 SERVINGS

When tomatoes are at the height of their season, I eat them, salted, with all sorts of cheese and herb combinations. Just as salting shredded root vegetables draws out their juices, so, too, it draws out the juices of fleshier vegetables like tomatoes.

Everybody knows the combination of tomatoes and basil—truly one from the gods—but any pungent herb combined with ripe tomatoes makes an equally profound statement. I happen to love the texture and flavor of fresh coriander seeds, which come from flowering cilantro. If you can't find fresh coriander seeds (from your own garden or at the farmers' market), use fresh cilantro leaves instead. Add a little finely sliced hot chili or thinly sliced scallions for more complexity, if you like. This dish is best served soon after it is prepared.

FLAVOR TIP: In the eastern Mediterranean, feta is traditionally made with sheep's milk, which produces a more complex and flavorful cheese than that made with cow's milk.

    4 large mixed red and yellow ripe tomatoes (about 2 pounds)
 1½ teaspoons fresh coriander seeds, crushed with the side of a knife,
       or ¼ cup fresh cilantro leaves, coarsely chopped
    1 teaspoon medium-coarse sea salt or fleur de sel, or more to taste
 1½ cups packed crumbled sheep's-milk feta cheese (about 5 ounces)
  ¼ cup extra-virgin olive oil
    1 tablespoon sherry vinegar, or more to taste
       Coarsely ground black pepper

Slice tomatoes into 8 wedges each and arrange on a serving platter. Sprinkle with fresh coriander seeds and salt; let sit for 5 minutes.

Sprinkle with feta and drizzle with oil and vinegar. Season with more salt and a bit more vinegar, if necessary, and a generous twist of the pepper grinder. Serve immediately.

SCALLOP CARPACCIO WITH LIME JUICE, SEA SALT, AND CHIVES

QUICK-COOK RECIPE / MAKES 4 SERVINGS

Carpaccio refers to thinly sliced raw ingredients—originally beef but now tuna, or even mushrooms or zucchini—dressed simply and served as an appetizer. In this version, salt and lime juice lightly and quickly "cook" thinly sliced scallops, while at the same time drawing out a touch of liquid to create a natural scallop *jus*.

Use the finest olive oil and sea salt you can get your hands on, and the freshest sea scallops. If possible, ask your fishmonger to let you taste them before buying—you'll know right away if they are worthy of eating raw. One of my favorite variations is to sprinkle cucumber-flavored borage blossoms over the scallops in place of the chives; you can also try chive blossoms.

FLAVOR TIP: When buying scallops, look for local (if possible) sea scallops, labeled "dry-packed" or "dry" (sometimes "diver" or "day-boat"), differentiating them from the preservative-treated "wet" scallops. When scallops are really fresh, they taste exquisitely rich and sweet.

> 1 pound dry-packed sea scallops
> 1/4 cup fresh lime juice
> Fleur de sel or other medium-coarse sea salt
> 2 teaspoons chopped fresh chives
> Aleppo pepper (see page 16) or other crushed dried red chili pepper
> Extra-virgin olive oil for drizzling

Remove tough foot from each scallop and cut scallops crosswise into 1/8-inch-thick slices. Toss with lime juice and salt to taste and let sit in a bowl for 1 minute.

Arrange scallop slices in a slightly overlapping fashion on four plates. Sprinkle each lightly with chives and chili, drizzle with oil, and spoon some lime juice from bowl lightly over the top. Sprinkle with more salt, and serve at once.

KIBBEH NAYE
(LAMB AND BULGUR TARTARE)

QUICK-COOK RECIPE / MAKES 8 SERVINGS

Kibbeh naye is classically served as part of a Lebanese cold *mezze*. The wonderful combination of raw lamb infused with bright citrus and sharp onion, crunchy romaine lettuce, and warm fresh pita is as much about texture as it is about flavor. The salt draws juices from the onion to mingle with the bulgur before it is mixed with the raw meat. The lemon juice softens the bulgur, and this initial seasoning step brings a depth to the finished dish that cannot be achieved by combining all the ingredients at once.

FLAVOR TIP: For extra freshness, grind the meat yourself if you can, or buy it from a reliable butcher who will grind it to order.

½	cup fine bulgur
1	small onion, minced
	Scant ½ cup fresh lemon juice
¼	cup cold water
1½	teaspoons fine sea salt
1	pound lean ground lamb, preferably from the leg
1	teaspoon Aleppo pepper (see page 16) or other crushed dried red chili pepper
¼	teaspoon ground allspice
2	tablespoons extra-virgin olive oil, plus more for drizzling
½	cup chopped fresh flat-leaf parsley
½	cup chopped fresh mint
	Medium-coarse sea salt
4	pita breads
2	romaine lettuce hearts, leaves separated and torn into 2-inch pieces

In a large bowl, mix together bulgur, onion, lemon juice, water, and ½ teaspoon salt. Let sit until bulgur has softened, about 45 minutes.

Add lamb to bulgur mixture and knead together until well combined. Add chili, remaining 1 teaspoon salt, and allspice. Knead again just to combine. Add oil and stir to combine.

Spread tartare on a platter, forming a 1-inch-thick patty. Sprinkle with herbs and sea salt, and drizzle with oil.

Warm pitas in a toaster oven or low oven, and cut into triangles. Serve *kibbeh* with warm pitas and romaine leaves on the side.

PAN-ROASTED ASPARAGUS WITH BACON

QUICK-COOK RECIPE / MAKES 4 SERVINGS

Pan-roasting asparagus caramelizes its natural sugars, deepening its flavor. You get nice crispy browned edges and a tender interior. And cooking the asparagus in bacon fat creates a deliciously rich dish. I use thick-cut country bacon. Look for good bacon, from pigs that were raised humanely and naturally, at the grocery store or your local farmers' market. (The photograph is on the previous page.)

FLAVOR TIPS: A set of cast-iron skillets is a worthwhile and inexpensive investment. Because these pans conduct and retain heat so well, the asparagus becomes evenly caramelized, which really makes the dish.

Snapping off the woody ends of asparagus is preferable to trimming them with a knife, since it allows each stalk to break where the tender part begins. Hold the stalk in your hands and gently bend the bottom until it snaps at its natural point.

NOTE: For the perfect hard-boiled egg (one with a bright yellow yolk with no greenish tinge), place the egg in a saucepan with cold water to cover by 1 inch. Bring the water to a full boil, then reduce to a medium boil and cook for 10 minutes. Immediately drain the egg and plunge into an ice water bath; leave it in for 5 to 10 minutes to cool completely. Very fresh eggs (straight from the hen) are much harder to peel than older ones, so this is a case where freshest isn't necessarily best.

4 slices thick-cut bacon

1 pound asparagus, tough ends snapped off

1 tablespoon unsalted butter

1 egg, hard-boiled (see Note), peeled, and pushed through a sieve

1 tablespoon fresh lemon juice

Cook bacon in a large cast-iron skillet over medium heat until fat is rendered and bacon is just crisp. Transfer bacon to a plate, leaving fat in pan.

Increase heat to high, place asparagus in skillet, and cook, turning asparagus occasionally, until golden and tender, 2 to 3 minutes for skinny pieces, up to 7 minutes for thicker ones; if you have spears of varying thickness, remove the thinner ones as they are done. Transfer asparagus to a serving plate.

Remove pan from heat, add butter, and swirl until melted. Sprinkle egg over asparagus, then pour pan juices over the top. Drizzle with lemon juice, top with bacon slices, and serve.

ASPARAGUS WITH OLIVE OIL AND QUESO IBERICO

QUICK-COOK RECIPE / MAKES 4 SERVINGS

Young, fresh, soft sheep's-milk cheeses—such as Queso Iberico, Manchego, and Pecorino Toscano—marry beautifully with the grassy spring flavor of asparagus. Young cheeses are preferable here to aged, which are firmer and more intense in flavor.

FLAVOR TIP: Since this dish is so simple, the quality of the ingredients is all-important. Buy fresh local asparagus and cook it as soon as possible for best flavor.

  1 pound asparagus, tough ends snapped off
    Fleur de sel or other medium-coarse sea salt
    About 4 ounces Queso Iberico or other young sheep's-milk cheese
    (see headnote)
  1 lemon
    Coarsely ground black pepper
  1½ tablespoons extra-virgin olive oil

Bring a large skillet of salted water to a boil. Add asparagus, cover, and cook until tender, 3 to 4 minutes (if you have spears of varying thickness, pull the skinny ones out earlier than the others). Drain, transfer to a large serving plate (or four smaller plates), and sprinkle with fleur de sel.

Using a cheese slicer or Y-shaped vegetable peeler, immediately shave enough cheese over hot asparagus to mostly cover it. Grate about ¼ teaspoon lemon zest over, season with pepper, and drizzle with oil. Serve at once.

WILTED COOKING GREENS

QUICK-COOK RECIPE / MAKES 4 TO 6 SERVINGS

Sautéed spinach is one of the simplest and most comforting dishes one can make. To create a more interesting version, I use the same technique with a mix of greens with different flavors and textures. Depending on the season, you can choose mustard or dandelion greens, Swiss chard, chicory, beet or turnip greens, mizuna, amaranth, escarole, and/or broccoli raab, as well as, of course, spinach. Sometimes I brown a little slivered red onion with the garlic or use slivered fresh chili pepper instead of dried. Toasted sesame seeds sprinkled over the top are nice, and when I'm in an Asian mood, I drizzle the greens with soy sauce and lime juice instead of olive oil and lemon.

Wilted greens make a great accompaniment to Slow-Roasted Pork Shoulder (page 318) or just about any main dish. They can also be pureed for a crostini topping or the basis for a quick soup or used to sauce short pasta such as penne or maccheroni (with toasted bread crumbs or a spoonful of creamy ricotta blended in).

FLAVOR TIP: Use a finer extra-virgin olive oil for drizzling and a less fancy oil for cooking.

- 3 pounds mixed cooking greens (see headnote)
- 1/4 cup extra-virgin olive oil, plus more for drizzling
- 2 garlic cloves, smashed and peeled
- 1 small dried red chili pepper
- Medium-coarse sea salt
- 1 lemon, halved

Strip leaves of greens from ribs and stems; discard ribs and stems. Cut leaves into 3-inch ribbons, wash, and partially spin-dry; leave a little moisture for cooking.

Gently heat oil and garlic in a Dutch oven or other heavy pot over medium-low heat, stirring occasionally, until garlic is golden, 5 to 7 minutes. Add chili and cook until lightly toasted, about 1 minute.

Add greens (in batches if necessary) and a good pinch of salt. Increase heat to medium, stir, and cover. Cook for 3 minutes, stir, and continue to cook, uncovered, turning with tongs, until greens are wilted and tender but still vibrant in color. Cooking time will vary, depending on what types of greens you are using.

Transfer cooked greens to a serving dish. Sprinkle with a little salt, drizzle with some really good olive oil, and give them a squeeze of lemon juice. Serve warm.

BAKED SPINACH AND EGGS

QUICK-COOK RECIPE / MAKES 4 TO 6 SERVINGS

This elaboration on wilted greens bakes eggs in sautéed spinach. With a glass of wine, a few slices of bread, and perhaps some good cheese, it's an easy one-dish farmhouse meal. You can make it with a mix of cooking greens, though I tend to return to spinach again and again. When it's cooked for a long time, its silky-soft texture is terrific with eggs.

- 3 pounds spinach, thick stems trimmed
- ¼ cup extra-virgin olive oil, plus more for drizzling
- 1 medium onion, coarsely chopped
- 2 garlic cloves, smashed and peeled
- Coarse sea salt
- 6 large eggs
- Coarsely ground black pepper
- 2 tablespoons freshly grated Parmigiano-Reggiano cheese

Heat oven to 325°F.

Wash spinach and drain in a colander (you want droplets of water on the leaves).

Heat oil in a large deep skillet with a lid or a Dutch oven over medium heat. Add onion, garlic, and a few pinches of salt; cook for 1 minute. Add as much spinach as fits in pan, cover, increase heat to medium-high, and cook until spinach is wilted enough so you can add more, about 3 minutes. Add remaining spinach in batches, stirring as you go, until all spinach is well wilted. Remove cover, raise heat to high, and cook until spinach is very tender, about 10 minutes.

Using tongs or a slotted spoon, transfer spinach to a 9-by-13-inch baking dish, leaving most of the liquid behind. Make 6 large equally spaced indentations in the spinach. Carefully crack an egg into each indentation, keeping yolk intact (you can crack each egg into a small bowl first to make sure yolk does not break, if you'd like).

Lightly sprinkle eggs with salt and pepper, and bake until they are set to your liking (I cook them for 25 to 30 minutes). Lightly drizzle with oil, sprinkle with cheese, and serve hot.

TEVERINA TINY-POTATO SALAD

QUICK-COOK RECIPE / MAKES 4 TO 6 SERVINGS

Fresh-dug potatoes have a very pleasing, slightly acidic flavor that marries well with the assertive herbs and other flavorings in this not-so-common potato salad. I remember the excitement of digging through my mother's garden in the Tuscan town of Teverina as a kid, pulling the potatoes out of the ground on hot summer days. Early in the season, the potatoes were so small that we most often tossed the boiled potatoes in vinaigrette to make this salad.

If you can't find tiny potatoes, cook larger ones, then cut into bite-sized pieces before tossing them with the vinaigrette.

FLAVOR TIP: Though you'll usually find potatoes in the market that are labeled "new," they may not be fresh-dug, which is what is best for this dish. As potatoes age, their skins thicken and their starch converts into sugar; older "new" potatoes have lost some moisture and are sweeter in flavor.

2 pounds tiny new potatoes ($1/2$ inch in diameter or smaller), preferably fresh-dug

4 tablespoons extra-virgin olive oil

2 tablespoons finely chopped onion

1 garlic clove, minced

$1^1/_2$ teaspoons Dijon mustard

$1/2$ teaspoon red wine vinegar

$1/3$ cup mixed chopped fresh herbs, such as flat-leaf parsley, tarragon, oregano, basil, mint, chervil, summer savory, and/or chives

Fine sea salt and coarsely ground black pepper

Place potatoes in a medium saucepan, cover with water, and bring to a boil. Cook until potatoes are tender but not falling apart, about 8 minutes.

While potatoes are cooking, heat 3 tablespoons oil in a small saucepan over medium heat. Add onion and garlic and cook, stirring occasionally, until onion is translucent, about 5 minutes. Remove from heat and whisk in mustard and vinegar, then whisk in remaining tablespoon oil to combine. Add herbs and stir to combine. Season to taste with salt and pepper.

Drain cooked potatoes and place in a large bowl. Add warm dressing and toss to combine. Season as needed with salt and pepper, and serve warm or at room temperature.

SLOW-COOKED CANNELLINI BEANS

SLOW-COOK RECIPE / MAKES 6 SERVINGS

The Tuscans are famed bean eaters, and so I defer to their knowledge when it comes to bean cookery. Soaking beans with aromatics (a head of garlic and herbs) and then cooking them in their soaking liquid results in an intensified flavor you can't achieve from a simple water soak-and-drain. Cooking time will depend on their age, so don't be surprised if they take a longer time; add more liquid if necessary.

When they're done, serve them traditionally as a side to pork. Or transform them into a soup by cooking them with aromatic vegetables, such as carrot, leek, and celery, and then pureeing them or by adding them to pureed Wilted Cooking Greens (page 37) and thinning the dish with some chicken stock.

2½ cups dried cannellini beans
1 head garlic
1 fresh sage, rosemary, or thyme sprig
1 teaspoon fine sea salt
Extra-virgin olive oil for drizzling
Medium-coarse sea salt and coarsely ground black pepper

Rinse beans, then place with garlic and herb sprig in a large saucepan and cover with water by 3 inches. Soak for 8 hours, or overnight.

Place saucepan over medium-low heat and bring liquid to a simmer; this will take about an hour. Cook at a bare simmer until beans are tender, about 45 minutes more. Stir in salt.

Serve with a drizzle of oil and a sprinkle of coarse salt and pepper.

FRESH SUMMER BEANS SIMMERED IN TOMATO SAUCE

SLOW-COOK RECIPE / MAKES 4 SERVINGS

Italians tend to prefer their vegetables very well done. The French like theirs barely cooked at all. I like them both ways. Here a slow simmering in tomato sauce brings out the sweetness of fresh beans while making them very tender. Serve this dish by itself or as a summer side.

FLAVOR TIP: Choose the herb you use based on the flavor profile you are looking for. Basil pushes the dish in an Italian direction, cilantro toward the Middle East. You can add some fresh or dried chili with the tomatoes, or stir in a little cilantro and harissa toward the end for a North African–style dish.

- 2 tablespoons extra-virgin olive oil
- 1 small onion, finely chopped
- 1 garlic clove, minced
- Medium-coarse sea salt
- 1 14-ounce can (or half a 28-ounce can) whole peeled San Marzano tomatoes, with their juices, run through a food mill
- 1 cup water
- 1 pound yard-long beans, romano beans, or green beans, trimmed
- 1 cup chopped fresh flat-leaf parsley, basil, or cilantro (see Tip)

Heat oil in a large skillet over medium heat. Add onion, garlic, and a pinch of salt. Cook until onion is translucent, about 5 minutes. Add tomatoes and water, bring to a brisk simmer, and cook for 10 minutes.

Add beans, reduce heat to low, cover, and cook for 10 minutes more. Uncover and stew gently until beans are tender and beginning to break apart, 25 to 30 minutes.

Stir in herbs and salt to taste. Serve warm.

RICOTTA-STUFFED SQUASH BLOSSOMS IN FRESH SUMMER TOMATO SAUCE

QUICK-COOK RECIPE / MAKES 6 SERVINGS

Stuffed or plain, squash blossoms fried in olive oil were one of the great gastronomic treats my family discovered during our early years in Italy. At home, gently braising the blossoms in a fresh tomato sauce is an easier way to prepare them and just as delicious. In this version, the squash blossoms act as a wrapper, encasing the savory ricotta while adding a light flavor all their own. As a bonus, the dish holds quite well at room temperature, so it can be prepared ahead on a hot summer day, if desired, and enjoyed later, far from the heat of the stove. The mild acidity of the fresh tomato sauce complements the flavors of the delicate blossoms and ricotta.

8	ounces fresh ricotta, preferably sheep's-milk
1/2	cup freshly grated Parmigiano-Reggiano cheese
1	large egg
1/2	teaspoon finely chopped fresh basil
1	teaspoon medium-coarse sea salt
	Coarsely ground black pepper
22–24	small squash blossoms or 18–20 large ones, stems trimmed
2	cups Fresh Summer Tomato Sauce (page 138)

Using a fork, combine ricotta, Parmesan, egg, basil, salt, and a few turns of the pepper grinder in a bowl. Transfer ricotta mixture to a large pastry bag or resealable plastic bag; if using a plastic bag, snip a tiny piece off one bottom corner and press ricotta mixture toward the opening.

Carefully open petals of one squash blossom and fill with ricotta mixture just up to the point where petals begin to split from one another. Gently twist top of petals together to seal blossom. Repeat with remaining blossoms.

Heat tomato sauce in a large skillet over medium heat until gently bubbling; reduce heat to medium-low. Carefully add squash blossoms to sauce and cook, turning them gently halfway through to lightly coat with sauce, until blossoms are heated through and stem ends are tender.

Carefully spoon blossoms and sauce onto plates and serve warm or at room temperature.

TABOULI WITH MANY GRAINS

QUICK-COOK RECIPE / MAKES 6 SERVINGS

Tabouli is one of my favorite foods, especially when made in true Lebanese fashion with a high ratio of chopped herbs to grain. When I returned to Beirut a few years ago with my mother, I learned to soften the bulgur in lemon juice, rather than cook it, as many recipes advise. This adds more flavor to the bulgur than water and allows the grain to retain a slightly crunchy texture. You need fine bulgur in order for this to work properly. If you can't find it, you can use a spice grinder to carefully pulse medium or coarse grains, just a couple times or so—do not grind them to a powder.

The mix of bulgur, millet, barley, and quinoa distinguishes this tabouli even further. If you don't have all of the grains on hand, that's okay; even two are enough.

FLAVOR TIP: I leave the seeds in the cucumber in this and many other recipes because they lend a fresh, grassy flavor and a nice "popping" texture.

- ½ cup fine bulgur (see headnote)
- ½ cup plus 3½ tablespoons fresh lemon juice (from 5–6 lemons)
- 1 tablespoon coarse sea salt
- ¼ cup millet
- ¼ cup quinoa
- ½ cup barley
- 1 cucumber, peeled and diced
- 8 radishes, cut into 8 wedges each
- 1 cup chopped fresh mint
- ½ cup chopped fresh flat-leaf parsley
- 3 scallions, thinly sliced
- ¼ cup plus 2 tablespoons extra-virgin olive oil
- 2 teaspoons pomegranate molasses (see page 20)
- ½–¾ teaspoon fine sea salt

Soak bulgur in ½ cup lemon juice for 45 minutes.

While bulgur is soaking, bring a large saucepan of water and 1 tablespoon coarse sea salt to a boil. Rinse millet and quinoa separately, discarding any grit or debris. When water comes to a full boil, add millet and cook for 5 minutes. Add barley and quinoa, bring water back to a full boil, and cook until grains are just tender yet still a bit firm, about 15 minutes more. Drain (do not rinse) and spread grains on a large plate to cool.

Transfer cooled grains to a large bowl. Add bulgur and any juices, cucumber, radishes, mint, parsley, scallions, oil, remaining 3½ tablespoons lemon juice, pomegranate molasses, and fine sea salt. Stir to combine, and serve.

RED ONIONS COOKED
IN ORANGE JUICE

QUICK-COOK RECIPE / MAKES 4 SERVINGS

This is my play on *cipollini in agrodolce,* or "sweet-and-sour onions." Browning the onions first caramelizes them, and the orange juice adds both tang, more commonly supplied by vinegar, and a little sweetness. I like to use red torpedo onions because they're nicely mild and slightly sweet, and because their rich color, once cooked, makes a gorgeous contrast to the burnt hue of the reduced orange juice, but you can also use small red onions, cipollini, or even pearl onions, leaving the smallest varieties whole. Enjoy these as they are, spoon them onto crostini for an easy cocktail snack, or top fish or game with them for a delicious main course.

1¼   pounds red torpedo or other small-to-medium red onions

3   tablespoons extra-virgin olive oil

Medium-coarse sea salt

1   cup fresh orange juice

2   tablespoons fresh lemon juice

1   bay leaf, preferably fresh

Piment d'Espelette (see page 16) or other crushed dried red chili pepper

Keeping root ends intact so that pieces will hold together, peel and quarter onions. Heat oil in a large skillet over medium-high heat. Add onions, cut side down, sprinkle with ¼ teaspoon salt, and reduce heat to medium. Cook until cut sides are golden, about 4 minutes per side.

Add orange juice, lemon juice, and bay leaf; reduce heat to low and simmer until juices are thickened and almost completely reduced to a glaze, about 30 minutes.

Sprinkle with chili and a little more salt, and serve warm.

MECHUIA
(TUNISIAN GRILLED CAPONATA)

QUICK-COOK RECIPE / MAKES 8 SERVINGS

Dishes combining eggplant, tomatoes, peppers, and onions are found all along the coast of the Mediterranean, but my favorite by far is this North African version. Here the vegetables are first grilled on a stovetop grill pan and then chopped together, rather then sautéed individually and simmered in olive oil, as they are in ratatouille or caponata. The heat from the chili, the bright acidity of the lime juice, and the cilantro result in crisp, clean flavors. *Mechuia* (meh-SHWEE-ah) can be scooped up with grilled or toasted pitas, served on crostini or alongside a tossed salad, or spooned over lamb chops, steaks, or oily fish, such as striped bass, mackerel, and tuna.

FLAVOR TIP: Never peel roasted peppers by holding them under running water, as you'll send the best flavor right down the drain. Instead, rub the skins off the peppers with your fingers, dipping your hands in a small bowl of water to rinse off the skin as you go.

1	red or yellow bell pepper
1	small jalapeño pepper
1½–2	pounds eggplant, cut into ½-inch-thick slices
3	tablespoons extra-virgin olive oil, plus more for brushing
	Medium-coarse sea salt and coarsely ground black pepper
2	medium zucchini, cut lengthwise in half
1	small red onion, cut crosswise into ¼-inch slices
3	plum tomatoes, cut crosswise in half
3	tablespoons fresh lime juice
2	garlic cloves, minced
½	cup coarsely chopped fresh cilantro

Heat a cast-iron grill pan over high heat. Grill bell and jalapeño peppers, turning occasionally until charred on all sides. Place in a bowl, cover tightly with plastic wrap, and let sit while you prepare remaining vegetables.

Lightly brush eggplant with oil and season with salt and pepper. Grill in the hot pan in batches, turning once, until charred and cooked through, 4 to 5 minutes per side. Place slices in a single layer on a baking sheet or large platter and set aside to cool to room temperature.

Repeat with zucchini and onion, grilling until well charred and tender but still firm, about 4 minutes per side, and transfer to a plate. Season and grill tomatoes until lightly charred, about 2 minutes per side.

Coarsely chop eggplant and place it in a large bowl. Remove peppers from bowl, rub charred skins off with your fingers, slice lengthwise in half, and remove and discard cores and seeds. Finely chop peppers together with zucchini and onion; add to bowl with eggplant.

Chop tomatoes and combine with rest of vegetables. Add 3 tablespoons oil, lime juice, and garlic and toss to combine. Season with 1 teaspoon salt, add pepper to taste, and stir in cilantro. Serve warm or at room temperature.

ROASTED RED PEPPERS
WITH GARLIC AND CELERY LEAVES

QUICK-COOK RECIPE / MAKES 6 SERVINGS

Basic roasted peppers don't show the full flavor potential of the vegetable, so after roasting and peeling the peppers, I like to continue cooking them, gently stewing them in their own juices with a little garlic and olive oil, until they are

meltingly sweet and tender. Celery leaves, with their slightly bitter bite, contrast with the sweetness of the peppers and perk up the dish.

When local red peppers are in season, this dish appears each time I put out a *mezze,* either on its own or with a hunk of cheese and some good bread. I also pair it with roast chicken or broiled or grilled striped bass or bluefish. Umbrians serve slow-cooked peppers with thin slices of black truffle on top—a heavenly combination that I encourage you to try.

- 6 large red or yellow bell peppers, or a combination
- 3 tablespoons extra-virgin olive oil
- 3 garlic cloves, smashed and peeled
-   Medium-coarse sea salt and coarsely ground black pepper
- ¼ cup water
- 2 tablespoons thinly sliced celery leaves or 1 tablespoon thinly sliced fresh lovage

Char peppers over a gas burner set on high or a hot charcoal fire, turning frequently, until skin is blackened and blistered on all sides. Transfer to a bowl and cover tightly with plastic wrap; let sit for 15 minutes.

Rub skins off peppers and discard cores and seeds. Slice peppers lengthwise into 1-inch-wide strips.

In a medium heavy saucepan, heat 2 tablespoons oil and garlic over medium heat, stirring occasionally, until garlic begins to color. Add peppers, a pinch each of salt and pepper, and water. Bring to a gentle simmer, reduce heat to low, and cook until peppers are very tender and liquid has reduced to a syrup, about 30 minutes. Remove from heat.

Stir in celery leaves and remaining tablespoon oil and season with salt and pepper to taste. Serve warm or at room temperature.

ROASTED CAULIFLOWER WITH TAHINI SAUCE

QUICK-COOK RECIPE / MAKES 4 TO 6 SERVINGS

The combination of tahini and cauliflower shows up often in Middle Eastern cookbooks. The vegetable is usually boiled or fried, but I love how the slight smokiness of the sesame seed paste, coupled with the sharp taste of garlic and zing of lemon, enhances the mellow flavor of roasted cauliflower. Great for a summer picnic or as part of a *mezze,* this is also a perfect side with grilled fish or roast chicken, or stuffed into a pita with lettuce for a vegetarian sandwich.

1	large head cauliflower, broken into florets
¼	cup plus 2 tablespoons extra-virgin olive oil
1½	teaspoons medium-coarse sea salt, or more to taste
¼	teaspoon coarsely ground black pepper
¼	cup plus 1 tablespoon tahini paste
¼	cup plus 2 tablespoons water
3	tablespoons fresh lemon juice
1	garlic clove, minced
¼	cup finely chopped fresh flat-leaf parsley

Heat oven to 400°F with a rack in center. Line a baking sheet with parchment.

Toss cauliflower with oil, 1¼ teaspoons salt, and pepper. Spread in a single layer on baking sheet and roast, stirring and turning once or twice, until cauliflower is tender and crispy brown in spots, about 45 minutes.

While cauliflower is roasting, puree tahini paste, water, lemon juice, garlic, and remaining ¼ teaspoon salt in a blender until combined. Transfer to a large bowl.

Remove cauliflower from oven, immediately add to bowl with tahini sauce, and toss with sauce and parsley. Season with more salt to taste if necessary, and serve warm, or let stand at room temperature for several hours before serving.

SWEET CORN SFORMATO

SLOW-COOK RECIPE / MAKES 6 SERVINGS

Sformato is a baked Italian custard, traditionally made with seasonal vegetables and ricotta cheese. Though sweet corn is not a common Italian ingredient, this recipe is a nice example of adapting a technique to local ingredients. Cream is infused with rich corn flavor, then combined with eggs, and the custards are gently baked in a water bath.

An elegant appetizer for any meal, *sformati* can be followed by a soup or salad to make a nice light meal. You can make the custards up to a day in advance and refrigerate them. Gently steam them in the molds to reheat, or enjoy them at room temperature or cold.

FLAVOR TIP: After cutting the kernels from each corncob, use the back of a knife to scrape the juices—and good corn flavor—from the cob into a bowl, and add to the cream mixture. If you like, you can gently simmer the cobs with onion, a little garlic, and fresh parsley, all just covered with water, to make a simple corn stock for risotto or soup.

3	medium to large mixed sweet and mildly spicy peppers, such as sweet banana and poblano (not bell)
1/4	cup extra-virgin olive oil
2	tablespoons chopped fresh flat-leaf parsley
1	tablespoon thinly sliced fresh basil leaves
1 1/2	teaspoons coarse sea salt, plus more for sprinkling
4	ears corn, shucked and kernels cut from cobs
3	cups heavy cream
9	large egg yolks
	Coarsely ground black pepper

Special equipment: six 5-ounce ramekins

Roast, peel, core, and seed peppers as for Roasted Red Peppers with Garlic and Celery Leaves (page 52), then slice lengthwise into ⅛-inch-wide strips. Place in a bowl and toss with oil, parsley, basil, and ½ teaspoon salt; set aside.

Heat oven to 275°F.

In a large heavy saucepan, combine corn, cream, and remaining 1 teaspoon salt. Bring to a boil, reduce to a simmer, and cook, stirring frequently, for 10 minutes. Puree mixture with a hand blender or in an ordinary blender, then strain through a fine sieve into a large bowl, pressing on solids to extract as much flavor as possible.

Lightly beat egg yolks in a large bowl. Slowly whisk in ½ cup warm cream mixture to temper yolks, then slowly whisk in remaining cream. Divide mixture among six 5-ounce ramekins, place them in a baking dish, and fill dish with enough hot water to come halfway up sides of ramekins.

Cover with foil and bake until *sformati* are just set, about 45 minutes. Remove from water bath.

Just before serving, top each custard with a tangle of peppers, a drizzle of the oil from peppers, and a sprinkle of salt and pepper. Serve *sformati* warm, at room temperature, or cold.

ROASTED CORN AND BRIOCHE PUDDING

SLOW-COOK RECIPE / MAKES 4 SERVINGS

Here a corn custard is used to soak the bread for a rustic, savory pudding. Half the corn is pureed with the cream; frying the remaining corn before folding it into the other ingredients is an important flavor step. By doing so, you infuse it with the olive oil and crisp it, to add a texture and toastiness to the dish. You can serve this as a warm appetizer on its own, or with a pile of lightly dressed bitter greens, or as a side to pan-roasted pork chops.

4 ounces brioche, cut into 1½-inch pieces (about 4 cups)

2 cups fresh corn kernels (from 2–3 ears of corn)

1 cup heavy cream

Fine sea salt

1 cup whole milk

2 large eggs

2 large egg yolks

1 tablespoon chopped fresh summer savory or thyme

1 tablespoon extra-virgin olive oil

1 tablespoon unsalted butter

¾ cup freshly grated Parmigiano-Reggiano cheese

Coarsely ground black pepper

Place brioche in a large bowl; set aside.

In a small saucepan, combine 1 cup corn kernels, cream, and 1 teaspoon salt. Bring to a boil, then immediately remove from heat and let cool slightly. Puree cream mixture in a blender until smooth. Transfer to a medium bowl and let cool.

In another medium bowl, whisk together milk, eggs, egg yolks, and savory.

Heat oil and butter in a large skillet over medium-high heat until butter has melted. Add remaining 1 cup corn kernels and a pinch of salt, reduce heat to medium, and cook, stirring occasionally, until kernels are golden and tender (they will pop a bit), 8 to 10 minutes. Remove from heat and add to cream mixture. Let cool.

Add cooled cream mixture to egg mixture, whisking to combine. Pour mixture over bread and toss to combine. Let bread sit at room temperature for 30 minutes.

Heat oven to 375°F.

Fold cheese and pepper to taste into bread mixture, and pour into a 2-quart baking dish. Bake until set, about 30 minutes. Serve hot or warm.

FRIED EGGPLANT BALLS

SLOW-COOK RECIPE / MAKES FORTY 1-INCH BALLS; 10 TO 12 SERVINGS

Fried eggplant balls are one of my favorite party appetizers. I roast the eggplant until cooked through and then, since it is a watery vegetable, drain it for at least 4 hours, leaving a thick, sweet, and smoky base to mix with the bread crumbs and egg and form into balls. Once you have fried up all of the balls, you can reheat them in a medium oven just before serving.

2 large eggplants (about 2¾ pounds)

1 large egg

2 cups medium-ground fresh bread crumbs (see Note, page 155)

1 cup freshly grated Parmigiano-Reggiano cheese, plus more for garnish

3 tablespoons chopped fresh flat-leaf parsley, plus more for garnish

3 garlic cloves, minced

½ teaspoon fine sea salt

Extra-virgin olive oil for shallow-frying

Heat oven to 375°F.

Prick each eggplant several times with a fork. Roast until cooked through, about 1 hour. Let cool.

Halve eggplants lengthwise, scrape flesh from skin, and place in a fine sieve set over a mixing bowl; discard skin. Drain for 4 hours at room temperature or overnight in the refrigerator.

Transfer eggplant flesh to a food processor (discard juices). Add egg, bread crumbs, cheese, parsley, garlic, and salt; pulse to combine. Transfer to a plate or bowl. Form into forty 1-inch balls.

Fill a large skillet with ¼ inch oil and heat to 360° to 365°F. Using a slotted spoon, add several eggplant balls to hot oil and cook until golden on all sides, about 5 minutes. Remove with slotted spoon and drain on paper towels. Repeat with remaining balls.

Serve eggplant balls hot, dusted with a little grated Parmigiano-Reggiano and chopped parsley.

PAN-ROASTED BRUSSELS SPROUTS, TURNIPS, AND BEETS WITH WARM FARRO

SLOW-COOK RECIPE / MAKES 4 TO 6 SERVINGS

Roasting beets, Brussels sprouts, and turnips unifies their disparate flavors while bringing out the unique sweetness of each. Farro, a hearty, nutty-tasting grain (one of my favorites), brings great texture to the dish. This is also a fantastic side for roast chicken or the Thanksgiving turkey.

The warmth of the roasted vegetable mixture melts the cheese just a bit, making it creamy, so be sure to add the cheese while the dish is hot, and then serve it right away. You could use a strong cheddar or a soft young Pecorino Toscano in place of the aged pecorino. For a simple variation, add pan-roasted carrots or chestnuts, or use as a substitute for one of the vegetables.

3 medium beets

¼ cup plus 3 tablespoons extra-virgin olive oil, plus more for beets
  Medium-coarse sea salt and coarsely ground black pepper

1 cup farro (see page 13)

6 small turnips, quartered (halved if using baby turnips)

8 ounces Brussels sprouts, bottoms trimmed and cut lengthwise in half

½ cup loosely packed fresh flat-leaf parsley leaves

2 tablespoons Vin Santo vinegar or other high-quality mild white wine vinegar

¼ cup thinly shaved aged Pecorino Toscano (see page 18)

Heat oven to 400°F.

Place beets in a baking dish. Add 1 inch water, drizzle with a little oil, and sprinkle with salt and pepper. Cover tightly with foil and bake until tender, 45 minutes to an hour. Remove beets from oven and drain, then let cool slightly and peel. Cut each one into eighths and place in a large bowl.

Meanwhile, when beets are almost finished cooking, bring a medium saucepan of salted water to a boil. Add farro and cook until just tender but still slightly firm to the bite, 10 to 15 minutes.

Drain farro and toss with beets.

Heat ¼ cup oil in a large skillet over medium-high heat. Add turnips and Brussels sprouts, cut side down, and a generous pinch each of salt and pepper (if you can't fit vegetables in a single layer, use two pans). Cook, turning occasionally, until vegetables are golden on all sides, about 5 minutes. Transfer to bowl with beets.

Add parsley, remaining 3 tablespoons oil, and vinegar; toss well. Season generously with salt and pepper and serve warm, topped with cheese.

MAINE SHRIMP PANFRIED IN OLIVE OIL

QUICK-COOK RECIPE / MAKES 4 SERVINGS

In the depths of winter, these tiny, festive pink shrimp filled with tasty roe make their appearance in Maine. Much more delicate in texture than regular shrimp, Maine shrimp are also prized for their sweet taste. They need little or no cooking (the Japanese serve them raw as *ama ebi*, or "sweet shrimp") and are best prepared simply. Here they're quickly fried, then lightly seasoned. Eat them crispy shells and all if you like—you can even eat the heads.

In our house, my mother would cover the table with newspaper and put down dishes of aïoli and cut lemons, then quickly steam the shrimp and pile them hot onto the newspaper. Everyone sat around, peeling or not, dunking the shrimp, enjoying the taste of the season, and making a happy mess. There is no substitute for Maine shrimp, so keep this as a seasonal recipe to look forward to.

1½   pounds fresh Maine shrimp

Extra-virgin olive oil for frying

Medium-coarse sea salt

Piment d'Espelette (see page 16), Aleppo pepper (see page 16), or other crushed dried red chili pepper

½   lemon, cut into wedges

Rinse shrimp under cold water and pat thoroughly dry with paper towels.

Line a large plate or baking sheet with paper towels. Fill a large deep skillet with 1 inch oil and heat over high heat to 350° to 365°F. Add shrimp 8 to 10 at a time and fry until crisp, about 1½ minutes. Using a slotted spoon, transfer shrimp to paper-towel-lined plate to drain. Place on a serving platter and sprinkle with salt and chili. Squeeze lemon over shrimp and serve immediately.

GRILLED SARDINES WITH ACCOMPANIMENTS

QUICK-COOK RECIPE / MAKES 4 SERVINGS

Alberto Avalle, the mad genius and co-owner of Il Buco restaurant in New York City, taught me so much about flavor, and he introduced me to the combination of sardines with pickled onions—ingredients that magically play off each other. I also love many of the other accompaniments traditionally served with the rich, oily fish, all of which are crisp and acidic: the chopped tomato salad of Morocco (page 66); shaved fennel and parsley leaves; and green olives and blood oranges. Salsa verde (see page 223) is also a lovely partner.

You can eat your sardines hot off the grill or dress them in olive oil and herbs, leave them to marinate at room temperature for a few hours, and then serve them with one of the following accompaniments. Mackerel and bluefish are equally rich, and their fillets can be given the same treatment. Cooking times may change depending on the thickness of your fillets.

FLAVOR TIP: Make sure you leave the skin on these fish—it chars and crisps up wonderfully.

12 fresh sardines, cleaned, leaving head and tail intact
   Fine sea salt and coarsely ground black pepper
   Extra-virgin olive oil for drizzling
1 lemon, cut into wedges

Build a hot fire in a charcoal grill.

Season sardines with salt and pepper and lay them on hottest part of grill. Cook until blistery and charred, about 2 minutes on the first side and 4 to 5 minutes on the second. Transfer to a plate, drizzle with oil, and serve with lemon wedges and one or more of the following condiments.

PICKLED PEARL ONIONS

QUICK-COOK RECIPE / MAKES ABOUT 1³/₄ CUPS; 7 TO 10 SIDE SERVINGS

This easy pickle recipe makes the perfect accompaniment to Grilled Sardines. Any extra onions are delicious dropped into cocktails, sliced over salads, or enjoyed with pâté or on their own as a snack.

- 1 cup white wine vinegar
- 1 cup water
- 1 tablespoon black peppercorns
- 1 bay leaf
- ³/₄ teaspoon fine sea salt
- 8 ounces red and/or white pearl onions or cipollini
- 2 large fresh thyme sprigs

Bring vinegar, water, peppercorns, bay leaf, and salt to a boil in a medium nonreactive saucepan. Add onions and return liquid to a simmer, then immediately remove from heat. Add thyme, stir, and let cool to room temperature.

Cover and refrigerate onions in their brine for at least 1 hour before serving. Onions will keep, covered and refrigerated (in the brine), for 2 to 3 weeks.

SHAVED FENNEL SALAD

QUICK-COOK RECIPE / MAKES 4 SIDE SERVINGS

Shave the fennel lengthwise from a narrow side, for smaller pieces that look the nicest. The thin slices will wilt a bit in the salt and lemon juice, just enough to pick up the flavors of the herb and chili pepper. This salad makes a small plate on its own and is also good on top of other fish or served with chicken.

1 large fennel bulb, trimmed and thinly shaved on a mandoline or other vegetable slicer (see headnote)

1 cup loosely packed fresh flat-leaf parsley leaves

1/4 cup fresh lemon juice

2 tablespoons extra-virgin olive oil

1/4 teaspoon piment d'Espelette (see page 16), Aleppo pepper (see page 16), or other crushed dried red chili pepper

1/4 teaspoon fine sea salt

Coarsely ground black pepper

Toss together fennel and parsley in a bowl. Add lemon juice, oil, chili, and salt; toss to combine. Add pepper to taste.

MOROCCAN SALAD

QUICK-COOK RECIPE / MAKES 4 SIDE SERVINGS

Classically paired with sardines at the outdoor grills along Morocco's Atlantic Coast, this chopped salad is delicious on its own, served in shallow bowls with grilled bread for dipping and sopping up the juices, or as a side to all sorts of grilled fish and meats. Like so many Mediterranean dishes, this one is limited in its variations only by your imagination. Add celery, carrots, radishes, or any other crisp vegetable. Puree leftovers in a blender, chill, and serve as Moroccan gazpacho.

8 ounces heirloom tomatoes, diced small

1 small yellow bell pepper, finely chopped

1 medium cucumber, peeled and finely chopped

1/2 small onion, finely chopped

1/4 cup chopped fresh flat-leaf parsley

2 tablespoons chopped fresh cilantro

2 tablespoons fresh lime juice

2 tablespoons extra-virgin olive oil

1 teaspoon fine sea salt

1/4 teaspoon ground cumin

Toss together tomatoes, bell pepper, cucumber, onion, parsley, cilantro, lime juice, oil, salt, and cumin. Serve with Grilled Sardines (page 64).

CHICKEN LIVER CROSTINI

QUICK-COOK RECIPE / MAKES 32 CROSTINI; 10 TO 12 SERVINGS

I make these Tuscan crostini again and again because they have the perfect balance of salty capers, acidic lemon, and sweet wine. Plumping the capers in sweet wine enriches both ingredients, bringing a deeper flavor to the dish as a whole. If you can't find Vin Santo, substitute any sweet dessert wine—Sauternes and port both work well.

- 3 tablespoons salt-packed capers (see page 12), rinsed several times and drained
- 3 tablespoons Vin Santo or other sweet dessert wine (see headnote)
- 3 tablespoons extra-virgin olive oil
- 1 small onion, chopped
- 2 garlic cloves, minced

  Fine sea salt
- ³/₄ cup water
- 1 tablespoon tomato paste, preferably double-concentrate (see page 19)
- 1¹/₂ teaspoons chopped fresh rosemary
- 1 pound chicken livers, preferably organic, rinsed, drained, and patted dry

  Finely grated zest of 1 lemon
- 32 ¹/₄-inch-thick slices country-style bread, lightly toasted

Combine capers and Vin Santo in a bowl and let sit until capers are plumped up a bit, about 10 minutes.

Heat 2 tablespoons oil in a large skillet over medium heat. Add onion, garlic, and ¹/₄ teaspoon salt and cook, stirring occasionally, until onion is softened, about 5 minutes. Add water and tomato paste, bring to a gentle simmer, and cook until most of the water has evaporated, about 20 minutes.

Drain capers, reserving wine. Add capers and rosemary to skillet, stir to combine, and cook for 1 minute. Push onion mixture to one side of pan; add livers and a pinch of salt to other side, reduce heat to medium-low, and cook until livers are almost cooked through, 10 to 12 minutes.

Stir livers and onion mixture together. Add reserved wine and stir to incorporate. With the back of a fork, mash and stir livers and onion mixture together, until livers are cooked through, about 5 minutes.

Stir in remaining tablespoon oil and lemon zest and immediately remove from heat. Season with more salt if necessary. Spread mashed chicken livers on crostini and serve warm.

SALAD

Nothing delights more than a salad of beautiful vegetables, raw or cooked—perhaps mixed with nuts, cheese, grains, or a little bit of protein (sliced grilled steak, smoked fish, or fine canned tuna)—drizzled with the finest olive oil, or sometimes nut oil, splashed with good vinegar or a squeeze of lemon, and seasoned with a few turns of the pepper grinder and a pinch of coarse sea salt. I could—and sometimes do—live off well-made salads.

A fresh head of Bibb lettuce is an easy beginning. A fine estate-bottled extra-virgin olive oil is next. Then you can build on this, depending on where the salad fits into your meal—as a light opener, in the American style; or after a heavy meal to cleanse and refresh the palate, as in Europe; or, with several added components, such as cheese or nuts, canned tuna, or avocado, as a meal in itself.

For a simple green salad, I begin by washing the greens in several changes of cold water, letting any dirt fall to the bottom of the bowl. Gently lifting the greens out of the water, I let them drain in a colander. Then I transfer them to a bowl lined with a clean dry cloth, fold the edges over the greens, turn them so the wet cloth is on top, and chill them for at least an hour in the fridge so they become exquisitely crisp.

When I am ready to eat, I dress the greens with a vinaigrette that I've made using some sharp mustard or with a 3:1 ratio of extra-virgin olive oil to acid (fresh lemon juice or vinegar). The oil and acid are added in a precise sequence: first the oil to coat the leaves, then salt, then the acid, which is buffered by the oil and won't wilt the leaves as it would if added first. Finally, a twist of the pepper grinder—and that's it.

For a slightly more involved salad, I add some avocado for richness, thin sliced scallion or shallot or chive blossoms for bite, carrots or radishes, ripe tomatoes if in season, and perhaps some leftover cooked farro for a toothsome texture and nutty flavor. If I have fresh leafy herbs kicking about, I might mix in whole basil or parsley leaves, using them like lettuce. A sprinkling of fresh herbs that are stronger in flavor, such as thyme, summer savory, and lovage, is also good. To turn my salad into a meal, I top with shavings of cheese or some smoked fish or canned tuna.

In the fall and winter, when root vegetables are dominant, I make salads of tart apples and shaved parsley root, or celery root with cabbage sliced razor-thin so that it wilts ever so slightly from the salt and acid.

Since a good salad stands or falls on the quality of its ingredients, there's no need to overdo it. If all you have access to is a nice head of lettuce, make a simple salad and leave it at that. Wait until your farmers' market or garden is in full swing to take it to the next level.

VINAIGRETTE

At its most basic, vinaigrette is mustard (an all-in-one acid, emulsifier, and flavor agent), vinegar (another acid and flavor agent), and oil (a fat, which offers body, and flavor agent) whisked together and seasoned with a dash of salt and pepper. By adding to these principal ingredients and/or varying them, you can change the flavor of a vinaigrette in countless ways, giving you myriad possibilities for fantastic salads.

For mustards, I favor French. I most often use Dijon, which in itself can be quite varied—smooth or grainy, spicy or mild. With vinegars, I like a mild red wine vinegar, an even milder white wine vinegar (like Vin Santo vinegar; see page 7), or sherry vinegar. Some of my favorite oils are olive, hazelnut, walnut, and cold-pressed sunflower oil, a slightly sweet, lightly nut-scented oil that also has some great health benefits.

Fresh herbs, citrus, garlic, onions (including red onion, shallots, scallions, chives, and others), and even capers, pickles, and chilies can bring a new dimension to a vinaigrette.

I encourage you to vary the three different recipes in this chapter at your whim, swapping out herbs, spices, and other flavorings. My cardinal rule is this: a good vinaigrette should be full of flavor and have a nice punch of acid and the right amount of salt.

SALAD

Fresh Herb Vinaigrette | 73

Cornichon, Caper, and
Parsley Vinaigrette | 74

Walnut Vinaigrette | 75

Crisp Bitter Greens with
Anchovy Vinaigrette | 76

Warm Escarole Salad
with Hot Anchovy Dressing | 77

Celery, Cherry Tomato,
and Bottarga Salad | 79

Raw Fava Bean Salad
with Pecorino | 80

Pear, Basil, and Pecorino
Toscano Salad | 82

Winter Root Salad with
English Farmhouse Cheddar | 85

Panzanella di Farro
(Tuscan-Style Tomato Salad
with Farro) | 86

continued

Fattouche
(Lebanese Salad with Pita) | 88

Green Beans with Shaved Onion, Fried
Almonds, and Parmigiano-Reggiano | 89

Beet, Arugula, and Cucumber
Salad with Yogurt Dressing | 91

Orange and Mint Leaf Salad
with Roasted Beets | 92

Smoked Trout Salad with
Spicy Arugula and Grapefruit | 94

"Dirty" Squid with Watercress | 96

Flank Steak Salad with Farro,
Arugula, and Fresh Horseradish | 98

FRESH HERB VINAIGRETTE

QUICK-COOK RECIPE / MAKES ²/₃ CUP

Make this robust-tasting vinaigrette a few hours before using, if time allows, and let sit at room temperature. The herbs will macerate and give up even more flavor to the dressing. You can then use it for a salad of sturdy lettuces (such as romaine), cucumbers, tomatoes, and celery leaves; toss it with cooked fresh lobster meat and mixed lettuces; or drizzle it over chunks of roast chicken and shaved fennel.

1 tablespoon red wine vinegar
1 teaspoon Dijon mustard
1 teaspoon whole-grain Dijon mustard
1 small garlic clove, minced
1 tablespoon minced shallot
2 pinches fine sea salt
½ cup extra-virgin olive oil
2 tablespoons minced fresh chives
2 tablespoons chopped fresh flat-leaf parsley
1 tablespoon chopped fresh tarragon
1 tablespoon chopped celery leaves from the heart
Coarsely ground black pepper

Whisk together vinegar, mustards, garlic, shallot, and salt. Let sit for 10 minutes.

Briskly whisk in oil in a slow, steady stream. Add chives, parsley, tarragon, and celery leaves. Stir to combine. Season with pepper. Vinaigrette can be stored in the refrigerator for up to 3 days.

CORNICHON, CAPER, AND PARSLEY VINAIGRETTE

QUICK-COOK RECIPE / MAKES ³/₄ CUP

This vinaigrette is reminiscent of Italian salsa verde—the pungent green condiment made of parsley, capers, and olive oil that is traditionally a garnish for boiled meats. Cornichons bring an extra level of acidity, making this assertive enough to stand up to robust greens and rich meats. Try it simply tossed with arugula or other bitter or spicy greens, serve it with pâté or Chicken Liver Crostini (page 67), or drizzle it over leftover cold roast pork—in a sandwich or on its own.

1 tablespoon fresh lemon juice

1 tablespoon minced shallot

2 teaspoons whole-grain Dijon mustard

Finely grated zest of ¹/₂ lemon

A good pinch of sea salt

¹/₂ cup extra-virgin olive oil

3 tablespoons chopped fresh flat-leaf parsley

6 cornichons, chopped (3 tablespoons)

1 tablespoon salt-packed capers (see page 12), rinsed several times, drained, and chopped

Coarsely ground black pepper

Whisk together lemon juice, shallot, mustard, lemon zest, and salt. Let sit for 10 minutes. Briskly whisk in oil in a slow, steady stream. Stir in parsley, pickles, and capers; season with pepper to taste. Vinaigrette can be stored in the refrigerator for up to 3 days.

WALNUT VINAIGRETTE

QUICK-COOK RECIPE / MAKES ²/₃ CUP

Nut oils have a mild, subtle flavor that best complements tender lettuces such as Bibb, oak leaf, and/or mesclun, or tender new leafy greens. This vinaigrette is perfect for a nice French salad with a little goat cheese, toasted walnuts, and croutons.

FLAVOR TIP: Use a good-quality walnut oil, one that smells strongly of nuts and is sold in a can rather than a glass jar (light is not good for any oil). Keep it—along with other nut oils—in the refrigerator, as it will quickly become rancid if left in the pantry.

1½ teaspoons Dijon mustard
1½ teaspoons whole-grain Dijon mustard
1 tablespoon red wine vinegar
1 tablespoon minced shallot
1 small garlic clove, minced
2 good pinches fine sea salt
½ cup walnut oil
¼ cup walnuts, chopped
Coarsely ground black pepper

Whisk together both mustards, vinegar, shallot, garlic, and salt. Let sit for 10 minutes. Briskly whisk in oil in a slow, steady stream. Stir in walnuts and season with pepper to taste. Vinaigrette can be stored in the refrigerator for up to 3 days.

CRISP BITTER GREENS
WITH ANCHOVY VINAIGRETTE

QUICK-COOK RECIPE / MAKES 4 SERVINGS

Though they sound similar, this recipe and the following one are quite different, in both flavor and technique. This one is a classic Roman recipe, made in Italy with puntarelle—the shoots of Catalonian chicory. In November, Rome's market stalls fill up with these beloved greens. The market ladies trim and discard the outer leaves, then slice the stems into long ribbons and soak them in ice water, which removes some of the bitterness and curls them. Dressed with anchovies and garlic and served chilled and crisp, *puntarelle alla romana* is a trattoria mainstay throughout the winter. Outside Italy, the greens are hard to come by, though they are occasionally available at farmers' markets (and a lot of work to prepare), so I substitute frisée or slivered endive. These greens need not be soaked, since they are not as bitter as puntarelle. While the result is not quite the same, it's still awfully good.

- 8 ounces mildly bitter salad greens, such as frisée or endive
- 5 oil-packed anchovy fillets
- 2 garlic cloves
- 2 tablespoons mild red wine vinegar
- 1/4 cup extra-virgin olive oil

Trim and wash greens. If using frisée, separate leaves. If using endive, thinly slice. Place in a large bowl.

Puree anchovies and garlic in a food processor or blender; add vinegar and pulse to combine. With machine running, add oil in a slow, steady stream. Gently toss greens with vinaigrette and serve.

WARM ESCAROLE SALAD
WITH HOT ANCHOVY DRESSING

QUICK-COOK RECIPE / MAKES 4 SERVINGS

Half-cooked as it is here, escarole makes a fine salad; I have always found it a little harsh raw. While this is a fairly simple dish, it's important that you heat the olive oil gently, so that it retains its delicate flavor, and follow the process step-by-step, or you will end up with fully cooked greens instead of a wilted salad. You can build on this by adding chopped hard-boiled egg or a sprinkling of shaved Parmigiano-Reggiano cheese.

1/2   French baguette or long Italian loaf, torn into 1-inch pieces
1 1/2 pounds escarole, leaves separated, washed, and dried
1/2   teaspoon fine sea salt
1/4   cup plus 2 tablespoons extra-virgin olive oil
4   garlic cloves, smashed and peeled
3   dried árbol chilies
3   anchovy fillets
2   tablespoons mild red wine vinegar

Heat oven to 375°F.

Place bread pieces on a baking sheet and bake until lightly toasted, about 10 minutes. Remove from oven and let cool.

Tear escarole into small pieces and place in a large bowl. Toss with toasted bread and salt.

Combine 2 tablespoons oil and garlic in a large skillet and cook over medium-low heat until garlic takes on some color, about 1 minute. Add chilies and cook until lightly toasted, about 30 seconds.

Remove pan from heat, add anchovies, and stir with a wooden spoon to break up anchovies and garlic. Add remaining 1/4 cup oil and vinegar to the pan, return to medium-low heat, and bring to a simmer.

Remove dressing from heat and pour over escarole and toasted bread; toss well. Place pan over high heat and, using tongs, grab a bunch of escarole and wipe pan with leaves until they start to wilt, about 30 seconds. Toss wilted escarole back into bowl and mix it around a bit; repeat 3 or 4 times, until most of lettuce is warm and wilted. Remove chilies, if desired, and serve immediately.

CELERY, CHERRY TOMATO, AND BOTTARGA SALAD

QUICK-COOK RECIPE / MAKES 4 SERVINGS

Alberto Avalle of Il Buco restaurant in New York City originally showed me this combination. The bitterness of the celery leaves, the sweetness of the tomatoes, the *pizzico* ("peppery taste") of the extra-virgin oil, and the salty fishiness of bottarga create an explosion of lively flavors in your mouth. It's a wonderfully complex salad to open a meal with, and I like to build the rest of the meal around it by serving very simple things afterwards. If you can't find bottarga, try smoked trout instead—not quite the same, but still tasty.

FLAVOR TIP: Use cherry tomatoes only if they come from the farmers' market, as the ones in the supermarket are generally very bland. Grape tomatoes, which you can find throughout the year at most supermarkets, are a good substitute.

1	celery heart (about 5 stalks), with leaves
2½	ounces *bottarga di muggine* (see page 11), any wax and thin skin peeled off
2	cups cherry or grape tomatoes, halved (see Tip)
¼	cup plus 2 tablespoons extra-virgin olive oil
1	teaspoon fleur de sel or other medium-coarse sea salt

Separate leaves from celery and place leaves in a large bowl. Trim base of celery heart, then, holding it together, thinly shave on a mandoline (or slice very thin with a knife). Add to bowl.

Using mandoline or a flat grater, shave bottarga over celery. Add tomatoes, oil, and salt and toss to combine. Serve immediately, as the moisture of the salad turns bottarga mushy and flat-tasting quite quickly.

RAW FAVA BEAN SALAD WITH PECORINO

QUICK-COOK RECIPE / MAKES 4 SERVINGS

In the springtime when plump green fava beans are finally ready to be harvested, Tuscans eat them with abandon. Sometimes they're served as a simple appetizer with home-cured salami that was made in the early days of January and is just ready to be eaten. At the end of a meal, it's common to pile favas onto the table alongside slices of soft young Pecorino Toscano. Everyone shucks the beans from the pods, eating handfuls with bites of cheese and washing it all down with young wine.

To be enjoyed raw, favas must be young, small, and exceedingly fresh. Otherwise, as with corn and sweet peas, their sugars rapidly convert to starch, and they become tough. I look for fava beans at the farmers' market when they first come into season and buy only those picked no earlier than the day before. If you can't get young favas, you can make this salad by blanching older ones in boiling water for 1 minute, shocking them in ice water, and peeling off the tough outer skin before proceeding.

FLAVOR TIP: Try swapping any of the herbs or lettuces for delicate aromatic herbs like lemon balm, chives, and tarragon; pea shoots and pea blossoms; or any edible flower or microgreen. In Tuscany, a splash of Prosecco is sometimes added, which is very nice if you have some around.

3 pounds young fava beans, removed from pods

6 ounces medium-aged Pecorino Toscano cheese (see page 18) or other mild semi-firm sheep's-milk cheese, cut into ¼-inch cubes

1 cup baby arugula or other microgreens

¾ cup loosely packed fresh basil leaves

½ cup loosely packed fresh flat-leaf parsley leaves

½ cup loosely packed fresh mint leaves

¼ cup extra-virgin olive oil

½ teaspoon fleur de sel or other medium-coarse sea salt

Coarsely ground black pepper

Toss fava beans, cheese, arugula, basil, parsley, and mint together in a large bowl. Add oil and salt and toss to combine. Season generously with pepper, and serve.

PEAR, BASIL, AND PECORINO TOSCANO SALAD

QUICK-COOK RECIPE / MAKES 4 SERVINGS

Fashion sweeps through restaurants in Italy as quickly and thoroughly as in all other aspects of life there. A few years ago, arugula, pear, and Pecorino salad turned up everywhere. I tried basil in place of arugula and loved the still pungent yet milder flavor. I start making this salad in the early fall with little juicy pears and aromatic end-of-the-season basil from the farmers' market. Later, as the first frost creeps down through the Hudson Valley and the basil disappears, I substitute thinly sliced hearts of celery and whole celery leaves (the celery is also wonderful along with the basil).

You can make this salad with many different cheeses; each one will change the flavor slightly. Look for a cheese that will keep its shape in a salad, such as an aged cheddar, Parmigiano-Reggiano, or a crumbly blue.

12	ounces Pecorino Toscano cheese (see page 18 and headnote)
4	ripe Bosc pears, cored and cut into eighths
1	cup packed fresh basil leaves
1/4	cup extra-virgin olive oil
1	tablespoon Vin Santo vinegar (see page 7) or other high-quality mild white wine vinegar
1/4	teaspoon fleur de sel or other medium-coarse sea salt, or more to taste
	Coarsely ground black pepper

Using the tip of a sharp paring knife, break cheese into irregular chunks about ½ inch in size.

Place cheese, pear slices, basil leaves, oil, vinegar, and salt in a large bowl and toss to combine. Season with pepper and more salt if needed. Serve at once.

WINTER ROOT SALAD
WITH ENGLISH FARMHOUSE CHEDDAR

QUICK-COOK RECIPE / MAKES 4 TO 6 SERVINGS

In New York City in the dead of winter, it's hard to scrounge up locally grown bright green leaves for salad. In Teverina, Tuscany, our neighbor Mita makes a winter salad of cabbage, shaved razor-thin and lightly wilted with salt and vinegar. It's a wonderful side dish for rich winter foods, but to jazz it up, I include a mix of root vegetables, good cheddar cheese, and a little parsley, which brings some green flavor to the plate.

FLAVOR TIP: English farmhouse cheddar is strong and assertive in flavor, with a crumbly texture that makes it perfect for this hearty vegetable salad.

¹/₂	small red cabbage, thinly sliced
1	small celery root, peeled and julienned or grated
2	medium carrots, julienned or grated
6	medium radishes, julienned or thinly sliced
1¹/₂	teaspoons fine sea salt, or more to taste
5¹/₃	ounces (¹/₃ pound) English farmhouse cheddar, such as Keen's or Montgomery's, both from Neal's Yard Dairy
1	tart apple, such as Granny Smith, unpeeled, julienned
1	cup loosely packed fresh flat-leaf parsley leaves
¹/₄	cup extra-virgin olive oil
2	tablespoons Vin Santo vinegar or other high-quality mild white wine vinegar
	Coarsely ground black pepper

Combine cabbage, celery root, carrots, and radishes in a large bowl. Add salt and toss to combine. Let sit for 5 minutes.

Crumble cheese into small bits and add to vegetables, then add apple, parsley, oil, and vinegar. Adjust salt if necessary, add pepper to taste, and serve.

PANZANELLA DI FARRO
(TUSCAN-STYLE TOMATO SALAD WITH FARRO)

QUICK-COOK RECIPE / MAKES 4 TO 6 SERVINGS

Panzanella is a Tuscan classic that makes use of stale leftover bread, marrying it with a few seasonal garden vegetables and a simple dressing of oil and vinegar. Substituting nutty-tasting farro for the bread makes the dish more complex. Purslane, a succulent wild green with a slight lemon flavor, is much beloved in the Mediterranean. It is packed with iron and other nutrients. Purslane is sold at farmers' markets in the summer months. When it is hard to come by, I substitute arugula.

   8 ounces purslane or arugula, thick stems discarded

   1 pint farmstand cherry tomatoes or grape tomatoes, halved or quartered if large

   1 medium cucumber, peeled if thick-skinned, halved lengthwise and sliced thinly on the bias into long half-moons

   5 radishes, thinly sliced

   2 scallions, thinly sliced on the bias

   ¼ cup plus 2 tablespoons extra-virgin olive oil

   2 tablespoons red wine vinegar

   2 teaspoons fine sea salt

   1 cup farro (see page 13)

   1 cup packed fresh basil leaves

      Coarsely ground black pepper

Bring a medium saucepan of salted water to a boil.

Toss together purslane, tomatoes, cucumber, radishes, and scallions in a large bowl. Add oil, vinegar, and salt and toss just to combine.

Add farro to boiling water and cook until tender but still firm to the bite, 10 to 15 minutes. Drain and spread on a baking sheet to cool to room temperature.

Add cooled farro and basil leaves to vegetable mixture; toss just to combine. Add pepper to taste, toss again, and serve.

FATTOUCHE (LEBANESE SALAD WITH PITA)

QUICK-COOK RECIPE / MAKES 4 SERVINGS

Essentially a Lebanese *panzanella*, *fattouche* is made with pita bread instead of a Tuscan loaf, lemon instead of vinegar, and lots of garlic and sumac. This is one of those dishes my family enjoyed when we lived in Lebanon—and forever after. The garlic-lemon dressing is the first recipe I learned to make as a child, taught to me by my mother. I made it so often that it became an official part of my chore list.

FLAVOR TIP: Sumac, a fine powder of the dried berries of a sumac tree, is a classic Lebanese seasoning that offers a wonderful astringency and color. If necessary, you can omit it, but it is worth tracking down (see Sources, page 357).

1	garlic clove, peeled
1	teaspoon coarse sea salt
1	tablespoon fresh lemon juice
3	tablespoons extra-virgin olive oil
1	large cucumber, peeled, quartered lengthwise, and cut into 1/2-inch wedges
1	bunch small radishes, quartered
1	large ripe tomato, cut into 3/4-inch cubes
1	pita bread, toasted and broken into small pieces
2	scallions, thinly sliced
12	ounces romaine hearts, washed and torn into pieces
1	teaspoon sumac (see Tip)

Crush garlic with the side of a chef's knife. In a salad bowl (ideally wooden), using the back of a wooden spoon, mash garlic with salt until you have a paste. Add lemon juice and stir together well. Whisk in oil.

Add cucumber, radishes, tomato, pita pieces, and scallions. Toss and let stand for 5 minutes so that bread softens and vegetables marinate a bit.

Add romaine, sprinkle with sumac, toss, and serve.

GREEN BEANS WITH SHAVED ONION, FRIED ALMONDS, AND PARMIGIANO-REGGIANO

QUICK-COOK RECIPE / MAKES 4 SERVINGS

Fresh-picked green beans are sublime and very different from not so fresh. In this dish, the onion is cooked just enough by the warmth of the beans to soften and sweeten its sharp piquancy. Even the cheese is transformed, as the warmth of the beans encourages it to give up its earthy tones to the dish.

You can vary this dish in many ways. Try adding torn basil or other herb leaves, using scallions in place of the onion, or substituting Manchego cheese or Queso Iberico for the Parmesan.

FLAVOR TIP: One of the simplest and best cooking techniques I learned in Italy is to toss vegetables just pulled from the oven or a pot of boiling water with a healthy pour of good extra-virgin olive oil. The heat of the vegetable brings out the perfume of the oil, allowing flavors to mingle in a way completely different from when a cold vegetable is dressed.

- 1/4 cup plus 2 tablespoons extra-virgin olive oil
- 1/2 cup whole raw almonds
- 1 teaspoon fleur de sel or other medium-coarse sea salt
- 1 pound green beans, trimmed
- 5 ounces Parmigiano-Reggiano cheese, any rind removed, cut into 1/3- to 1/2-inch irregular chunks
- 1 small red onion, thinly sliced or shaved on a mandoline or vegetable slicer
- 1/2 cup loosely packed fresh flat-leaf parsley leaves

Heat 2 tablespoons oil in a small skillet over medium heat. Add almonds and cook, shaking pan back and forth occasionally, until nuts are golden and start to pop, about 4 minutes. Remove from heat, sprinkle with 1/2 teaspoon salt, and stir. Remove nuts from oil with a slotted spoon and drain on paper towels, then coarsely chop.

Bring a large saucepan of well-salted water to a boil. Add beans and cook until crisp-tender, about 5 minutes. Drain, transfer to a large bowl, and immediately toss beans with remaining 1/4 cup oil and 1/2 teaspoon salt.

Add cheese, onion, and parsley; toss well. Let sit for a few minutes, then toss with almonds and serve.

BEET, ARUGULA, AND CUCUMBER SALAD
WITH YOGURT DRESSING

QUICK-COOK RECIPE / MAKES 4 SERVINGS

This salad is an extrapolation of the classic eastern Mediterranean dip made from yogurt, mint, and cucumbers, Greek *tzatziki* or Turkish *cacik*. I love the warm roasted beets with the cool, refreshing cucumber. The arugula acts as both an herb and a leafy green, adding a peppery bite that's the perfect foil for the tanginess of the yogurt. Enjoy this dish on its own or put it on the table *mezze*-style with other salads and small plates.

3	medium beets
6	tablespoons extra-virgin olive oil
	Fine sea salt
1/4	cup plain nonfat yogurt
1	tablespoon red wine vinegar
1	garlic clove, thinly sliced
	Coarsely ground black pepper
1	large bunch arugula, washed and torn
1	cucumber, peeled, halved lengthwise, seeded, and cut into 1/4-inch half-moons

Heat oven to 400°F.

Place beets in a baking dish with 1 inch water; drizzle with 1 tablespoon oil and sprinkle with salt. Cover tightly with foil and bake until tender, 45 minutes to an hour. Remove beets from oven, drain, and let cool slightly, then peel and cut into eighths.

While beets are cooking, whisk together remaining 5 tablespoons oil, yogurt, vinegar, and garlic in a large bowl. Add 2 or 3 drops of warm water to smooth and emulsify dressing if needed. Season with salt and pepper.

Add beets, arugula, and cucumber to dressing and toss gently. Season with salt and pepper to taste, and serve.

ORANGE AND MINT LEAF SALAD
WITH ROASTED BEETS

QUICK-COOK RECIPE / MAKES 4 SERVINGS

Roasted beets and mint is a classic Pugliese dish; the oranges make it mine. I use blood oranges because they are tarter than other varieties. If you can't find them, use regular oranges and add a little lemon juice to the dressing. For an easy variation, add a little feta cheese. The sweet, tart flavors of this dish make it a comforting hearty winter salad or small plate.

- 9 medium red beets
- 4 tablespoons extra-virgin olive oil
- Fine sea salt
- 4 blood oranges (see headnote)
- 1 small red onion, thinly sliced
- 1 cup loosely packed fresh mint leaves
- 1 teaspoon mild white wine vinegar
- Coarsely ground black pepper

Heat oven to 400°F.

Place beets in a baking dish with 1 inch water; drizzle with 1 tablespoon oil and sprinkle with salt. Cover tightly with foil and bake until tender, 45 minutes to an hour.

While beets are cooking, using a sharp paring knife, trim off tops and bottoms of oranges. Stand each fruit on end and carefully cut peel and pith from flesh, following curve of fruit from top to bottom. Trim away any remaining pith. Cut each section away from membranes, cutting as close to membranes as you can, and place in a large bowl.

When they are tender, remove beets from oven, drain, and let cool slightly.

While beets are cooling, add onion and a pinch of salt to oranges and toss gently to combine. Let stand for 10 minutes.

While they are still warm, peel beets and cut into quarters. Add warm beets, mint, remaining 3 tablespoons oil, and vinegar to oranges and gently toss to combine. Season with salt and pepper to taste, and serve.

SMOKED TROUT SALAD
WITH SPICY ARUGULA AND GRAPEFRUIT

QUICK-COOK RECIPE / MAKES 4 SERVINGS

Greens and a tangy lemon dressing are a great complement to salty smoked fish. Here arugula adds a little bite, and the grapefruit brings another acidic element into play.

FLAVOR TIP: Try using a mandoline to (carefully) slice the shallot as thin as possible. As with any onion, the thinner you slice it, the sweeter and less sharp the flavor.

- 1 tablespoon Dijon mustard
- 1 tablespoon red wine vinegar
- 1 tablespoon fresh lemon juice
- 1 large shallot, thinly sliced (see Tip)
- 1 garlic clove, cut into fine julienne
- Fine sea salt and coarsely ground black pepper
- 1 pink grapefruit
- 1/3 cup extra-virgin olive oil
- 8 ounces smoked trout, flaked into small pieces
- 2 bunches arugula, washed and torn
- 1/2 small red onion, very thinly sliced

Whisk together mustard, vinegar, lemon juice, shallot, garlic, 1/2 teaspoon salt, and 1/8 teaspoon pepper; let sit for 10 minutes.

Meanwhile, using a sharp paring knife, trim off top and bottom of grapefruit. Stand fruit on end and carefully cut peel and pith from flesh, following curve of fruit from top to bottom. Trim away any remaining pith. Cut each section away from membranes, cutting as close to membranes as you can, and place in a medium bowl.

Whisk oil into vinegar mixture in a slow, steady stream.

Add trout, arugula, and onion to grapefruit and toss gently. Add dressing and toss to combine. Season to taste with salt and pepper, and serve.

"DIRTY" SQUID WITH WATERCRESS

QUICK- COOK RECIPE / MAKES 4 SERVINGS

"Dirty" is what I call squid that still has its deep purplish thin outer skin. Spaniards prize it for the rich flavor it adds. This hearty salad could be a light dinner on its own. If you want to serve it as part of a larger meal, bracket it with simpler one-note dishes, such as Slow-Cooked Cannellini Beans (page 42) and Vellutata di Carote (Velvety Carrot Soup; page 111). A good fishmonger should be able to procure "dirty" squid, and you can also get it in Chinatown.

FLAVOR TIP: Slowly braising squid makes it tender. Searing it gives a nice crisp edge.

2 bunches watercress or arugula, washed and thick stems discarded

2 pounds squid with its outer purple skin (see headnote)

Fine sea salt and coarsely ground black pepper

1/2–1 cup water

5 tablespoons extra-virgin olive oil

2 garlic cloves, thinly sliced

2 tablespoons fresh lemon juice

1 tablespoon harissa (see page 16)

Place greens in a large bowl. Set aside.

Separate squid bodies from tentacles and remove quills and beaks. Season squid with salt and pepper. Put squid and ½ cup water in a large skillet and bring to a simmer over medium-high heat, then reduce heat and cook at a gentle simmer, stirring occasionally, until squid is tender, about 20 minutes; add more water if necessary so liquid comes halfway up squid.

Using a slotted spoon, transfer squid to a cutting board. Increase heat to high and cook until pan juices are thick, syrupy, and reduced to about 3 tablespoons. Remove from heat and set aside.

While juices are reducing, slice squid bodies into 1-inch-wide rings or ribbons if large (if small, leave whole). Slice large tentacles in half.

In another large skillet, heat 2 tablespoons oil over high heat. Add squid pieces in a single layer and cook until golden and crisp on underside, about 5 minutes. Transfer to bowl with greens.

Add garlic and 1 tablespoon oil to skillet, reduce heat to medium-low, and cook until garlic is golden, about 2 minutes. Remove pan from heat, whisk in lemon juice, harissa, remaining 2 tablespoons oil, and squid pan juices. Add to greens and squid, toss, and serve.

FLANK STEAK SALAD WITH FARRO, ARUGULA, AND FRESH HORSERADISH

QUICK-COOK RECIPE / MAKES 4 TO 6 SERVINGS

The warmth of just-cooked farro and grilled steak wilts the greens a bit and releases the perfume of the olive oil. The bite of the fresh-grated horseradish and arugula is a notable contrast to the richness of the meat and, as is often the case, the tang of lemon lends a fresh brightness and pulls all the flavors together. You can substitute watercress for the arugula, or lentils for the farro, and you could certainly grill the steaks over charcoal. You can also use any cut of steak, cooked medium-rare and thinly sliced. If radish sprouts are not available, bump up the arugula a bit.

FLAVOR TIP: The juices released from the meat, which become part of the dressing, are a key element here, as is fresh horseradish.

- 6 large radishes, cut into thin matchsticks
- 1 cup radish sprouts (optional; see headnote)
- 5 tablespoons extra-virgin olive oil
- 8 ounces flank steak
  Fleur de sel or other medium-coarse sea salt
  Coarsely ground black pepper
- 1 cup farro (see page 13)
- 1 small bunch arugula, washed and torn
  Juice of 1 lemon (about 2½ tablespoons)
- 2 tablespoons freshly grated horseradish

Mix together radishes and radish sprouts in a large bowl.

Heat a grill pan or large cast-iron skillet over medium-high heat. Brush with 2 tablespoons oil, then add steak and brown for 4 to 5 minutes. Season with salt and pepper, turn, and season other side. Cook for about 5 minutes more for medium-rare. Transfer steak to a plate or a carving board with a moat (so that you can collect the juices that will be released) and let rest for 5 minutes.

While steak is cooking and resting, bring a medium saucepan of salted water to a boil. Add farro and cook until just tender but still firm to the bite, about 10 minutes. Drain (do not rinse).

Slice steak into ¼-inch-thick pieces on the bias. Add steak, warm farro, and reserved meat juices to radish mixture, then add arugula, remaining 3 tablespoons olive oil, lemon juice, horseradish, and a pinch or two of salt. Toss well to distribute the horseradish evenly. Season to taste with pepper and with more salt if desired, and serve at once.

SOUP

Odd as it may sound to most Americans, soup is my favorite dish to eat for breakfast. I lightly brown a little garlic in olive oil in a small saucepan and add some chopped cooking greens; a scoop of leftover beans, chickpeas, or lentils; and a ladleful of homemade chicken stock. Once it's heated through, I finish it with a squirt of lemon or lime juice, a drizzle of olive oil, and maybe a sprinkle of Aleppo pepper or slivered fresh hot chili. Poured over a thick piece of grilled bread or eaten just as is, this nutritious dish is an energy booster at any time.

Whenever I make soup—whether it's a simple Vellutata di Carote (Velvety Carrot Soup), a hearty Farro and Kale Soup, or a refreshing summer gazpacho made by blending raw fruits or vegetables with olive oil and yogurt and a small spoonful of heady vinegar—layering the flavors in steps is key. Many Italian dishes begin with a *battuto,* usually a mixture of finely minced onions, celery, and carrot. The ingredients I choose for my *battuto* lay the foundation for the rest of the soup. A simple mix of onions, garlic, and parsley, for example, is a light-tasting base on which to build a delicate broth or fish stew. Add bits of prosciutto fat, celery, leek, carrot, and rosemary, and you have an appropriate beginning to a more hearty grain and greens soup.

Once the *battuto* has cooked, I begin to put in the other ingredients, depending on how much cooking time they require, adding the longer-cooking ingredients first and working from there. I give the soup just enough liquid (water or broth) to cover the vegetables but not drown them. By slowly, gently poaching vegetables, you bring out their sweetness, which also helps to build flavor. A touch of an acidic ingredient, like vinegar or fresh lemon or lime juice, will add subtle depth when stirred into a soup while it is cooking, and a fresh zing if drizzled in just before serving.

Although homemade broths are great to have on hand for certain soups like Parmesan Broth with Pea Shoots, not all soups need them. You can make an amazing soup with little more than potato, celery, and leeks, using just water. In fact, water-based soups are much tastier than ruining your fresh vegetables and herbs with commercial broths. The gentle, slow cooking of the vegetables allows the water to become concentrated with flavor, similar to what occurs when you make broth. To add richness, simply add a little cream or drop in an egg and poach it before serving. Ingredients like olive oil, salt, and chili pepper added at the finish lift and intensify the soup. Skip this step, and you'll miss a big part of the flavor.

Once you learn a few techniques, you'll start to think of soup as a spontaneous, flexible dish. Last night's Slow-Cooked Cannellini Beans, for example, can be brightened with a bit of olive oil, slivered garlic, fresh rosemary, and a little broth or water, then pureed and served garnished with a dash more oil, freshly grated Parmesan, coarsely ground black pepper, and coarse sea salt—a perfect and perfectly easy soup (and a good excuse for making a double batch of beans). Flexibility reigns when you make Ribollita, a Tuscan vegetable and bread soup that can be comprised of all sorts of root vegetables in all kinds of variations.

This chapter begins with elemental soups—many of which can be enjoyed as a first course or light main course or served in tiny cups or glasses at the beginning of a meal—and then moves on to more complex combinations and heartier soups. Made with nutrient-rich grains and legumes, these can easily serve as a whole meal, with a good hunk of bread, a few nice cheeses, and a favorite bottle of wine.

SOUP

White Almond Gazpacho | 104

Cantaloupe Gazpacho
with Jamón Serrano | 106

Rich Chicken Broth | 108

Green Garlic Soup | 110

Vellutata di Carote
(Velvety Carrot Soup) | 111

Turnip, Apple, and
Jerusalem Artichoke Soup | 113

Sweet Pumpkin and Rice Bean
Soup with Crème Fraîche and
Crispy Seeds | 114

Parmesan Broth
with Pea Shoots | 117

Ribollita
(Tuscan-Style
Vegetable and
Bread Soup) | 118

Cabbage and
Chickpea Soup | 121

Lentil Soup | 123

White Bean Soup
with Ramps | 124

Rich Chicken Soup
with Greens | 126

Potato, Celery, and
Leek Soup | 129

Farro and Kale Soup | 130

WHITE ALMOND GAZPACHO

QUICK-COOK RECIPE / MAKES 4 TO 6 SERVINGS

Although almonds in a soup may seem unusual, the result is delicious. The nuts provide mellow flavor and also act as an emulsifier. Thick, rich, and quite garlicky, white gazpacho is often enjoyed at the midday meal on hot summer days in Spain, followed by a nice long siesta. The traditional garnish is peeled grapes, but when I can find gooseberries, I use them. Sweet and tart, with a flavor slightly reminiscent of raspberries, gooseberries show up in farmers' markets and some specialty markets in midsummer. Although I like the soup so thick you can stand a spoon up in it, you can add extra ice water to thin it to your liking.

- 1 cup blanched almonds
- 2 garlic cloves
- 2 cups plus 2 tablespoons ice water
- 2 tablespoons sherry vinegar
- 3/4 teaspoon fine sea salt
- 2 1/2-inch-thick slices stale bread, cut into 1/2-inch cubes (2 cups)
- 1 cup extra-virgin olive oil, plus more for drizzling
- 1 cup gooseberries or peeled green or red grapes (optional)

Finely chop almonds and garlic in a blender. With motor running, slowly add 1 cup water, sherry vinegar, and salt, blending to incorporate. Add bread in 2 batches, blending well (some of the bread will not be entirely incorporated until the next step; this is okay). With motor running, slowly add 1/2 cup oil, followed by remaining 1 cup plus 2 tablespoons water, followed by remaining 1/2 cup oil.

Transfer to a bowl, cover, and chill in the refrigerator for at least 2 hours.

Serve in individual bowls, sprinkled with gooseberries, if using, and drizzled with oil.

CANTALOUPE GAZPACHO WITH JAMÓN SERRANO

QUICK-COOK RECIPE / MAKES 6 SERVINGS

Sweet cantaloupe served with salty cured prosciutto is a classic Italian appetizer. Thinking of Spain's traditional tomato gazpacho, which is garnished with little batons of jamón and other good things, I came up with this Italian-inspired variation. Serve it as a light midday meal or in little glasses as the opener to a nice lunch or dinner.

FLAVOR TIP: It's important to cut the ham into thick strips (think squared-match-stick size). The subtle flavor of thinly sliced ham would get lost in the soup.

1 cantaloupe (2³/₄–3 pounds), peeled, seeded, and cubed
1 medium cucumber, peeled, halved lengthwise, and seeded
1 cup plain low-fat yogurt
3 tablespoons sherry vinegar
1 tablespoon minced shallot
¹/₂ teaspoon fine sea salt
1 cup extra-virgin olive oil, plus more for drizzling
1 ¹/₈-inch-thick slice serrano ham or prosciutto, cut into short matchsticks
   Aleppo pepper (see page 16) or coarsely ground black pepper

Puree melon and cucumber in a blender. Transfer half of mixture to a large bowl.

Add yogurt, vinegar, shallot, and salt to blender and puree until combined. With motor running, add oil in a slow, steady stream. Whisk into melon mixture in bowl. Cover and chill in the refrigerator for at least 3 hours or up to 1 day.

Before serving, stir gazpacho well and adjust seasonings if necessary. Serve topped with ham, a drizzle of oil, and a sprinkling of pepper.

RICH CHICKEN BROTH

SLOW-COOK RECIPE / MAKES ABOUT 4½ QUARTS

The older the chicken, the better the broth. If you can find a stewing or soup chicken, by all means go ahead and use that. Otherwise, two small chickens will do just fine.

FLAVOR TIP: Leaving the skin on the onion and garlic and browning all the vegetables well to pull out their sugars adds golden color and deeper flavor.

¼ cup extra-virgin olive oil

5 medium carrots, coarsely chopped

4 celery stalks, coarsely chopped

1 large unpeeled onion, cut into eighths

1 head garlic, cut horizontally in half

1 7- to 7½-pound soup chicken, cut into 8 parts, or 2 small chickens, cut into 8 parts each, plus neck(s)

1 large bunch flat-leaf parsley

1 leafy fresh savory or thyme sprig (optional)

1 cup dry white wine

About 4½ quarts water

Heat oil in a large stockpot over high heat. Add carrots, celery, onion, and garlic and cook, stirring occasionally, until vegetables are browned, about 8 minutes. Add chicken, parsley, savory (if using), and wine, then add water to just barely cover the chicken and vegetables, about 3 quarts. Reduce heat to medium-low. When broth comes to a bare simmer, add 2 more cups cold water and reduce heat to low.

Allow broth to cook away at a very slight simmer, checking every half hour or so to skim foam and fat and add water as needed to just barely cover the chicken and vegetables, until stock is very rich, about 4 hours. Remove pot from heat and strain broth. Store in the refrigerator for up to 3 days or in the freezer for up to 6 months.

RICH CHICKEN BROTH

If you've got some homemade broth tucked away in the freezer, a soup or risotto is never very far away. I like to make chicken broth on a rainy Sunday afternoon, using either a whole chicken or leftover meat and bones from a roast chicken or goose. Since it doesn't require much supervision, I can while away the time reading the Sunday paper or flipping through cookbooks as the broth slowly simmers. Once it's made, strained, and cooled, I pack it into quart or half-quart containers, label, and stow it away in the freezer.

My basic rules for a truly rich chicken broth are (1) Add only enough water at any one time to just cover the bones and the vegetables. (2) Never let the broth come above a bare (I mean *very slight*) simmer: a few bubbles should just barely rise slowly from the bottom of the liquid to the top. (3) Skim religiously (this helps keep the broth clear and clean-tasting). (4) Gently simmer the broth for a minimum of 4 hours. (5) Never add salt, because you don't know how you'll be using the broth in the future—you may want to put in other salty ingredients, like cheese, anchovies, capers, and olives, later.

There are a couple of different ways to defat the broth. The easiest is to chill the finished broth for several hours. During this time, the fat will congeal on the surface; you can then simply remove it with a spoon. A quicker way, though you may end up leaving a bit of fat in the pot (which is fine), is to gently lower a large shallow spoon to just barely below the surface of the warm soup and then tip the spoon slightly inward, allowing the fat to flow slowly in, and discard the fat. Don't be discouraged if your technique is a little sloppy at first, and you seem to be re-moving more soup than fat. The process requires a soft touch and may take a few practice tries. Skim until you are satisfied with how much fat you've removed. Since fat contains a tremendous amount of flavor, leaving some behind as droplets in your broth is akin to drizzling a little olive oil or sprinkling a bit of cheese into it.

That's it. A few ingredients and a little attention and time, and you have a broth that can't be equaled.

GREEN GARLIC SOUP

QUICK-COOK RECIPE / MAKES 6 SERVINGS

At outdoor markets in Italy and at New York City's Union Square farmers' market, where I do much of my shopping, young "green" garlic makes a much-anticipated though short-lived appearance in the early spring. It's mild, and you can use both the bulb and a good part of the stalk rather than just the cloves. The tender bulb does not need to be peeled. I prefer this *vellutata* on the thick side, but you can thin this with water as you wish.

1½	pounds green garlic (about 15 stalks)
2	tablespoons unsalted butter
2	tablespoons extra-virgin olive oil, plus more for drizzling
¾	teaspoon fine sea salt
3½–4	cups water
1¼	pounds Yukon Gold potatoes (about 2 large), peeled and cut into ¼-inch cubes
	Freshly grated Parmigiano-Reggiano cheese
	Coarsely ground black pepper

Chop off and discard all but 5 inches of garlic stalks. Cut remaining stalks into ⅓-inch pieces. Split bulbs lengthwise in half and cut into ⅓-inch-thick slices.

Heat butter and oil in a large Dutch oven or other heavy pot over medium heat until butter is melted. Add garlic and salt, stir, and cook for 1 minute. Add ½ cup water, reduce heat to low, cover, and cook, stirring once halfway through, until garlic is softened, about 10 minutes.

Add potatoes and 3 cups more water; stir. Cover and continue to cook over low heat until potatoes are tender, about 45 minutes.

Puree soup in a blender until smooth. Thin with extra water if desired, then reheat. Serve garnished with grated Parmesan cheese, a drizzle of olive oil, and a sprinkling of pepper.

VELLUTATA DI CAROTE (VELVETY CARROT SOUP)

SLOW-COOK RECIPE / MAKES 4 SERVINGS

Cooking carrots with onions highlights the sweet taste of both vegetables, and lovage, which is a little bitter, adds contrast. If you can't find lovage, you can use the pale green leaves from the center of a bunch of celery instead. Drizzle the soup with extra-virgin olive oil or add a bit of cream or a swirl of crème fraîche at the finish for a hint of richness, if you like.

- 2 tablespoons extra-virgin olive oil, plus more for drizzling
- 2 tablespoons unsalted butter
- 1³/₄ pounds carrots (2 large bunches), coarsely chopped
- Medium-coarse sea salt
- 1 small onion, finely chopped
- 1 medium Yukon Gold potato, peeled and coarsely chopped
- 1 tablespoon lovage leaves or 2 tablespoons tender celery leaves, finely sliced
- Coarsely ground black pepper

VELLUTATA

"Velvety" is the literal translation of *vellutata*—the Italian term for the smooth vegetable puree whose variations seem limitless. This soup, Green Garlic Soup (opposite page), and Turnip, Apple, and Jerusalem Artichoke Soup (page 113) are all examples of this style, and they build from the most straightforward in flavor and texture to a more complex version. The fresher and more local your produce, the more delicious the soup. Adding a little cooked potato to a *vellutata* is a classic Italian technique that gives it extra smoothness.

Heat oil and butter in a large saucepan over medium-high heat until butter is melted. Add carrots and a pinch of salt and cook, stirring occasionally, until carrots begin to take on a little color, about 10 minutes. Add onion and another pinch of salt. Reduce heat to medium-low and cook until onion becomes translucent, 6 to 8 minutes.

Add potato and enough cold water to come to just below top of vegetables. Bring to a boil, then reduce to a very gentle simmer and cook, stirring occasionally and adding water as necessary to maintain the same level of liquid, until vegetables are very tender and beginning to fall apart, about 50 minutes.

Puree mixture in a blender and season with salt to taste. If you like your soup a bit thinner, add more water little by little until you reach desired consistency; adjust salt if necessary.

Ladle soup into bowls and garnish with lovage leaves, a drizzle of extra-virgin olive oil, and a sprinkling of salt and pepper.

TURNIP, APPLE, AND JERUSALEM ARTICHOKE SOUP

SLOW-COOK RECIPE / MAKES 6 TO 8 SERVINGS

Sweet and bitter at once, turnips lend themselves to many different preparations raw or cooked. Though good in summer, they show their best flavor when fresh-dug in the early fall and winter months. Here they are paired with apple and Jerusalem artichoke—a gnarled, potato-like tuber that has a mild artichoke flavor.

- 1 leek, trimmed
- 1 small onion, coarsely chopped
- 1 garlic clove
- ¼ cup extra-virgin olive oil, plus more for drizzling
  Medium-coarse sea salt
- 2½ cups water
- 2½ pounds turnips, peeled and diced
- 1¼ pounds Jerusalem artichokes, peeled and diced
- 2 tart apples, peeled, cored, and diced
  Coarsely ground black pepper or Aleppo pepper (see page 16)

Cut leek lengthwise in half and rinse well. Finely chop leek together with onion and garlic.

Heat oil in a large Dutch oven or other heavy pot over medium heat. Add leek mixture and cook, stirring occasionally, until vegetables begin to soften, about 3 minutes. Add a pinch of salt and ½ cup water. Bring to a gentle simmer, reduce heat to medium-low, and cook until water is almost completely evaporated, about 15 minutes.

Add turnips, artichokes, and remaining 2 cups water. Cover and simmer until vegetables are very tender, about 1 hour and 20 minutes.

Add apples and a generous pinch of salt to pot, cover, and simmer until apples are soft and flavors have blended, about 30 minutes more.

Puree soup in batches in a blender until smooth. Add salt to taste. Serve drizzled with oil and sprinkled with pepper and coarse salt.

SWEET PUMPKIN AND RICE BEAN SOUP WITH CRÈME FRAÎCHE AND CRISPY SEEDS

SLOW-COOK RECIPE / MAKES 6 SERVINGS

Pumpkin soup on its own is a little rich. Small white rice beans at once cut the richness of the pumpkin and add a pleasing textural contrast (cannellini beans, though larger, can be substituted). My favorite pumpkin is kabocha, a Japanese variety also called Japanese pumpkin or kabocha squash. It has sweet, dry, dense orange flesh that makes for a voluptuous soup. You could also try buttercup squash. In the Tuscan manner of letting nothing go to waste, I like to use the seeds as a crisp, salty contrast to the smooth soup.

NOTES: White rice beans, Southeast Asian in origin, are shaped like long-grain rice but are much wider. They do not need to be soaked before using, but when I have time, I do soak them, covered by 2 inches of water, for 1 to 2 hours (drain and discard the water before cooking). They seem to cook more evenly and a little faster this way, but you'll still have a great soup without the soak.

To remove the pulp from the pumpkin seeds easily, place them in a bowl and fill it with water. Using your fingers, separate the seeds from the pulp, removing the larger pieces of pulp as you go. Drain, discard any remaining pulp, and pat the seeds dry.

- 1 cup white rice beans (6 ounces; see Notes; see Sources, page 357)
- 2 unpeeled garlic cloves
- 1 celery stalk, cut into 3 pieces
- 1 unpeeled shallot, cut in half
- 1/2 teaspoon black peppercorns
- 1 3¼- to 3½-pound Japanese pumpkin (kabocha squash)
- 1/4 cup plus 2 tablespoons extra-virgin olive oil
- 4 tablespoons (½ stick) unsalted butter
- 1 tablespoon coarse sea salt, plus more for sprinkling
- 1 small onion, finely chopped
- 2 cups water
  Crème fraîche
  Coarsely ground black pepper

Rinse beans and place in a medium saucepan with garlic, celery, shallot, and peppercorns. Cover with water by 2 inches, place over medium-low heat, and slowly bring to a very gentle simmer; this will take about 30 minutes. Simmer gently until beans are tender, about 45 minutes more, depending on age of beans (older beans require a longer cooking time). Drain beans, reserving cooking liquid. Discard aromatics.

While beans are cooking, peel squash. Remove and reserve seeds, and cut flesh into 1-inch pieces. Heat ¼ cup oil and 2 tablespoons butter in a large Dutch oven or other heavy pot over high heat until butter is melted. Add squash and cook, stirring occasionally, for 5 minutes. Add 1 teaspoon salt and continue to cook until squash begins to color, about 5 minutes more.

Push squash to one side of pot, add remaining 2 tablespoons butter and onion, and let onion cook in butter for 1 minute. Stir squash and onion together. Add water and bring to a simmer, then reduce heat to medium-low, cover, and cook until squash is beginning to soften, 15 to 18 minutes. Remove lid and continue cooking until squash is completely tender, about 12 minutes more. Remove from heat, and puree in a blender until smooth.

While squash is cooking, prepare seeds. Heat oven to 350°F.

Remove squash pulp from seeds (see Notes) and toss seeds with remaining 2 tablespoons oil and 1 teaspoon salt. Spread seeds on a baking sheet and bake, stirring occasionally, until golden, 18 to 20 minutes. Remove from oven and let cool.

Return pureed soup to rinsed-out pot and add cooked beans plus 1 to 1½ cups reserved cooking liquid, to thin soup to your liking. Add remaining 1 teaspoon salt, stir to combine, and set over medium heat to heat through, stirring occasionally.

Serve soup hot with a dollop of crème fraîche swirled in and a sprinkling of crispy seeds, salt, and pepper.

PARMESAN BROTH WITH PEA SHOOTS

SLOW-COOK RECIPE / MAKES 4 TO 6 SERVINGS

Growing up, whenever I ate tortellini or pasta in broth in Italy, I wondered why the broth tasted so wonderfully cheesy. Then I learned that the Italians save their Parmesan rinds and use them to add richness.

If you have cheese rinds and some homemade chicken broth on hand, this soup is very easy to assemble. It's amazing how the rinds build the broth into a unique soup. Serve this as an elegant opener to a meal or add a little cooked pasta or rice to make a light summer supper.

Look for baby pea shoots at the farmers' market or a good grocer. The larger ones you find at Asian markets work well too, but they need to simmer in the broth for a minute or two longer, until tender.

FLAVOR TIP: As you use up hunks of Parmesan cheese, put the rinds in a sealed bag in the freezer; they add flavor to broths and soups (remove them before serving).

    8 cups Rich Chicken Broth (page 108)
    8 ounces Parmigiano-Reggiano rinds
    4 cups loosely packed pea shoots (3 ounces), preferably baby-sized
       Fleur de sel or other medium-coarse sea salt
    1 lemon
       Coarsely ground black pepper

Combine broth and rinds in a saucepan and slowly bring to a very slight simmer over medium-low heat. Reduce heat to low (you want the liquid just barely bubbling up from the bottom) and simmer very gently until broth is reduced to 6 cups, about 2 hours.

Strain broth and discard rinds. You can refrigerate broth for up to 3 days or freeze for up to 4 months.

When you are ready to serve, bring broth to a simmer, just to heat through; immediately remove from heat. Divide pea shoots among bowls, sprinkle with a pinch of salt, and top with broth. Finely grate a bit of lemon zest over each bowl, add a few grinds of pepper, and serve immediately.

RIBOLLITA
(TUSCAN-STYLE VEGETABLE
AND BREAD SOUP)

SLOW-COOK RECIPE / MAKES 8 TO 10 SERVINGS

This classic soup is more complex in flavor than most Tuscan dishes. Traditionally, *ribollita*—a true farmhouse dish—is enjoyed as a three-day affair: a thick vegetable soup is served on the first day, then bread is added to extend the soup on the second day, and finally it is reheated slowly in a skillet on the third day so the bread forms a crust to create a "crispy soup." The flavors build and deepen as the days progress. In this version, the bread is added immediately after the vegetables are cooked so it softens in the soup, a fair amount of olive oil is stirred in, and the bread blends with the vegetables.

Many recipes for *ribollita* call for canned tomatoes, but I prefer to limit the tomato to just a little bit of paste and let the flavors of the root vegetables and the sweetness of the beans shine through. Since this soup requires more effort than many of the others here, I make a large batch to share with friends or to have leftovers to enjoy "crispy" later in the week.

The soup is a great one for varying. I put in as many different root vegetables as possible, although you could also make it with just kale, a little pumpkin, potato, and beans. Try to keep an equal balance between sweet root vegetables (like carrots and parsnips) and bitter ones (such as celery root, turnips, and rutabaga). Parsley root, from a vegetable that is a cousin of common parsley, has the same texture as parsnips but an earthier flavor. It can be found at farmers' markets in fall and winter. The greens can change too; keep a balance between firm, tough greens (such as cabbage, kale, and mustard greens) and more tender ones (escarole, chicory, and Swiss chard). If lacinato kale (aka Tuscan kale, cavolo nero, or dinosaur kale) is available, use it.

NOTE: Start the beans soaking the night before.

FLAVOR TIP: If you have leftovers and want to try "crispy soup," heat a bit of olive oil in a nonstick skillet, add 1 or 2 servings of soup, and let cook gently, uncovered, over the lowest possible heat until a crispy crust is formed on the bottom. This will take about 30 minutes.

1 cup dried white beans (6 ounces)

About 8 cups water

4 unpeeled garlic cloves

1 fresh sage sprig

3/4 cup extra-virgin olive oil, plus more for drizzling

2 celery stalks, finely chopped

1 medium carrot, finely chopped

1 small onion, finely chopped

1 leek, trimmed, rinsed, and finely chopped

Medium-coarse sea salt

5 cups cubed mixed Yukon Gold potatoes, turnips, parsnips, and celery root or parsley root (see headnote)

2 teaspoons tomato paste, preferably double-concentrate (see page 19)

5 cups chopped sturdy greens, such as stemmed regular kale or lacinato kale, or 4 cups chopped Savoy cabbage

8 cups torn tender cooking greens, such as chicory, escarole, dandelion, and/or Swiss chard

8 ounces stale thick slices of bread, cubed (about 4 cups) and lightly toasted

Coarsely ground black pepper

Rinse beans well and transfer to a medium saucepan. Add 2 cups water, 3 garlic cloves, and sage and soak overnight.

Set pan of beans over medium-low heat and cook at a bare simmer, adding water by the ½ cupful as necessary to keep liquid just covering beans, until beans are tender, about 2 hours. Remove from heat, and remove garlic cloves; let them cool slightly.

When garlic is cool enough to handle, squeeze pulp into beans and bean liquid; stir to combine. Discard sage.

Smash and peel remaining garlic clove. Heat ¼ cup oil in a large Dutch oven or other heavy pot over medium-low heat. Add garlic clove, celery, carrot, onion, leek, and a pinch of salt and stir to combine. Cook, stirring occasionally, until vegetables begin to soften, about 5 minutes. Add ½ cup water, increase heat to medium-high, and cook until water is almost evaporated, about 5 minutes.

Add potatoes and other root vegetables and enough water to just cover vegetables (about 4 cups). Add tomato paste and stir to dissolve. Bring to a gentle simmer and cook until vegetables are very tender, about 45 minutes.

Add sturdy greens and simmer until just tender, about 15 minutes. Add tender greens and cook until all greens are tender, about 5 minutes more. Add beans and their liquid, stir to combine, and cook until heated through.

Remove from heat, add bread, stir, and let sit until bread is softened, about 5 minutes.

Add remaining ½ cup oil, whisking well to break up bread so that it blends into soup, and season with salt to taste. Serve hot, drizzled with oil and sprinkled with salt and pepper to taste.

CABBAGE AND CHICKPEA SOUP

SLOW-COOK RECIPE / MAKES 8 SERVINGS

Careful cooking can make even the most humble ingredients taste exceptionally good. Delicious and packed with nutrients, but sadly underappreciated, cabbage can shine through either the technique used to prepare it or the companions it's cooked with. Here, gently simmering it in just a small amount of water mellows its strong flavor.

You can vary this soup in several ways with a quick hunt through the fridge or pantry. I often use leftover cooked chickpeas or beans. Try substituting Savoy cabbage or spinach, kale, or escarole for the green cabbage (adjust the cooking time depending on the chosen green), adding a touch of harissa or a chili, or grating a good Pecorino Toscano or Parmigiano-Reggiano cheese over the top.

NOTE: You'll need to soak the chickpeas the night before.

FLAVOR TIP: Simmering the minced garlic in a bit of water before adding the remaining ingredients softens its flavor.

1½ cups dried chickpeas

4 garlic cloves, 2 unpeeled, 2 minced

1 fresh rosemary sprig

6–7 cups water

2 tablespoons extra-virgin olive oil

1 2½- to 2¾-pound green cabbage, cored and thinly sliced (about 10 cups)

1 teaspoon medium-coarse sea salt, or more to taste

Coarsely ground black pepper

Rinse chickpeas well and remove any stones. Place in a large bowl with 2 whole garlic cloves and rosemary, cover with 2½ cups cold water, and soak overnight.

Pour soaked chickpeas and their liquid, garlic, and rosemary into a medium saucepan; add 2 cups water. Bring to a gentle simmer and cook until chickpeas are tender, adding water in ½-cup increments as necessary to keep chickpeas just submerged, about 2 hours. Remove from heat (do not drain).

Remove garlic cloves and let cool slightly, then squeeze pulp from skin and stir into chickpeas. Discard rosemary sprig.

Heat oil in a large Dutch oven or other heavy pot over medium heat. Add minced garlic and cook, stirring, for 1 minute. Add ¼ cup water, bring to a simmer, and cook for 4 minutes. Add cabbage and cook, stirring, just until it starts to wilt, about 1 minute. Add 1 cup water and salt, bring to a simmer, and cook until cabbage starts to become tender, about 10 minutes.

Add chickpeas and their liquid and simmer until cabbage is tender and flavors are blended, about 20 minutes more. Adjust salt as necessary. Finish with a grinding of pepper.

LENTIL SOUP

QUICK-COOK RECIPE / MAKES 4 TO 6 SERVINGS

Eating this soup at a local trattoria in Naples years ago, I was astonished at how good the barely adorned dish was. A great deal of chopped parsley was stirred in at the end, which gave the lentils brightness and dimension. I like to use the tiny Castelluccio or Colfiorito lentils (both are from Umbria), but the more common small ones, such as French lentils du Puy or Spanish pardina (also known as Spanish brown lentils), are great too.

FLAVOR TIP: Be sure to use small lentils (as opposed to common brown lentils), since they taste better and hold their shape.

1¹/₂	cups small lentils (about 12 ounces; see headnote)
1	small red onion, coarsely chopped
1	small carrot, coarsely chopped
1	celery stalk, coarsely chopped
1	garlic clove
¹/₄	cup extra-virgin olive oil, plus more for drizzling
1	small dried red chili pepper
¹/₂	cup dry red wine
4¹/₂	cups water
³/₄	cup chopped fresh flat-leaf parsley
1	teaspoon medium-coarse sea salt, or more to taste

Rinse lentils and discard any stones or other debris.

Pulse onion, carrot, celery, and garlic in a food processor until just minced. Heat oil in a large Dutch oven or other heavy pot over medium-high heat. Add vegetable mixture and crumble in chili, then reduce heat to medium and cook, stirring occasionally, until vegetables are tender, about 8 minutes.

Add wine and cook until mostly evaporated, about 6 minutes. Add water and lentils, bring to a gentle simmer, and cook until lentils are tender, about 35 minutes. Stir in parsley and salt.

Serve soup hot, drizzled with olive oil and sprinkled with additional salt to taste.

WHITE BEAN SOUP WITH RAMPS

SLOW-COOK RECIPE / MAKES 6 SERVINGS

One warm fall day in Tuscany, my brother, Nico, and I loaded up an old demijohn into the back of our run-down Fiat and crossed over the Valdichiana Plain in search of the winery where, back in the seventies, our parents bought *vino sfuso* ("loose wine") to fuel their rustic, intellectual life. By the time we arrived in the nearby medieval hill town of Montalcino, it was lunchtime and the winery was shut, so we stepped into the bar for lunch. Like so many classic Tuscan *osterias* (few of which still exist), this one was warm with the smell of good food and dense with cigarette smoke. Peasant farmworkers sat about with aristocratic winery owners eating pureed white bean soup, served with a cruet of fluorescent-green new olive oil and a whole raw scallion for dipping. In the end, we got the wine, but the trip would have been worth it just for the soup.

In this recipe, I use ramps (wild leeks), one of the first vegetables to come up in the spring. You can substitute 1 medium leek in the soup and use 4 thinly sliced scallions for garnish when ramps are not available.

NOTE: Start the beans the night before.

1 pound dried white beans (2 1/2 cups)

About 10 cups water

1 whole head garlic, plus 2 peeled garlic cloves

1 fresh sage sprig

5 nice-sized ramps (2 1/2 ounces), whites and greens separated (see headnote)

1 small onion, coarsely chopped

1 medium carrot, coarsely chopped

1 celery stalk, coarsely chopped

1/4 cup plus 1 tablespoon extra-virgin olive oil, plus more for drizzling

8 ounces new potatoes or Yukon Gold potatoes, peeled and cut into 1/4-inch pieces

Coarsely ground black pepper

Rinse beans well. Soak in 8 cups water with whole garlic head and sage overnight.

Finely chop ramp whites, onion, carrot, celery, and 2 peeled garlic cloves together, or process in a food processor. Heat ¼ cup oil in a large Dutch oven or other heavy pot over medium-high heat. Add ramp mixture, reduce heat to medium, and cook, stirring occasionally, until vegetables are softened, about 5 minutes.

Add soaked beans, with their liquid, garlic head, and sage. Reduce heat to medium-low; bring to a very gentle simmer. Cook, adding water by the ½ cupful as needed to keep level of liquid just covering beans, until beans are becoming tender, 2 hours or so, depending on their age (older beans require a longer cooking time).

Add potatoes, stir, and cook until potatoes and beans are very tender, about 1 hour more, adding water as necessary to keep liquid just above bean mixture. Remove and discard sage and squeeze the garlic from the head into the soup.

Meanwhile, when soup is just about ready, heat remaining tablespoon oil in a medium skillet over medium-high heat. Add ramp greens, reduce heat to medium, and cook, stirring occasionally, until softened, about 5 minutes. Remove from heat and set aside.

Pass soup through a food mill. Thin with a little water, if desired, and serve garnished with sautéed ramp greens, a drizzle of oil, and a good sprinkling of pepper.

RICH CHICKEN SOUP WITH GREENS

SLOW-COOK RECIPE / MAKES 8 SERVINGS

I originally discovered this dish while traveling in Naples with my mother one Christmas. She was on assignment doing a story for a food magazine, and I went along as her unofficial tasting assistant. We both fell in love with Naples, with its people, tough and gritty; its culture and beauty; and its warm Mediterranean character. The original soup, *minestra maritata,* or "married soup"—presumably referring to the perfect union of meats and bitter greens—calls for pork, chicken, and veal, plus a variety of obscure wild greens not often found outside of Naples. My version is much simpler, just chicken, the broth it's cooked in, and any number of easily found greens.

This soup can be varied in countless ways. You can toss in cooked lentils, white beans, barley, or farro when you return the chicken to the broth; add cubed potatoes and turnips (or carrots and parsnips) and simmer with the chicken until just tender before adding the greens; or ladle the hot soup over a poached egg on a thick slice of crunchy toast.

1/4	cup extra-virgin olive oil, plus more for drizzling
2	carrots, chopped into 3 or 4 pieces each
2	celery stalks, chopped into 3 or 4 pieces each
1	medium onion, quartered
1	leek, trimmed just above the green, sliced lengthwise in half, rinsed thoroughly, and halves cut crosswise into 3 pieces
1	head garlic, sliced horizontally in half
1	tablespoon plus 1 teaspoon fine sea salt
1/2	cup dry white wine
1	3 1/2- to 4-pound chicken, cut into 6 pieces
1/2	bunch fresh flat-leaf parsley
	About 10 cups water
6	cups packed shredded cooking greens, including one or more of the following: spinach, escarole, beet greens, dandelion greens, chicory, Swiss chard, and mustard greens

Coarsely ground black pepper

1 small lemon, cut into wedges

¹/₂–1 cup freshly grated Parmigiano-Reggiano cheese

Heat oil in a large stockpot over high heat. Add carrots, celery, onion, leek, garlic, and 1 tablespoon salt. Cook, stirring occasionally, until vegetables are well browned on all sides, about 10 minutes.

Add wine and bring to a simmer; scrape up any browned bits from bottom of pot. Add chicken, parsley, and water to just cover. Cover and heat just until liquid comes to a simmer, about 10 minutes. Remove cover, reduce heat to low, and cook at a bare simmer, occasionally skimming foam, until broth is rich-tasting, about 1 hour and 45 minutes.

Remove from heat, pull chicken pieces out and reserve, and strain broth through a fine strainer or cheesecloth. Discard all vegetables except for ½ head garlic. When chicken is cool enough to handle, pull meat off bones; discard bones and skin.

Remove fat from surface of broth (see page 109). Put broth and chicken meat in a large clean saucepan and bring to a simmer. Press garlic pulp from reserved ½ head garlic through a fine strainer into broth, scraping every bit you can get into the liquid; stir garlic into broth to combine; discard garlic skins. Add remaining teaspoon salt and greens and simmer just until greens are wilted, about 6 minutes.

Serve immediately, with a drizzle of oil, a grinding of pepper, a squeeze of lemon juice, and a sprinkle of Parmigiano-Reggiano.

POTATO, CELERY, AND LEEK SOUP

SLOW-COOK RECIPE / MAKES 4 TO 6 SERVINGS

This soup is a classic "poor dish," which, in Mediterranean peasant culture, refers to a meal made with common kitchen-garden ingredients and without expensive meat or other luxurious items. And yet, as simple as these ingredients are, they make a surprisingly sumptuous soup. Parmigiano-Reggiano cheese offers just the right touch of fat and a bit of wealth.

Perfect in winter, when local vegetables are limited, this soup is also good in spring, when sweet wintered-over potatoes bring depth to the dish.

FLAVOR TIP: Use a good extra-virgin olive oil and alert leeks and celery.

6	medium leeks, white parts only
2	tablespoons extra-virgin olive oil, plus more for drizzling
5	celery stalks, finely minced
1½	teaspoons fine sea salt
2	pounds Yukon Gold potatoes, peeled and cut into ¼-inch cubes
3¼	cups water
	Freshly grated Parmigiano-Reggiano cheese
	Coarsely ground black pepper

Slice leeks into ¼-inch rounds and soak in a large bowl of water to get rid of dirt and grit. Pull leeks out of water with your hands, leaving dirt settled at bottom of bowl. Rinse leeks in a sieve under cold water.

Heat oil in a large Dutch oven or other heavy pot over high heat. Add leeks, celery, and salt and cook, stirring frequently, until vegetables are softened, about 9 minutes. Add potatoes and water. Bring to a simmer, then reduce to a bare simmer and cook, stirring occasionally, until vegetables are tender, about 40 minutes.

Using the back of a large wooden spoon, press half of potatoes against side of pot to crush them, then stir back into soup. Continue cooking until soup is richly flavored, about 20 minutes more.

Serve drizzled with oil and sprinkled with cheese and pepper.

FARRO AND KALE SOUP

QUICK-COOK RECIPE / MAKES 8 SERVINGS

The rustic flavors of kale and farro make for a hearty soup. A Tuscan farmwife might add a little bit of prosciutto fat to her *battuto* (the aromatic vegetable mixture) and perhaps toss in a diced fresh-dug potato to cook with the farro. Try this soup with a soft poached egg on top, drizzled with extra-virgin olive oil, for a complete meal.

1	leek, white and light green parts only
2	celery stalks, coarsely chopped
1	large carrot, coarsely chopped
1	small onion, coarsely chopped
1	garlic clove
1/4	cup extra-virgin olive oil, plus more for drizzling
	Medium-coarse sea salt
6	cups water
2	teaspoons tomato paste, preferably double-concentrate (see page 19)
1 1/2	cups farro (see page 13)
3	bunches lacinato kale, stemmed and chopped into 1/2-inch-wide strips
	Freshly grated Parmigiano-Reggiano or Pecorino Romano cheese for serving
	Coarsely ground black pepper

Cut leek lengthwise in half and rinse well; coarsely chop. Pulse leek, celery, carrot, onion, and garlic in a food processor until finely chopped.

Heat oil in a large Dutch oven or other heavy pot over medium-high heat. Add chopped vegetables and a generous pinch of salt; cook, stirring occasionally, until vegetables start to soften, about 4 minutes. Add 1 cup water and tomato paste, and stir to dissolve paste. Continue to cook, stirring occasionally, until liquid has almost evaporated, about 20 minutes.

Add remaining 5 cups water, farro, and kale, bring to a simmer, and cook, stirring occasionally, until farro and kale are tender and flavors have blended, 20 to 25 minutes. Season to taste with salt.

Serve with a drizzle of olive oil, a little grated cheese, and a sprinkle of coarse salt and pepper.

PASTA, RISOTTO, AND POLENTA

As delicious as various noodles from around the world are, I am unapologetically chauvinistic when it comes to the incredible flavors and multifaceted nature of Italian pasta.

From the philosophies that govern the type of wheat used to make pasta to those that dictate how to cook it, proper sauce-to-pasta ratios, and which type and shape of pasta goes best with which sauce, Italians have perfected the dish. Once you begin to learn about pasta, you realize that even a simple plate of penne tossed with tomato sauce and Parmesan cheese is more than just the sum of its parts. With a little focus on a few basic pasta flavor principles, you'll soon be cooking better pasta and appreciating it more than you ever have.

In Italy, the standard day-to-day pasta is *pasta secca*, "dried pasta," made from *semola*, or durum wheat flour. When I was a kid, everyone there ate Barilla and Buitoni, the megabrands of Italy. Italian law dictated (and still does) that *pasta secca* must be made from hard durum wheat flour, which makes for a good firm noodle.

Then, in the eighties, artisanal dried pastas—made as they had been at the turn of the century—started appearing. Artisanal pastas are made from select grains, extruded through bronze rather than Teflon dies, and slow-dried for as long as seventy-two hours, as opposed to being blast-heat-dried for five minutes.

The bronze dies give a rougher texture to the surface of the pasta, which allows it to hold on to and absorb sauces better than the smoother mass-produced types. The long drying process enhances flavor and makes for a sturdier pasta with a truer al dente texture when cooked properly.

For feast days and special occasions, there is *pasta fresca*, "fresh pasta," made with eggs and soft white flour and available in myriad shapes, sizes, and packages for whatever sauce or filling anyone could possibly dream up. Fresh pasta is something Mita, our Tuscan neighbor, makes with eggs from her own chickens for Sunday lunch or harvest feasts. She rolls it by hand either into tagliatelle or, if she is firing up the bread oven, lasagna sheets. Either way, it is cooked within hours of being made, and the condiments are always the same: meat ragù and Parmesan cheese, and a little *besciamel* if she is making lasagna.

Tuscany, where bread, polenta, and beans have always been more common as everyday fare than pasta, is on the far southern reach of Northern Italy's classic egg-rich fresh pasta traditions. But you still find plenty of pasta there, fresh and dried. One of my favorites, *pici*, is fresh and made from just flour and water, no eggs. The dough is kneaded until smooth, and long strands are quickly rolled out under the heel of the cook's hand on a lightly floured wooden board. The soft, irregularly shaped noodles marry perfectly with the gamy ragùs of the region. In its day, *pici* was such poor food it was sauced with nothing more than fried bread crumbs and olive oil. In a strange twist of fate, today it is nearly impossible to find true handmade *pici*, because the cost of the labor involved is prohibitive.

When it comes to cooking pasta, the first lesson I teach a new pasta cook is: don't overcook it, and don't oversauce it. When cooking pasta, use a nice large pot. Fill it three-quarters full with generously salted water; the water should taste salty. Bring the water to a vigorous boil. When the water is at a full boil, quickly add the pasta all at once, stir, and immediately cover the pot to bring the water back to a boil; uncover it partially before the water has a chance to boil over. The water should be at a rolling boil at all times so that the pasta cooks quickly and evenly until al dente—firm, or, literally, "to the tooth."

Cooking times vary for different types and shapes of pasta. For packaged pastas, use the time on the box only as a guide, and begin tasting the pasta several minutes early. You want the pasta to be toothsome. Especially when using high-quality artisanal pasta, try draining it when you think it is nearly al dente. Eat it like this a few times, and you're likely to make it your standard. (I'm sometimes amazed at how firm some Italians will eat their pasta.) The minimal cooking helps the pasta retain its flavor. However, it's important to note that the technique of cooking pasta to the lower limits of al dente does not work as well with lesser-quality brands, which, instead of being toothsome, end up crunchy.

When the pasta is ready, drain it, but never, ever rinse it. The heat and the residual starch on the surface of the noodles are what will help your delicious sauce bond with the pasta, ensuring that each strand or tube is evenly coated. To this end, you want to toss the hot pasta with the sauce as soon as it is drained, so have the sauce ready and hot before you cook your pasta. If cheese or bread crumbs are part of the equation, add them after the first toss of pasta and sauce, and then toss again. Add the cheese in two batches so that it blends thoroughly with the sauce and pasta.

If I'm using fresh herbs, I like to toss them in last, allowing the heat to just wilt them and bring out their aroma and flavor. To add a little richness, you can also toss in a tablespoon of butter or olive oil as well. Once that's all done, get your beautiful pasta right into a bowl and deliver it to the table—diners ready and waiting. In Italy, you're expected to start eating your food, especially if it is a hot dish, the moment it lands on the table in front of you. Waiting until everyone is served or the cook sits down is considered an insult, so throw away your mannerly notions and start eating.

The more good pasta you eat, the more you'll understand this: for Italians, a pasta dish is about the pasta itself—the flavor of the wheat and the texture of the dough. The sauce is a condiment. It can be as simple as garlic, olive oil, and dried chili or as complex as a wine-marinated wild boar ragù, but it should never upstage or drown the pasta. When I finish eating a bowl of pasta, I like there to be just enough sauce left in the bowl that I can take a walnut-sized morsel of bread and sop up the last remnants, and then the bowl is clean—more than that, and the pasta is oversauced.

Matching the right shape to the right sauce is important as well, but not restrictive. There are hundreds of pasta shapes and sizes. I categorize them into four types: dried short, long, and soup (the tiniest shapes, such as ditalini and orzo) pasta and fresh pasta, and I generally find that if one pasta goes with a sauce, another of that type will as well. Spaghetti, spaghettini, bucatini, and others like these are safely interchangeable; maccheroncini and penne function more or less the same way; and fresh egg pasta noodles can pretty much go with anything. Stuffed pastas like cannelloni, ravioli, and tortellini are less versatile, since their fillings are generally paired with specific sauces.

Risotto, though it is a rice dish, shares the place of pasta in the sequence of a traditional Italian meal. It lends itself to a great many variations, depending on what is available or in season. Because of its popularity here, risotto is a dish that many people think they know. But until you taste it made with homemade broth and prepared properly from start to finish, you have not truly experienced it.

In this chapter, you'll find classics such as Slow-Cooked Tomato Sauce and Homemade Lasagna, along with others, like Pasta with Sweet Corn, that are modern twists or adaptations using local American ingredients in an Italian way.

PASTA, RISOTTO, AND POLENTA

Fresh Summer
Tomato Sauce | 138

Slow-Cooked Tomato Sauce | 140

Spaghettini with
Burst Cherry Tomatoes | 142

Penne with Zucchini
and Mint | 144

Short Pasta with
Mushrooms and Mint | 146

Pasta with Sweet Corn | 148

Short Pasta with Leeks and
Prosciutto | 149

Long Pasta with Bacon,
Red Cabbage, Walnuts, and
Rosemary | 150

Pasta with Roasted
Cauliflower, Olives,
Capers, and Bread Crumbs | 153

Toasted Seasoned
Bread Crumbs | 155

Maccheroni with
White Beans, Mustard Greens,
and Anchovy | 156

Pasta Shells with
Many Cheeses | 158

Pasta Carbonara | 159

Spaghetti with
Lemon Sole, Almonds,
Capers, and Parsley | 160

Pasta with Bottarga | 162

Spaghettini with Ground
Lamb, Yogurt, and Mint | 164

Spaghetti with Chicken Livers,
Rosemary, and Lemon | 166

Classic Central
Italian Meat Ragù | 168

Southern Italian
Pork Ragù | 170

Braised Guinea
Hen Ragù | 172

Braised Rabbit Ragù | 174

Tuscan Wild Boar Ragù | 176

Homemade Lasagna | 178
    Fresh Pasta Dough | 180
    Besciamel Sauce | 181

Maine Shrimp Risotto | 184
    Shrimp Broth | 186

Sweet Pea and
Squash Blossom Risotto | 187

Strawberry Risotto | 190

Bacon and Ramp Risotto | 192

Potato Gnocchi | 194

Classic Tuscan Eggplant
Parmesan | 197

Polenta with Aromatic
Herb Butter | 199
    Aromatic Herb
    Butter | 200

FRESH SUMMER TOMATO SAUCE

QUICK-COOK RECIPE / MAKES 4 CUPS,
ENOUGH TO SAUCE ABOUT 1½ POUNDS PASTA

During my first summer as a cook, I worked at La Chiusa, a countryside restaurant near Siena, and lived upstairs with the owners. The bread was baked with flour milled from their own grain, and each November they geared up the olive mill to press their own olives. Below the restaurant were the kitchen gardens, and in the afternoons, between lunch and dinner, the gardener brought in crates of warm sun-ripened plum tomatoes. It was my job to peel, seed, and dice them for this sauce. The tomatoes were so perfectly ripe that you could peel them with nothing more than a paring knife.

TOMATO SAUCE

There are probably as many recipes for tomato sauce as there are cooks in Italy. Like meat ragù, it is a ubiquitous default sauce for pasta, always good, always there. A great comfort food, it's universally loved by children, and it's easy to turn to when there's nothing else around to cook. The most basic tomato sauce is easy to make with pantry ingredients: Italian canned tomatoes, garlic, onions, olive oil. With pasta in the pantry as well, and some Parmesan cheese, in just about 20 minutes, you can have a tasty and nutritious meal that's good any time of the day.

Depending on what I'm after and the season, I have a few different recipes for tomato sauce. In the summer, when tomatoes are ripe, I make a quick light sauce with plum tomatoes, a little garlic, basil, and butter, and another one using tiny sweet tomatoes that burst and caramelize when cooking. When fresh tomatoes are unavailable, I make a slower-cooked sauce that can be varied depending on what goes into the vegetable base; garlic and parsley can be added, for example, or carrot and celery, or even a whole dried chili.

Use the ripest farm-fresh plum tomatoes you can get your hands on for this recipe. Your reward will be a lovely, light, and incredibly fresh sauce that is just as good spooned over hot buttered bread as it is tossed with pasta.

FLAVOR TIP: Plum tomatoes are best for this sauce, as the ratio of pulp to seed is much higher than in other types. With less water to give up, they also require less cooking time than other tomatoes.

- 5 pounds ripe plum tomatoes
- 3 tablespoons extra-virgin olive oil
- 2 tablespoons unsalted butter
- 2 garlic cloves, minced
- 2 teaspoons fine sea salt
- 1/3 cup thinly sliced fresh basil leaves

Bring a large saucepan of water to a boil. Set up a large bowl filled with ice water. Add tomatoes to boiling water and blanch for 45 seconds; immediately drain and shock in ice water.

Drain tomatoes and, using a serrated paring knife, cut an X in the bottom of each one. Peel, then cut tomatoes lengthwise in half and cut out and discard core. Push out and discard seeds, and chop tomatoes into 1/4-inch pieces.

Heat oil and butter in a wide heavy saucepan over medium-high heat until butter is melted. Add garlic, reduce heat to medium-low, and cook for 30 seconds. Add tomatoes and salt, increase heat to medium-high, and cook, stirring frequently, until juices have reduced and sauce is flavorful, 18 to 20 minutes. Remove from heat and stir in basil. Toss with hot pasta, or let cool and store for up to 4 days in the refrigerator or for up to 3 months in the freezer.

SLOW-COOKED TOMATO SAUCE

SLOW-COOK RECIPE / MAKES 3 CUPS,
ENOUGH TO SAUCE ABOUT 1 POUND PASTA

This is a favorite recipe I use most of the year, when good fresh tomatoes are unavailable. The slow-cooking saps the canned tomatoes of their acidity. Despite the large quantity of onions in this sauce, you don't get an overwhelming oniony flavor. Gently cooking them in water softens their bite and makes them sweet.

Every Italian has his or her own recipe for this basic, which is used for saucing pasta, simmering beans, and making eggplant Parmesan, lasagna, and a myriad of other dishes. This elementary version can be spiced up with fresh or dried chilies or flavored with fresh herbs. Toss it with any pasta shape, along with toasted bread crumbs (see page 155), grated Parmesan cheese, or fresh sheep's-milk ricotta with a little Parmesan and fresh parsley. The more slowly you cook it, the sweeter it will be. The sauce can easily be doubled or tripled.

FLAVOR TIP: The food mill is a classic European tool, and one that I highly recommend. It involves a little more elbow grease than an immersion blender or a food processor, but that's not the major difference. Rather then pulverizing everything together, the food mill holds back unwanted skins, bitter seeds, pulp, and larger pieces of food, leaving you with smooth sauces or soups. The flavor difference, though subtle, is worth the effort.

- 3 tablespoons extra-virgin olive oil
- 2 medium onions, finely chopped
- 2 garlic cloves, sliced
- 1 cup water
- 1 35-ounce can whole peeled San Marzano tomatoes, with 2 tablespoons of their juices
- 1/2 teaspoon fine sea salt

Heat oil in a large saucepan over medium heat. Add onions and cook for 2 minutes to help soften. Add garlic, reduce heat to medium-low, and cook for 10 minutes. Add ½ cup water and cook for 15 minutes.

Add remaining ½ cup water and cook until onions are well stewed and softened and there are about 2 tablespoons liquid left in pan, about 10 minutes more.

Add tomatoes, juices, and salt, stirring and breaking up tomatoes with a wooden spoon. Bring to a very gentle simmer and cook, stirring occasionally, for 1 hour. Remove from heat.

Pass sauce through a food mill. Toss with pasta, or let cool and store in the refrigerator for up to 3 days or in the freezer for up to 3 months.

SPAGHETTINI WITH BURST CHERRY TOMATOES

QUICK-COOK RECIPE / MAKES 4 SERVINGS

This is the sauce to make during the hot, muggy days of summer, when local farmstands are overflowing with ripe cherry tomatoes. As the tomatoes lightly brown in olive oil in a hot skillet, their skins burst and their juices caramelize, giving this quick sauce a depth that one usually encounters only in slower-cooked versions. I like to use a mix of varieties and colors, though my absolute favorite is the small, intensely flavorful currant tomato.

- 1/4 cup extra-virgin olive oil
- 2 pints mixed heirloom cherry tomatoes, currant tomatoes, and grape tomatoes
- 1/2 teaspoon fine sea salt
- 2 garlic cloves, thinly sliced
- 1 pound spaghettini or spaghetti
- 1/3 cup thinly sliced fresh basil leaves
- 1 1/2 cups freshly grated Parmigiano-Reggiano cheese
- Coarsely ground black pepper

Bring a large pot of salted water to a boil.

Heat oil in a large skillet over medium-high heat until very hot but not smoking. Add half of tomatoes, sprinkle with salt, and cook, tossing occasionally, until tomatoes start to blister and collapse, about 3 minutes. Add remaining tomatoes and cook, tossing once, for 2 minutes more.

With a wooden spoon, push tomatoes to one side of pan to make room for garlic. Add garlic and cook until fragrant, 3 to 4 minutes, then stir gently to mix garlic and tomatoes together. Continue cooking, stirring occasionally and gently pressing tomatoes to release juices, until all tomatoes have collapsed and sauce is juicy and thick, about 4 minutes more. Remove from heat.

Cook pasta until al dente. Meanwhile, gently reheat sauce. Drain pasta and immediately toss with sauce and basil. Add 3/4 cup of cheese and toss; add remaining 3/4 cup cheese and toss again. Season with pepper and serve at once.

PENNE WITH ZUCCHINI AND MINT

QUICK-COOK RECIPE / MAKES 4 SERVINGS

This and the three recipes that follow are all vegetable pastas made with a similar simple technique. They begin with a quick sauté of onions or garlic. Whichever vegetable is in season is added to the pan, then everything is tossed with Parmesan and whatever fresh herbs and pasta go best with it. This version offers a balance of different squash textures and flavors, providing you can get yourself some squash blossoms and even tendrils—but it is also perfectly delicious made with only grated zucchini.

Cucuzza squash is a long curly variety much beloved by Sicilians and the only one I know of with edible tendrils. Though rare in this country, the squash can be found at some farmers' markets.

FLAVOR TIP: Separating the green base from the petals of the squash blossom allows you to cook and soften the sturdier base without overcooking the delicate petals, which need only a gentle wilting at the end.

2	tablespoons extra-virgin olive oil
5	tablespoons unsalted butter
2	shallots, finely minced
4	medium zucchini, grated or julienned on a mandoline
4	medium yellow zucchini, grated or julienned on a mandoline
2	teaspoons medium-coarse sea salt
1	cup coarsely chopped cucuzza squash tendrils (optional; see headnote)
5⅓	ounces (⅓ pound) squash blossoms, trimmed, green bases separated from flower petals and petals reserved (optional)
¼	cup thinly sliced fresh mint leaves
1	pound penne
	Coarsely ground black pepper for serving
	Freshly grated Parmigiano-Reggiano cheese for serving

Bring a large pot of salted water to a boil.

Heat oil and 3 tablespoons butter in a large saucepan over medium-high heat until butter is melted. Add shallots, reduce heat to low, and cook until just softened, 1 to 2 minutes. Add zucchini and salt; stir. Increase heat to medium-high and cook until vegetables are tender and their liquid has evaporated, about 15 minutes.

Add squash tendrils and squash blossom greens, if using, and cook, stirring occasionally, until greens are tender, 5 to 7 minutes. Remove from heat. Add squash blossom petals, if using, and mint. Stir well and set aside.

Cook pasta until al dente. Drain and immediately toss with remaining 2 tablespoons butter and vegetable mixture. Serve at once, with pepper and cheese.

SHORT PASTA WITH MUSHROOMS AND MINT

QUICK-COOK RECIPE / MAKES 4 SERVINGS

In Tuscany, prized porcini mushroom caps are seasoned with garlic and wild mint, then grilled or sautéed. That combination of bracing flavors inspired this dish. Use a short pasta, such as penne, maccheroncini, or even shells, to catch the sauce.

FLAVOR TIP: If you forage for or otherwise have access to true wild mushrooms, such as morels or porcini, their flavor is so special you'll want to savor it without distraction from other types. Otherwise, a combination of interesting store-bought varieties works well. That said, I avoid portobello and cremini mushrooms, which won't lend much flavor to the dish.

1½   pounds mixed mushrooms, such as shiitake, bluefoot, oyster, chanterelle, and/or hedgehog

¼   cup plus 2 tablespoons extra-virgin olive oil

     Fine sea salt and coarsely ground black pepper

2   tablespoons unsalted butter

2   garlic cloves, minced

1½   teaspoons finely chopped fresh thyme

1   pound penne

3   tablespoons coarsely chopped fresh mint

2   cups freshly grated Parmigiano-Reggiano cheese

Bring a large pot of salted water to a boil.

Cut stems from shiitake and bluefoot mushrooms, if using, and discard. Leave caps whole or, if very large, cut into halves or quarters. If using oyster, chanterelle, and/or hedgehog mushrooms, trim tough bases and halve lengthwise if large.

In a large heavy skillet, heat oil over medium-high heat. Slowly feed mushrooms into pan; add a handful in a single layer, lightly season with salt and pepper, and let mushrooms start to brown, about 3 minutes, before pushing them to side of pan and adding more. When you've added all mushrooms and they are nicely browned around edges, add butter and let it foam. Add garlic and thyme, stir, and remove from heat.

Cook pasta until al dente. Drain and immediately toss with mushroom mixture. Add mint and half of cheese. Toss, then add remaining cheese; toss and season with salt and pepper. Serve at once.

PASTA WITH SWEET CORN

QUICK-COOK RECIPE / MAKES 4 SERVINGS

Fresh corn, with all its magnificent sweetness, caramelizes in the pan when sautéed in butter. Use the freshest corn you can get (never frozen), and cook it as soon as possible. Corn sugars quickly convert into starch once the corn is harvested. The more sugars the corn retains, the sweeter, more delicious a sauce you will have. For this recipe, you'll need a small pasta shape—anything with curls that will trap the corn kernels.

- 4 tablespoons (½ stick) unsalted butter
- 2 tablespoons extra-virgin olive oil
- 8 medium ears corn, shucked and kernels cut from cobs
  Coarse sea salt
- 1 medium onion, finely chopped
- 2 tablespoons chopped fresh summer savory or thyme
- 1 pound fusilli, capricci, cavatappi, or small shell-shaped pasta (see headnote)
  Coarsely ground black pepper
- 1½ cups freshly grated Parmigiano-Reggiano cheese

Bring a large pot of salted water to a boil.

Heat 2 tablespoons butter and oil in a large skillet over medium-high heat until butter is melted. Add corn and a pinch of salt and cook, stirring occasionally, until corn is softened, about 8 minutes. Add onion, stir, and cook until softened, about 5 minutes. Remove from heat and toss with savory.

While corn sauce is finishing, cook pasta until al dente. Drain pasta, place in a large bowl, and immediately toss with remaining 2 tablespoons butter. Add sauce, a sprinkle of salt and pepper, and ¾ cup cheese. Toss well, stir in remaining ¾ cup cheese, and serve at once.

SHORT PASTA WITH
LEEKS AND PROSCIUTTO

QUICK-COOK RECIPE / MAKES 4 SERVINGS

I love to add a little bit of salty meat to pastas made with fresh seasonal vegetables—things like applewood-smoked bacon, pancetta, prosciutto, and guanciale (cured pig jowl). The saltiness of the meat complements sweet vegetables like corn, peas, and leeks, and in a restaurant, it's a good way to use up the end pieces from a whole ham.

2 tablespoons extra-virgin olive oil

1 $1/4$-inch-thick slice prosciutto, cut into $1/4$-inch-wide strips

3 tablespoons unsalted butter

6 medium leeks, white and light green parts only, cut into $1/4$-inch slices, washed well, and drained

1 tablespoon chopped fresh thyme

1 teaspoon medium-coarse sea salt

1 cup water

1 pound penne or other short tubular or curly pasta

2 cups freshly grated Parmigiano-Reggiano cheese

2 teaspoons coarsely ground black pepper

Heat oil in a large skillet over medium heat. Add prosciutto and cook, stirring occasionally, until crisp and golden, about 5 minutes. Reduce heat to low, add 2 tablespoons butter, leeks, thyme, and salt. Cook, stirring occasionally and adding water in $1/3$-cup increments when leeks look dry, until they are very tender, about 30 minutes. Remove from heat.

Meanwhile, bring a large pot of salted water to a boil. Cook pasta until al dente.

Drain pasta, transfer to a large bowl, and immediately toss with remaining tablespoon butter. Add half of leek sauce and toss to combine. Add half of cheese and toss. Repeat with remaining leek sauce and then remaining cheese. Toss one last time with pepper, and serve at once.

LONG PASTA WITH BACON, RED CABBAGE, WALNUTS, AND ROSEMARY

QUICK-COOK RECIPE / MAKES 6 SERVINGS

In the spirit of making do with what you've got, this is a pasta dish comprised almost completely of basic winter ingredients. It is creamy and rich, so small portions are best. For variation, try it with 1 cup of Toasted Seasoned Bread Crumbs (page 155) in place of the cheese.

FLAVOR TIP: When purchasing nuts, buy them from a good shop with high turnover. Store the unused portion, well sealed, in the freezer, to keep the nuts tasting fresh. When stored in the pantry, nuts, like nut oils, quickly turn rancid.

 1 tablespoon unsalted butter
 3/4 cup chopped walnuts
 2 tablespoons chopped fresh rosemary
 2 tablespoons extra-virgin olive oil
 4 slices thick-cut bacon, cut into 1/4-inch-wide strips
 1 small head red cabbage (1 1/2 pounds), cored and very thinly sliced
 1 teaspoon fine sea salt
 1 cup heavy cream
 1 cup water
 1 pound spaghetti or bucatini
 2 cups freshly grated Parmigiano-Reggiano cheese
    Coarsely ground black pepper

Melt butter in a medium skillet over medium-low heat. Add walnuts and rosemary and cook, stirring occasionally, until nuts are toasted, about 4 minutes. Remove from heat and set aside.

Line a plate with paper towels. Add oil and bacon to a large skillet and cook over medium-low heat, stirring occasionally, until fat is rendered from bacon, about 8 minutes. Using a slotted spoon, transfer bacon to paper towels to drain.

Increase heat under pan to medium-high. Add a large handful of cabbage and 1 teaspoon salt and cook, stirring, until cabbage is wilted and you have room in skillet to add more. Continue adding cabbage in batches and cooking until it is all wilted. Then cook, stirring occasionally, until cabbage is tender and lightly browned around edges, about 10 minutes.

Bring a large pot of salted water to a boil.

Add cream and walnut mixture to cabbage, and cook for 1 minute. Add ½ cup water and cook, stirring, for 2 minutes more. Add remaining ½ cup water and bring to a gentle simmer; then reduce heat to medium and cook until sauce is thick and flavors are well blended, 8 to 10 minutes. Stir in reserved bacon and remove from heat.

Cook pasta until al dente. Drain, transfer to a large bowl, and immediately toss with cabbage sauce. Add half of cheese and toss; add remaining cheese and toss once more. Season generously with pepper, and serve at once.

PASTA WITH ROASTED CAULIFLOWER, OLIVES, CAPERS, AND BREAD CRUMBS

SLOW-COOK RECIPE / MAKES 4 TO 6 SERVINGS

Olives and capers thrive in arid Mediterranean conditions and frequently show up as a flavor combination in southern Mediterranean dishes—the pungent brininess of the capers plays off the bitter, acid notes in the olives. I like to add salty anchovy to the mix, which goes particularly well with the sweetness

of roasted cauliflower. In the fall, when I can find it, I use beautiful celadon-colored Romanesco cauliflower.

I like the mildness of the Spanish arbequina olives, but the much stronger cured black olives will work too; just use half as many. This is the sort of dish I rarely make the same way twice. You can try it with more capers or none at all, leave out the anchovy, and vary the olives any way you like.

2 medium heads cauliflower, cored and broken into florets

¼ cup plus 2 tablespoons extra-virgin olive oil

Coarse sea salt and coarsely ground black pepper

2 tablespoons unsalted butter

1 garlic clove, smashed and peeled

½ cup pitted mild olives, such as arbequina, coarsely chopped (see headnote)

2 tablespoons salt-packed capers, rinsed several times and drained

1 medium dried red chili

2 large anchovy fillets

1 pound strozzapreti, pennette, maccheroncini, or similar pasta

1 cup freshly grated Parmigiano-Reggiano cheese

⅓ cup chopped fresh flat-leaf parsley

1 cup Toasted Seasoned Bread Crumbs (recipe follows)

Heat oven to 400°F with a rack in center. Line a baking sheet with parchment.

Toss cauliflower with 2 tablespoons oil and season with salt and pepper. Spread on baking sheet and roast, stirring and turning once or twice, until tender and crispy brown in spots, about 45 minutes. Remove from oven and let cool.

Bring a large pot of salted water to a boil.

Heat remaining ¼ cup oil and butter in a large Dutch oven or other heavy pot over medium-low heat until butter is melted. Add garlic and cook, stirring occasionally, until lightly browned, about 4 minutes. Add olives, capers, and chili and cook for 2 minutes more. Add anchovies, stirring until dissolved. Add roasted cauliflower and stir well. Remove from heat.

Cook pasta until al dente. Drain and immediately toss with cauliflower mixture. Add half of cheese and parsley; toss. Add bread crumbs and remaining cheese, toss again, and serve at once.

TOASTED SEASONED BREAD CRUMBS

QUICK-COOK RECIPE / MAKES 3 CUPS

Get into the habit of making your own bread crumbs. It's a thrifty way to use up less-than-fresh bread, and you'll find they're much fresher and better-tasting than store-bought.

These keep well in the freezer for quite some time. I like to make a batch often so that I always have them on hand.

NOTE: To make homemade bread crumbs, tear or cut a fresh or day-old loaf of bread into 2-inch pieces and spread on a baking sheet. Bake at 325°F, tossing occasionally, until lightly toasted and dried, about 20 minutes. Remove from oven and let cool, then break into smaller pieces. Place in a resealable bag and crush with your hands for coarse crumbs, or buzz in a food processor for fine crumbs.

- 1/4 cup extra-virgin olive oil
- 2 garlic cloves, finely chopped
- 1/3 cup chopped fresh flat-leaf parsley
- 2 medium dried red chilies, crumbled
- 3 cups coarse fresh bread crumbs (see Note)

Heat oil in a large heavy skillet over medium-high heat. Add garlic and cook until just lightly browned, about 2 minutes. Remove skillet from heat, add parsley and chilies, and stir together.

Add bread crumbs, return skillet to heat, increase heat to high, and cook, stirring constantly, until crumbs are crisp, 5 to 7 minutes. Transfer to a bowl to cool. Store in a sealed container in the refrigerator for up to 3 days or in the freezer for up to 4 months.

MACCHERONI WITH WHITE BEANS, MUSTARD GREENS, AND ANCHOVY

QUICK-COOK RECIPE / MAKES 4 SERVINGS

This is a combination of that Italian-American classic *pasta fazool* and the Pugliese tradition of pairing pasta with bitter greens. In place of maccheroni, you can use pennette, ziti, or orecchiette. Toasted Seasoned Bread Crumbs (page 155) sprinkled over the top make a nice addition.

2	tablespoons extra-virgin olive oil
2	tablespoons unsalted butter
2	garlic cloves, gently smashed and peeled
3	anchovy fillets
2	small dried árbol chilies
1	pound mustard greens, trimmed, washed, and coarsely chopped
1½	cups water
	Fine sea salt
1	cup cooked cannellini or flageolet beans (see page 42)
12	ounces maccheroni
¾	cup freshly grated Parmigiano-Reggiano cheese
	Coarsely ground black pepper

Bring a large pot of salted water to a boil.

Heat oil and 1 tablespoon butter in a large deep skillet over medium heat until butter is melted. Add garlic and cook until lightly browned, about 2 minutes. Add anchovies and chilies, remove pan from heat, and stir with a wooden spoon to dissolve anchovies.

Return pan to heat, add one third of greens, water, and 1 teaspoon salt, and increase heat to high. As soon as greens wilt and you have room in pan, add remaining greens, in 2 batches if necessary. When all greens have been added to pan and are wilted, add beans. Cook until greens are tender and liquid has reduced by half, about 12 minutes.

While greens are cooking, cook pasta until al dente.

Drain pasta, place in a large bowl, and toss immediately with remaining tablespoon butter, greens, and cheese. Season generously with pepper and more salt, if desired. Serve at once.

PASTA SHELLS WITH MANY CHEESES

QUICK-COOK RECIPE / MAKES 6 TO 8 SERVINGS

I came up with this dish in a frugal attempt to make something tasty out of scraps left behind from a fancy cheese board. The critical cheese types are: a blue that is strong and sheepy, such as Roquefort; a nutty high-alpine cheese, such as Gruyère or Comté; a good Italian Fontina for melting; and a sharp cheddar for pungent flavor. Nice variations include adding a pinch of crushed dried red chili pepper, using a combination of thyme and oregano, and stirring in crumbled toasted walnuts just before serving.

FLAVOR TIP: Don't use more than 4 ounces Roquefort or blue cheese, or the flavor will dominate the dish and the subtleties of the other cheeses will be lost.

1½ cups heavy cream

2 tablespoons finely chopped fresh thyme

Pinch of freshly grated nutmeg

1 pound small pasta shells or fusilli

2 pounds mixed cheeses, at least 6 and as many as 10 (such as Roquefort, see Tip; aged Gouda; Mimolette; English cheddar; Fontina; Comté; goat's-milk Gouda; Gruyère; Emmenthaler; Beaufort; Italian sharp provolone; and/or Manchego), grated or crumbled

Coarsely ground black pepper

Bring a large pot of salted water to a boil.

In a medium saucepan, bring cream, thyme, and nutmeg to a simmer over medium heat; cook until thickened and slightly reduced, about 5 minutes.

Once cream is reduced, add pasta to water and cook until al dente. While pasta is cooking, reduce heat under cream to lowest setting and, stirring with a wooden spoon, begin adding cheese in handfuls, allowing each addition to melt and blend with cream before adding the next, until all of the cheese is used and you have a thick sauce.

Drain pasta, transfer to a large bowl, add cheese sauce, and toss together. Season with pepper and serve immediately.

PASTA CARBONARA

QUICK-COOK RECIPE / MAKES 4 TO 6 SERVINGS

Pasta carbonara, originally a dish of the gritty postwar working-class trattorias that fed Rome's inner-city inhabitants, is traditionally made with guanciale (cured hog jowls), lots of coarsely ground black pepper, and raw eggs beaten with grated Pecorino Romano cheese. The heat of the just-cooked pasta thickens the egg and cheese mixture to a creamy unctuousness that coats each strand of pasta. I like to combine Pecorino Romano (its salty taste gives an authentic Roman flavor) and Parmigiano-Reggiano. I make this with guanciale, pancetta, or good bacon—whatever I have. Carbonara purists would scowl at my use of sautéed shallots, but I think they bring a welcome sweetness to the dish.

5   slices good thick-cut bacon, cut into ¼-inch-wide strips

2   tablespoons extra-virgin olive oil

2   large shallots, minced

5   large eggs

2   cups freshly grated Pecorino Romano cheese

2   cups freshly grated Parmigiano-Reggiano cheese

1   tablespoon coarsely ground black pepper

1   pound bucatini or spaghetti

Bring a large pot of salted water to a boil.

Cook bacon in oil in a medium skillet over low heat, stirring occasionally, until fat is rendered, about 10 minutes. Add shallots and continue to cook, stirring occasionally, until softened, 5 to 7 minutes. Remove from heat.

In a large, wide bowl, whisk together eggs, Pecorino Romano, Parmesan, and pepper.

Cook pasta until al dente. Drain and immediately toss with egg mixture. Add bacon mixture, toss well, and serve at once.

SPAGHETTI WITH LEMON SOLE, ALMONDS, CAPERS, AND PARSLEY

QUICK-COOK RECIPE / MAKES 4 SERVINGS

Capers, parsley, and lemon are a common pairing with fish in the Mediterranean. Flaked with a few turns of the fork, the fish and its flavorings become an unexpected, delicious sauce for pasta. Coarsely chopped almonds add texture and flavor. This recipe works well with any white-fleshed fish, especially flaky types like sole and flounder.

FLAVOR TIP: For a spicy dish, add a pinch or two of crushed dried red chili pepper or piment d'Espelette (see page 16) with the butter.

- ¼ cup plus 3 tablespoons extra-virgin olive oil, plus (optional) extra for drizzling
- 1 pound lemon sole, fluke, or flounder fillets (see headnote)
- 2 tablespoons unsalted butter
- 1 cup whole raw almonds, coarsely chopped
- 2 tablespoons salt-packed capers, rinsed several times and drained
- 3 garlic cloves, thinly sliced
- ½ cup chopped fresh flat-leaf parsley
  Finely grated zest and juice of 1 lemon
- 1 pound spaghetti
  Coarsely ground black pepper

Bring a large pot of salted water to a boil.

Heat ¼ cup oil in a large cast-iron skillet over high heat. Add fish and cook, tilting pan occasionally and using a spoon to baste fish with hot oil, until bottom has formed a golden crust, about 4 minutes. Transfer fish to a large bowl.

Pour oil from skillet and discard; return skillet to medium-high heat. Add butter, almonds, capers, and garlic and cook until fragrant, about 30 seconds. Add parsley, stir, and transfer mixture to bowl with fish. Using a fork, break fish into bits and toss with other ingredients. Add lemon zest and juice and gently stir to combine; cover to keep warm while you cook pasta.

Cook pasta until al dente. Remove ½ cup cooking water, then drain. Immediately add hot pasta, cooking water, and remaining 3 tablespoons oil to fish. Toss and season with pepper. Finish with a drizzle of oil, if desired, and serve at once.

PASTA WITH BOTTARGA

QUICK-COOK RECIPE / MAKES 4 TO 6 SERVINGS

I ate this pasta one summer day in Castelvetrano, Sicily, at the home of Gian Franco Becchina, the producer of one of the region's finest olive oils, Olio Verde. Like many Italians, Gian Franco is passionate about his heritage and his food—two things that are always combined in the Italian mentality. If you are Sicilian, then Sicilian food is the most important cuisine in Italy; if you are Roman, Roman food is.

The scirocco (the hot desert wind that comes from the Sahara and sometimes makes it as far as Tuscany) had been blowing for a few days, and the fishermen had been hesitant to go out, so the market was slim pickings.

Bottarga, a staple of the Sicilian pantry, provided an easy solution for lunch. The salted and air-dried egg sac of tuna or gray mullet, it has a unique slightly bitter, salty fish flavor.

Extra-virgin olive oil for shallow-frying

4 garlic cloves, smashed and peeled

2 cups small torn-up pieces of plain country loaf bread

3/4 cup chopped fresh flat-leaf parsley

Grated zest of 1 lemon

1/2 teaspoon crushed dried red chili pepper

Juice of 2 lemons (5–6 tablespoons)

1/4 cup your best extra-virgin olive oil

3½ ounces *bottarga di muggine* or *bottarga di tonno* (see page 11), any wax and thin skin peeled off

1 pound spaghetti

Bring a large pot of salted water to a boil.

Pour 1/8 inch oil into a large skillet and heat over medium-high heat. Add garlic and cook until garlic starts to brown, about 1 minute. Add bread, parsley, lemon zest, and chili pepper and cook, stirring constantly, until bread is lightly golden and fragrant, about 2 minutes. Remove from heat.

Combine lemon juice and ¼ cup oil; set aside. Grind bottarga in a food processor until coarsely ground; add bread mixture and process until finely ground.

Cook pasta until al dente. Drain and immediately toss with lemon juice and oil. Add bottarga mixture, toss, and serve at once.

SPAGHETTINI WITH GROUND LAMB, YOGURT, AND MINT

QUICK-COOK RECIPE / MAKES 4 TO 6 SERVINGS

This may be the only pasta I make that is not Italian-inspired, but it's one that I really love. The flavor of cool, tangy yogurt with hot lamb, good as it is in a kebab-type sandwich, is just as terrific in this unusual recipe, which is originally from Turkey. Other long pastas also work well here, especially spaghetti, bucatini, and fresh tagliatelle.

2 cups tangy plain whole-milk yogurt, such as Old Chatham sheep's-milk yogurt

½ teaspoon Aleppo pepper (see page 16) or crushed dried red chili pepper

3 garlic cloves, minced

1 cup coarsely chopped mint leaves

2 tablespoons extra-virgin olive oil

1 medium onion, minced

Medium-coarse sea salt

¼ cup pine nuts

1 tablespoon unsalted butter

2 pounds ground lamb

1 pound spaghettini or other long pasta

Coarsely ground black pepper

Bring a large pot of salted water to a boil.

Stir together yogurt, Aleppo pepper, two thirds of garlic, and half of mint in a medium bowl.

Heat oil in a large skillet over medium heat. Add onion, remaining garlic, and a pinch of salt and cook, stirring occasionally, until onion is becoming translucent, about 2 minutes. Add pine nuts and butter and cook until nuts begin to color, about 2 minutes more. Transfer mixture to bowl with yogurt.

Add one third of lamb to skillet, increase heat to high, and cook until lamb starts to brown, about 5 minutes. Add remaining lamb in 2 batches, then cook, stirring occasionally, until well browned, crispy in spots, and cooked through, about 5 minutes more. The lamb should give off some liquid, but if not, add ¼ cup or so water, to give a little moisture, and stir to blend. Remove from heat.

Meanwhile, when lamb is close to done, cook pasta until al dente.

Drain, transfer hot pasta to a large bowl, and immediately toss with half of lamb and half of yogurt mixture. Add remaining mint, lamb, and yogurt mixture and toss again. Season with salt to taste and abundant black pepper, and serve at once.

SPAGHETTI WITH CHICKEN LIVERS, ROSEMARY, AND LEMON

QUICK-COOK RECIPE / MAKES 4 TO 6 SERVINGS

I've always loved the flavor of liver, even as a child. Paired with rosemary and lemon, ingredients that are always a good match for liver, it makes a quick, deliciously rich pasta sauce. I discovered this recipe while hanging out in Dario Cecchini's famous butcher shop in Panzano in Chianti, browsing through his collection of Italian and Tuscan cookbooks and listening with half an ear to the tales being told around me. I buy organic chicken livers and encourage you to do the same.

FLAVOR TIP: When liver is cooked just through, it has a pleasing sweetness. Be careful not to overcook it, or it will become bitter.

- 1 lemon
- 2 tablespoons chopped fresh rosemary
- 1 garlic clove
- 1 pound chicken livers, preferably organic
  Fine sea salt and coarsely ground black pepper
- 2 tablespoons extra-virgin olive oil
- 2 tablespoons unsalted butter
- 1/4 cup water
- 1 pound spaghetti

Bring a large pot of salted water to a boil.

Using a paring knife or vegetable peeler, cut peel from lemon, avoiding the bitter pith. Finely mince peel together with rosemary and garlic; set aside. Juice lemon and set aside.

Rinse and drain chicken livers, and blot dry with paper towels. Season liberally with salt and pepper. Heat oil in a large cast-iron skillet over high heat. Feed livers slowly into pan, to maintain temperature, and brown well, 3 to 4 minutes per side. Transfer livers to a cutting board (set pan aside) and coarsely chop.

Return skillet to heat and reduce heat to medium-low. Add 1 tablespoon butter and heat until melted. Add rosemary mixture and cook until fragrant, about 2 minutes. Add chopped liver and water and cook, stirring and smushing up the liver a bit to make a creamy sauce, until liver is just cooked through, about 4 minutes (do not overcook). Remove from heat and stir in lemon juice.

Meanwhile, cook pasta until al dente. Drain, transfer to a large bowl, and immediately toss with remaining tablespoon butter and liver sauce. Season to taste with salt and pepper, and serve at once.

CLASSIC CENTRAL ITALIAN MEAT RAGÙ

SLOW-COOK RECIPE / MAKES 9 CUPS

Simmering mild-flavored meats in their own juices with lots of aromatic vegetables gives this ragù its wonderfully delicate taste; no one ingredient comes to the forefront. When properly cooked, the sauce has a kind of melt-in-your-mouth quality. Commonly served with soft fresh egg noodles, the ragù works well over any shape or form of pasta, and it is also perfect for Homemade Lasagna (page 178). It's a time-consuming recipe, but it makes a large quantity, so you can use some for a pasta or lasagna and freeze the rest. As long as you use a variety of meats, feel free to vary the proportions to suit your own taste. My Tuscan neighbor Mita even adds a little chicken liver, which brings a subtle rich touch.

2	carrots, cut into 1-inch pieces
2	celery stalks, cut into 1-inch pieces
1	medium onion, quartered
2	garlic cloves
1/4	cup extra-virgin olive oil
2	tablespoons fine sea salt, or to taste
1½	cups water
1	tablespoon tomato paste, preferably double-concentrate (see page 19)
1½	pounds ground beef
1½	pounds ground pork
1½	pounds ground veal
1	35-ounce can whole peeled San Marzano tomatoes, with their juices

In a food processor, pulse carrots, celery, onion, and garlic until finely minced.

Heat oil in a large Dutch oven or other heavy pot over high heat. Add vegetable mixture and 1 teaspoon salt. Cook, stirring once or twice, until vegetables start to soften, about 1 minute. Add 1 cup water and tomato paste, stirring with a wooden spoon to dissolve paste. Bring to a boil and cook, stirring frequently, until about 2 tablespoons liquid remain, about 7 minutes.

Add beef, pork, and veal, stirring to break meat into smaller clumps, then stir constantly (you want to be sure to break up the meat here to achieve a nice texture) for 10 minutes. Add 2 teaspoons salt, reduce heat to low, and simmer for 40 minutes.

While meat is cooking, pass tomatoes and their juices through a food mill.

Add remaining ½ cup water to pot with meat, stir, and cook for 10 minutes. Add pureed tomatoes, stir, and simmer until ragù is thick and flavorful, about 2 hours more.

Season with 1 tablespoon more salt, or to taste. Serve, or let cool and store in the refrigerator for up to 5 days or the freezer for up to 6 months.

MEAT RAGÙS

Meat ragù is Italian cooking at its frugal best—tough meat scraps slowly cooked with aromatic vegetables and herbs, and perhaps a little tomato. Pair it with pasta or polenta, and you have a fine meal. The famous Bolognese is perhaps the best known of all ragùs, so much so that restaurants all over Italy refer to whatever ragù they make as "Bolognese." But, in fact, meat ragù changes from house to house, village to village, province to province, and north to south. There are the rich game ragùs of Tuscany, made with wild boar, venison, hare, or squab; assertive spicy pork ragùs from Southern Italy, made with seasoned sausage as well as fresh pork; the delicate three-meat ragù of the North, very slowly cooked until the meat is very tender; and even ragùs with no tomato.

A ragù can faithfully follow traditional regional recipes—my wild boar ragù is as classically Tuscan as they come—but it is also a perfect sauce for the resourceful and inventive cook, made with whatever scraps, leftovers, and herbs are available. I often take the leftover meat from a roast and stew it slowly with some aromatic vegetables, fresh rosemary, sage, or marjoram, and a little tomato.

In making a ragù, every cooking decision is a flavor prospect: brown the meat or not (browning is best for robust-style ragùs); brown the vegetables or not; choose the herbs to use; marinate the meat overnight or not; add extra pork fat or not; add tomato paste, canned tomatoes, or no tomatoes at all; use ground meat or meat cut into small cubes that will fall apart through the long, slow cooking. I usually add water and a small amount of tomato paste to the vegetables and simmer them before adding the meat; this step softens the flavor of the vegetables, allowing them to fade into the background somewhat and blend harmoniously with the meat.

Generally, you'll need 4 cups of ragù to sauce 1 pound of pasta. Ragùs freeze beautifully, so you can double a recipe and save some for later.

SOUTHERN ITALIAN PORK RAGÙ

SLOW-COOK RECIPE / MAKES 6 CUPS

Southern ragùs are heavier affairs than the ragùs of central Italy. They're more assertive and richer, because of the cooking technique and the stronger-flavored meats, such as highly seasoned sausage or lamb. Browning the meat and aromatic vegetables before adding the rest of the ingredients intensifies the flavors of this sauce. For a more gamy, Southern Italian–style sauce, use ground lamb in place of the ground pork and the sausage. I like this sauce with short, tubular pastas—penne, maccheroncini, ziti, and the like.

FLAVOR TIP: For the most authentic flavor, use either dried wild Mediterranean oregano, which you can find in Greek food shops and gourmet stores, or 1 teaspoon finely chopped fresh oregano.

1	medium onion, cut into quarters
1	large carrot, cut into large chunks
1	celery stalk, cut into 4 pieces
4	garlic cloves
1½	pounds hot Italian pork sausage, removed from casings
½	cup extra-virgin olive oil
1½	pounds ground pork
1	tablespoon tomato paste, preferably double-concentrate (see page 19)
¾–1¼	cups water
1	28-ounce can whole peeled San Marzano tomatoes, with their juices
2	teaspoons dried oregano (see Tip)
	Fine sea salt

In a food processor, pulse onion, carrot, celery, and garlic until finely minced.

Cook sausage in a large Dutch oven or other heavy pot over medium heat, breaking it up just a little bit with a wooden spoon, until fat is rendered, any juices have reduced, and sausage is browned, about 20 minutes.

Add ¼ cup oil to pot, then add ground pork in 4 or 5 batches, stirring and cooking each one for a minute or so before adding next. Once all pork has been added, cook for 5 minutes more, stirring constantly to break up meat.

Remove all but ¼ cup meat from pot and reserve. Add remaining ¼ cup oil and minced vegetables to pot and cook, stirring occasionally, until vegetables are tender and golden, about 10 minutes. Add reserved meat to pot and cook, stirring occasionally, for 5 minutes.

Dissolve tomato paste in ¾ cup water and add to meat mixture, along with tomatoes and their juices, oregano, and a pinch of salt. Bring to a gentle simmer, reduce heat to low, and cook, stirring occasionally, adding up to ½ cup more water if ragù appears dry, until thick and flavorful, about 4 hours. Season with salt to taste.

Serve, or let cool and refrigerate for up to 5 days or freeze for up to 6 months.

BRAISED GUINEA HEN RAGÙ

SLOW-COOK RECIPE / MAKES 4 CUPS

Guinea hen, available from specialty butchers (see Sources, page 357), has a more pronounced flavor than chicken. Here the meat is browned before being braised in red wine; the caramelized meat juices add depth of flavor, while the wine gives complexity. Add a bit of grated Parmesan when you toss this ragù with pasta.

The technique for this ragù works with any poultry. Simply adjust the cooking time—less for chicken, more for duck or goose—and braise until the meat is tender and the flavors have melded to your liking. When using duck or goose, remove the very fatty skin before cooking; the leaner guinea hen benefits from the skin, though. For a nice variation, add sautéed wild mushrooms.

FLAVOR TIP: Try white wine in place of the red for a more delicate flavor.

2–2¼	pounds guinea hen legs and thighs (about 4 pieces; see headnote)
	Fine sea salt and coarsely ground black pepper
¼	cup extra-virgin olive oil
2	carrots, cut into ½-inch pieces
1	celery stalk, cut into ½-inch pieces
1	medium onion, coarsely chopped
3	garlic cloves, smashed and peeled
3	leafy fresh thyme, rosemary, or sage sprigs, leaves removed from stems and coarsely chopped and stems discarded
1	cup dry red wine
1	tablespoon tomato paste, preferably double-concentrate (see page 19)
1½	cups water
2	tablespoons chopped fresh flat-leaf parsley

Heat oven to 300°F.

Season guinea hen generously with salt and pepper.

Heat oil in a large Dutch oven or other heavy ovenproof pot over medium-high heat. Brown hen pieces, about 5 minutes per side, removing them to a plate as they brown.

Add carrots, celery, onion, garlic, herb, and 1 teaspoon salt to pot. Cook, stirring occasionally, until vegetables start to brown, about 10 minutes. Remove from heat. Drain vegetables and hen pieces in a colander, and discard fat from pot.

Return hen and vegetables to pot, then add wine and tomato paste, stirring to dissolve paste. Bring to a simmer, then add 1 cup water and return to a simmer. Cover and braise in oven until meat is tender, about 40 minutes. Remove pot from oven and let cool.

Pull meat from bones in large chunks; discard skin and bones. Puree vegetables with braising liquid in a food processor or blender. Return to pot, along with meat, add remaining ½ cup water, and bring to a simmer over low heat. Cover and cook for 30 to 45 minutes more to allow flavors to meld.

Remove from heat and stir in parsley. Serve, or let cool and refrigerate for up to 5 days or freeze for up to 6 months.

BRAISED RABBIT RAGÙ

SLOW-COOK RECIPE / MAKES SCANT 5 CUPS

The rabbit meat here is browned, as are the vegetables, before they are braised together. The use of white or rosé wine rather than red reflects the more delicate character of rabbit meat. All the classic Tuscan flavors are here: rosemary, garlic, and delicious braised game. This chunky ragù is most often served with pappardelle, but any wide flat pasta will work well.

1 2½-pound rabbit
 Fine sea salt and coarsely ground black pepper
¼ cup plus 3 tablespoons extra-virgin olive oil
3 celery stalks, cut into 1-inch pieces
2 large carrots, cut into 1-inch pieces
1 medium onion, cut into 1-inch pieces
3 garlic cloves, smashed and peeled
1 tablespoon chopped fresh rosemary
1 tablespoon tomato paste, preferably double-concentrate (see page 19)
1 cup dry rosé or white wine
1 cup water

Cut rabbit in half lengthwise, then cut crosswise into about 14 roughly equal pieces. Season generously with salt and pepper. Heat 3 tablespoons oil in a large Dutch oven or other heavy pot over medium-high heat. Add only as many rabbit pieces as fit in pot without crowding and brown on all sides, about 6 minutes per side. Remove to a large bowl, and repeat with remaining rabbit.

Add remaining ¼ cup oil, celery, carrots, onion, and garlic to pot and cook, stirring occasionally, until vegetables are browned, about 8 minutes. Using a slotted spoon, transfer vegetables to bowl with rabbit. Pour all but about 1 tablespoon of oil out of pot.

Add rosemary to pot and cook over medium heat until fragrant, about 1 minute. Dissolve tomato paste in wine and add to pot, scraping up browned bits. Add vegetables, rabbit pieces, and water and bring to a gentle simmer. Reduce heat to low, cover, and cook until meat is tender, about 1½ hours.

Remove lid and continue cooking at a gentle simmer until sauce is reduced and slightly thickened, about 25 minutes more. Remove from heat, and transfer rabbit to a bowl.

Puree vegetables with braising liquid in a blender or food processor until smooth. Return sauce to pot.

Pull meat from bones, tearing it into small chunks but not shredding it; discard bones. Mix meat into sauce and reheat and serve, or let cool and refrigerate for up to 5 days or freeze for up to 6 months.

TUSCAN WILD BOAR RAGÙ

SLOW-COOK RECIPE / MAKES 4 CUPS

Wild boar are ubiquitous in Tuscany, where they cause grave damage to vine-yards and home gardens. From September to April, the hills of Teverina echo with the sounds of hunting horns, barking dogs, rifle shots, and cursing men. Needless to say, the meat turns up in a lot of dishes, and as kids, we never tired of hunkering down to a big plate of it.

True wild boar, like all wild game, has a tasty funkiness to it. Even the do-mesticated version that we get in America has a stronger, more pronounced flavor than ordinary pork. Marinating the meat overnight in red wine with assertive fla-voring agents like bay leaf, peppercorns, juniper, and garlic before cooking boosts its richness. In fact, this marinating technique is a great one for any game.

Game ragùs are classically served with fresh pappardelle or tagliatelle, but they do equally well with short tubular dried pastas, such as penne and rigatoni, and are also good spooned over plain soft polenta. I like to add a little chopped fresh rosemary or even sage just before tossing with pasta and a bit of grated Parmesan or aged Pecorino Toscano.

You can substitute any kind of strong game, such as venison, hare, or squab, for the boar.

MARINADE

1 carrot, cut into 1-inch pieces

1 celery stalk, cut into 1-inch pieces

1 medium onion, quartered

3 garlic cloves

1 shallot, quartered

2 fresh rosemary sprigs

8 juniper berries

2 bay leaves

1 tablespoon black peppercorns

2½ cups dry red wine

2–2¼ pounds bone-in boar shoulder, cut into 1-inch pieces (reserve bone to make stock, if desired); see headnote

RAGÙ

1 carrot, cut into 1-inch pieces

1 celery stalk, cut into 1-inch pieces

1 medium onion, quartered

1 garlic clove

1 fresh rosemary sprig, leaves only

Fine sea salt and coarsely ground black pepper

¼ cup extra-virgin olive oil

2 cups water

1 tablespoon tomato paste, preferably double-concentrate (see page 19)

1 28-ounce can whole peeled San Marzano tomatoes, with their juices

FOR THE MARINADE: Combine carrot, celery, onion, garlic, shallot, rosemary, juniper berries, bay leaves, peppercorns, and wine in a large bowl. Add boar, cover, and marinate in the refrigerator for at least 12 hours, or overnight.

FOR THE RAGÙ: In a food processor, pulse carrot, celery, onion, garlic, and rosemary until finely minced.

Drain boar, pat dry, and discard marinade. Season boar generously with salt and pepper. Heat oil in a large Dutch oven or other heavy pot over medium-high heat. Add boar, slowly feeding it into pot to keep pan temperature from dropping too much, and cook until you have a good sear on one side, about 10 minutes. Move browned pieces to side of pot and continue until all meat is seared. Transfer meat to a plate.

Add vegetable mixture and 1 teaspoon salt to pot and cook, stirring occasionally, until vegetables start to brown, about 7 minutes. Return meat to pot, then add water and tomato paste, stirring to dissolve paste. Cover and simmer gently for about 2 hours.

Add tomatoes and juices and simmer for another hour or so, until meat is very tender, gently breaking meat into chunks with a wooden spoon as it becomes tender. Remove from heat and let cool.

Remove meat from pot and shred with your fingers (this will give you a country-style ragù that will coat your pasta in the appropriate way). Return meat to pot and reheat gently before serving, or let cool and refrigerate for up to 5 days or freeze for up to 6 months.

HOMEMADE LASAGNA

SLOW-COOK RECIPE / MAKES 8 SERVINGS

Tuscan lasagna is very different from what most Americans think of as lasagna. Like most Italian pastas, it is as much about the pasta as the sauce. This is traditionally a farmhouse dish—its delicate layers of thinly rolled sheets of fresh pasta, with the merest skimming of sauce and Parmesan cheese between, are stacked as high as possible in a battered aluminum roasting pan and then put into the cooling wood oven, once the bread has come out, to slowly bake for Sunday lunch.

You can roll out the pasta sheets by hand, as I describe here, or use a pasta machine to roll out thin lasagna noodles (use the thinnest setting on the machine). Yes, this is a time-consuming recipe, but you can prepare the ragù ahead and keep it refrigerated or frozen until your lasagna-making day arrives.

FLAVOR TIPS: Making the final layer heavy on the *besciamel* and light on the tomato sauce helps you to get the characteristic golden brown crust. Be sure the entire top of the lasagna is covered with *besciamel*. Apart from flavoring the dish, it will seal in the cooking juices, making for a moist final dish.

After assembling the lasagna, don't trim the dough around the edges of the pan too carefully—you want to leave a little overhang to brown up and add a nice crisp texture to every serving.

2½ pounds Fresh Pasta Dough (page 180)
All-purpose flour for dusting
Besciamel Sauce (page 181)
3 cups Classic Central Italian Meat Ragù (page 168)
1¾ cups freshly grated Parmigiano-Reggiano cheese
Coarsely ground black pepper
1 tablespoon unsalted butter

Pull off a workable-sized piece of pasta dough, about one sixth of what you have; keep the rest of the dough covered. Lightly dust the piece of dough with flour and roll out with a rolling pin on a lightly floured surface to a rectangle about 12 by 18 inches. Trim to a 10½-by-17-inch rectangle. Lay pasta sheet flat and cover with a clean dish towel; repeat with remaining dough, covering each piece with a clean towel or plastic wrap as you go.

Heat oven to 375°F with a rack in center.

Bring a large pot of salted water to a boil. Fill a large bowl with ice and water. Add 1 lasagna sheet to the boiling water (if you used a pasta machine to roll sheets, you can add several at a time), cover, and cook for 1 minute. Transfer sheet to ice water for 30 seconds, then lay flat on a dish towel and repeat with remaining sheets, covering each with a towel as you go.

TO ASSEMBLE LASAGNA: Spread together about ⅓ cup *besciamel* and about ¼ cup ragù over the bottom of a 9-by-13-inch glass or ceramic baking dish. Top with 1 pasta sheet (or with a layer of 2 lasagna noodles if you rolled the pasta with a machine). Top pasta with ⅔ cup *besciamel* and ½ cup ragù and spread together evenly over pasta, then sprinkle with ¼ cup cheese and pepper to taste. Continue layering until last sheet of pasta is in pan. Top with remaining 1⅓ cups *besciamel*, ¼ cup ragù, and ½ cup cheese. Trim overhang just a bit if needed, but leave enough of the edges so they are crispy.

Dot top of lasagna with butter and bake until golden brown and bubbly, about 45 minutes. Let rest for 10 minutes before cutting.

FRESH PASTA DOUGH

QUICK-COOK RECIPE / MAKES 2¹/₂ POUNDS PASTA; ABOUT 10 SERVINGS

This simple dough of flour and eggs is lightened with a little water, and some olive oil is kneaded in at the end to give it elasticity. My Tuscan neighbor Mita makes fresh pasta only for feast days, using it in one of two ways: cut into ribbons for tagliatelle, to be served with a meat ragù, or cut into sheets, to be layered with meat ragù, *besciamel*, and Parmigiano-Reggiano for classic Tuscan lasagna. I have used the dough to make just about every shape there is, from ravioli to tortellini to cannelloni.

5¹/₂ cups all-purpose flour

6 large eggs

¹/₂ cup water

1¹/₂ teaspoons extra-virgin olive oil

Mound flour in a large mixing bowl; create a well in center and add eggs and water. Using a fork, gently break up eggs and start slowly incorporating flour from inside rim of well until liquid is absorbed (about half of flour will be incorporated). Then knead dough in bowl until it comes together in a mass.

Transfer dough to a lightly floured board and knead until you have a smooth, compact dough, about 8 minutes more. Drizzle oil over top and knead for about 1 minute to incorporate. Wrap tightly in plastic and let rest for 15 minutes at room temperature, or for up to 6 hours in the refrigerator, before rolling out as desired.

BESCIAMEL SAUCE

SLOW-COOK RECIPE / MAKES 5 CUPS

Besciamel is one of the mother sauces of classic French cuisine (it is *béchamel* in French), but Italians use it frequently as well. Infusing the milk with a rich assortment of herbs and aromatic vegetables adds depth of flavor. In addition to or in place of the herbs, you can also try fresh chives, oregano, savory, and/or just the tiniest amount of lovage. Since I use this version of the sauce for Classic Tuscan Eggplant Parmesan (page 197) and Homemade Lasagna (page 178), I whisk Parmigiano-Reggiano into the *besciamel* as a final step, to reflect the cheese in those dishes.

NOTE: You'll need to use the *besciamel* right away, since it solidifies as it cools and won't spread evenly.

6	cups whole milk
2	celery stalks, cut into 4 pieces each
1	medium unpeeled onion, quartered
1	leek, trimmed, cut lengthwise in half, and washed well
1	carrot, cut into 4 pieces
2	garlic cloves, peeled
1/3	bunch fresh flat-leaf parsley
5	fresh sage sprigs
4	bay leaves
1/2	teaspoon black peppercorns
7	tablespoons unsalted butter
3/4	cup all-purpose flour
1	teaspoon fine sea salt
1/4	teaspoon freshly grated nutmeg
1	cup freshly grated Parmigiano-Reggiano cheese

Combine milk, celery, onion, leek, carrot, garlic, parsley, sage, bay leaves, and peppercorns in a large saucepan over medium heat and bring to just under a boil. Remove from heat and let steep for 1 hour.

Strain milk into another saucepan; discard solids. Bring milk back to a gentle simmer, and remove from heat.

Melt butter in a large heavy saucepan over medium heat. Add flour and, using a wooden spoon, stir rapidly to incorporate. Cook, stirring constantly, for 3 minutes. Add milk ½ cup at a time, stirring well and making sure to scrape corners of pan after each addition. Add salt and nutmeg and cook, stirring occasionally, for 5 minutes. Add cheese and cook, stirring, for 2 minutes more. Reduce heat to low and cook, stirring occasionally, until sauce is thickened and flavorful, about 10 minutes more.

RISOTTO

Risotto is a Northern Italian dish, in which short-grain rice gradually releases its starch to bond with and absorb the flavors of its fellow principal ingredients. These must always include good olive oil, butter, homemade broth, and, more often than not, the best cheese you can find. The rest is up to you. Once you understand how risotto works, you have a blank slate that can be endlessly varied.

I mastered risotto-making in part by reading Burton Anderson's book, *Treasures of the Italian Table,* which describes in loving detail the traditional foods of Italy and the vanishing culinary artisans who make them. In the risotto chapter, Anderson explains how the dish is made in the Po River Valley, Italy's largest agricultural plain and main rice-producing region.

Though the dish is actually very simple, there are a few key factors involved in making risotto that seem to flummox people.

Short-grain rice is essential. There are several varieties used in Italy for risotto, including Baldo, Vialone Nano, and Carnaroli, as well as the more common Arborio. All work quite well, but Carnaroli, which I prefer, makes the most luxurious, creamy risotto. (In a pinch, I've made the dish successfully with Spanish paella rice.)

Your broth should be homemade, ideally, and be kept hot so that as you add it, you will not cool the rice. This ensures even cooking. Since the broth is the main ingredient you are "feeding" to the rice, it has to be superior; an inferior product will produce inferior results, no matter how good your technique. Commercial broth does not have the proper flavor, richness, and body for risotto;

better to wait until you have the real thing on hand. If you must use store-bought, which is saltier than homemade, go lightly when adding salt to season your dish. If you like, you can infuse the broth with an ingredient that reflects the main flavor of the dish; pea pods from freshly shucked peas in the broth for pea risotto, the naked corncobs for corn risotto, and so on.

The first step in cooking risotto, and a critical one to understand, is the *tostatura,* the toasting of the rice in hot fat (butter and/or oil, or bacon fat) for at least 5 minutes; some say as long as 10. This forms a crust around each kernel of rice, which seals in the starch so that as the cooking process progresses, the starch is only gradually released. Adding the stock in small increments and stirring fairly constantly is also important. This allows the rice to cook evenly and the starch to be slowly drawn out so it bonds with the liquid, forming a creamy sauce around the rice.

There are several different schools of thought as to how dry or how soupy the finished risotto should be. The Venetian ideal, which tends toward a more liquid version, referred to as *all'onda* ("with waves"), is achieved by finishing the dish with a little more broth than you would for a drier style. I vary my risotto based on ingredients or mood, sometimes preferring a drier risotto and sometimes preferring a wetter one. Try both and see which you prefer.

I like to cook risotto until the rice is just al dente, then cover it and let it steam for a final 5 minutes off the heat. I've found that this results in a tender, yet not overcooked, dish.

MAINE SHRIMP RISOTTO

QUICK-COOK RECIPE / MAKES 4 MAIN-COURSE SERVINGS

The sweet little Arctic shrimp that come into season in Maine in December or January are perfect for this straightforward risotto. The shrimp are stirred in at the last minute so that just the heat from the rice cooks them and they keep their tender texture. A simple stock made with their heads and shells enriches the flavors of the dish. You can substitute 1 to 1¼ pounds small regular shrimp for the Maine, but try to get them with heads on.

- 3 tablespoons extra-virgin olive oil
- 1 small onion, finely chopped
- Fine sea salt
- 2 cups Carnaroli rice
- ⅔ cup dry white wine
- 3¾ cups Shrimp Broth (recipe follows), heated to a simmer
- 1 pound Maine shrimp, peeled, shells (and heads, if you have them) reserved for stock (see headnote and Sources, page 357)
- ¼ cup chopped fresh chives
- Coarsely ground black pepper

Heat oil in a large saucepan over medium heat. Add onion and a pinch of salt and cook, stirring occasionally, until onion is translucent, about 5 minutes. Add rice and cook, stirring constantly, until it is chalky-looking and a white dot is visible in center of each grain, about 5 minutes.

Add wine and stir constantly until mostly absorbed, about 1 minute. Add 1 cup broth and cook, stirring, until mostly absorbed, 2 to 3 minutes. Add ½ cup more broth and cook, stirring, until mostly absorbed. Repeat, adding liquid in ½-cupfuls, until rice is tender yet still slightly firm to the bite.

Add remaining ¼ cup broth, shrimp, and chives, stir, and remove from heat. Cover and let sit for 5 minutes.

Season risotto with salt and pepper to taste, and serve immediately.

SHRIMP BROTH

QUICK-COOK RECIPE / MAKES 4½ CUPS

You can make a perfectly good broth simply with shrimp heads and shells, onion, celery, and carrot. But for Maine Shrimp Risotto (page 184), where the broth is the primary flavoring in the dish, I use additional ingredients, including saffron, tomato paste, and fennel, for a deeper, richer base.

FLAVOR TIP: Shrimp heads add richness and depth. If you can't get head-on shrimp, add ¼ pound shrimp with shells on to the broth.

¼	cup extra-virgin olive oil
	Shells (and heads, if possible) from 1 pound Maine shrimp (see Tip)
1	medium carrot, cut into 4 pieces
1	celery stalk, cut into 4 pieces
1	small onion, quartered
1	small fennel bulb with fronds, stalks cut into 3 pieces each, bulb quartered
1	bay leaf
1½	teaspoons tomato paste, preferably double-concentrate (see page 19)
½	cup dry white wine
5½	cups water
¼	bunch fresh flat-leaf parsley
¼	teaspoon saffron threads
½	teaspoon black peppercorns

Heat oil in a large Dutch oven or other heavy pot over medium-high heat. Add shrimp shells, and heads, if using, and cook, stirring, until shells become opaque, 3 to 4 minutes. Add carrot, celery, onion, fennel, and bay leaf and cook, stirring frequently, until vegetables become fragrant and lightly golden, about 6 minutes.

Dissolve tomato paste in wine and add to pot, scraping up any browned bits from bottom of pot. Cook for 1 to 2 minutes. Add water, parsley, saffron, and peppercorns and bring to a boil, then reduce to a gentle simmer and cook for 30 minutes.

Remove broth from heat and allow to steep for 15 minutes, then strain. Broth can be refrigerated for up to 2 days or frozen for up to 3 months.

SWEET PEA AND SQUASH BLOSSOM RISOTTO

QUICK-COOK RECIPE / MAKES 4 MAIN-COURSE SERVINGS

This risotto is based on the Venetian classic *risi e bisi* ("rice and peas"). Infusing the chicken broth with the pea pods intensifies the flavor of the dish. The squash blossoms add a special touch, beautiful color, and nice texture, but they have a short season. You can make a great dish without them just as well.

FLAVOR TIP: This recipe depends on fresh peas from the pod; once they are shelled, the pods are used to create the delicate broth that flavors the rice. Fresh peas are, like corn, most flavorful and sweet when used as quickly as possible after picking, before their sugars have a chance to convert to starch. Buy these vegetables at your local farmers' market and use them the same day, whenever possible.

4⅓ cups Rich Chicken Broth (page 108)

2 pounds fresh peas in the pod, stripped from their pods; 2 handfuls pods reserved

4 ounces squash blossoms (optional)

2 tablespoons extra-virgin olive oil

3 tablespoons unsalted butter

1 medium onion, finely chopped

Medium-coarse sea salt

2 cups Carnaroli rice

½ cup dry white wine

1 cup freshly grated Parmigiano-Reggiano cheese, plus more shaved Parmesan for serving

Coarsely ground black pepper

Bring broth and reserved pea pods to a simmer in a medium saucepan. Remove from heat, strain pods from broth, and discard pods. Return broth to heat and keep at a bare simmer.

Cut green bottoms from squash blossoms, if using, and reserve; cut blossoms lengthwise in half.

Heat oil and butter in a large saucepan over medium-high heat until butter is melted. Add onion and a pinch of salt, reduce heat to medium-low, and cook until onion is translucent, about 5 minutes. Add rice, increase heat to medium, and cook, stirring constantly, until it is chalky-looking and a white dot is visible in center of each grain, about 5 minutes.

Add wine and stir constantly until mostly absorbed, about 1 minute. Add 1 cup broth and cook, stirring constantly, until mostly absorbed, about 2 minutes. Add ½ cup broth and cook, stirring continuously, until mostly absorbed. Add peas and ½ cup more broth and cook, stirring, until broth is mostly absorbed. Repeat, adding broth by ½-cupfuls, until you have only ⅓ cup broth left. Add final ⅓ cup broth and squash blossom bottoms, if using, and cook until broth is absorbed and rice is tender yet still slightly firm to the bite, 2 to 3 minutes more. Stir in squash blossom flowers, if using, and cheese, remove from heat, cover, and let risotto sit for 5 minutes.

Season with salt to taste and serve immediately, with extra cheese and a grinding of pepper.

STRAWBERRY RISOTTO

QUICK-COOK RECIPE / MAKES 4 MAIN-COURSE SERVINGS

When my family lived in Rome, one of our favorite places to eat was a small neighborhood trattoria nestled away in a warren of streets between the Tiber and Piazza Navona. As in so many family-run spots, the wife managed the front of the house and the husband was in the kitchen. But the food—though perfectly Roman—was cooked with more imagination than in most places. It was here that we first encountered *risotto con le fragole* ("risotto with strawberries"), a dish that by the mid-eighties was all the rage in every Roman restaurant and then, just as quickly, disappeared.

Strange as it sounds, this is a wonderful, deeply flavored dish that is not at all sweet. I always make it in the summer with fresh-picked local strawberries, as their flavor most closely resembles that of the little berries of the Roman countryside, but it is surprisingly good with just about any flavorful strawberry you find.

2	tablespoons extra-virgin olive oil
2	tablespoons unsalted butter
1	small onion, finely chopped
	Fine sea salt
2	cups Carnaroli rice
10	ounces strawberries, hulled and cut in half or into quarters, depending on size (1³/₄ cups cut berries)
1	teaspoon sugar
¹/₂	cup dry red wine, such as Chianti
3¹/₄ – 3¹/₂	cups Rich Chicken Broth (page 108), heated to a simmer
1¹/₂	cups freshly grated Parmigiano-Reggiano cheese, plus (optional) more for serving
2	tablespoons chopped fresh chives
	Coarsely ground black pepper

Heat oil and butter in a large saucepan over medium-low heat until butter is melted. Add onion and a pinch of salt and cook until onion is translucent, about 5 minutes. Add rice, increase heat to medium, and cook, stirring constantly, until it is chalky-looking and a white dot is visible in center of each grain, about 5 minutes.

Add strawberries and sugar, stir to combine, and cook until berries soften slightly, 1 to 2 minutes. Add wine and cook, stirring, until wine has mostly been absorbed, about 1 minute. Add 1 cup broth and cook, stirring, until mostly absorbed, about 4 minutes. Add ½ cup more broth and cook, stirring, until mostly absorbed. Repeat with 3 more ½-cupfuls broth, then add ¼ cup broth and cook, stirring, for 1 to 2 minutes, until rice is tender but still firm to the bite. Add final ¼ cup broth only if necessary. Remove risotto from heat, add cheese, stir to combine, cover, and let sit for 5 minutes.

Sprinkle with chives and pepper, and serve immediately, passing extra Parmesan, if desired.

BACON AND RAMP RISOTTO

QUICK-COOK RECIPE / MAKES 4 MAIN-COURSE SERVINGS

Ramps, or wild leeks, make their appearance in the Northeast in midspring. Their pungent, garlicky-onion flavor makes them a perfect companion to the smoky, fatty taste of bacon. I use the flat broad greens of the plant like fresh herbs, chopping and tossing them into the risotto just before serving.

    2 tablespoons extra-virgin olive oil

    2 tablespoons unsalted butter

    2 slices thick-cut bacon, cut into ¼-inch-wide strips

    8 ounces ramps (about 2 bunches),
       whites thinly sliced, greens coarsely chopped
       (keep whites and greens separate)

    2 cups Carnaroli rice

    1 cup dry white wine

    5 cups Rich Chicken Broth (page 108), heated to a simmer

 1½ cups freshly grated Parmigiano-Reggiano cheese,
       plus more for serving (optional)

       Fine sea salt and coarsely ground black pepper

Heat oil and 1 tablespoon butter in a medium saucepan over medium-high heat until butter is melted. Add bacon and cook, stirring constantly, until it starts to crisp, about 2 minutes. Add ramp whites and cook, stirring, until they start to wilt and pick up a bit of color, about 1 minute. Reduce heat to medium, add rice, and cook, stirring constantly, until it is chalky-looking and a white dot is visible in center of each grain, about 5 minutes.

Add wine and cook, stirring, until mostly absorbed, about 1 minute. Add 1 cup broth and cook, stirring constantly, until liquid is mostly absorbed, about 3 minutes. Add ½ cup broth and cook, stirring, until mostly absorbed. Continue adding broth by ½-cupfuls, stirring constantly, until you have 1 cup broth left. Add ramp greens and ½ cup broth. Cook, stirring constantly, until broth is mostly absorbed, then add remaining ½ cup broth and cook, stirring, for 1 to 2 minutes more. Rice should be tender yet still slightly firm to the bite.

Remove risotto from heat, add cheese and remaining 1 tablespoon butter, and stir to combine. Cover and let sit for 5 minutes.

Season risotto to taste with salt if needed. Serve immediately, with a grinding of pepper, and extra Parmesan, if desired.

POTATO GNOCCHI

QUICK-COOK RECIPE / MAKES 4 SERVINGS

When my family first arrived in the Tuscan village of Teverina, we were exotic strangers and the objects of much curiosity. Everyone welcomed us into their homes, insisting on inviting us over for as many meals as we could manage. Our neighbor Mita often made these gnocchi for lunch when we ate with her and her family; in fact, we think "gnocchi" was my brother's first word.

The first time we were invited for gnocchi was a great lesson in rural Italian hospitality. As Americans, we assumed that "come to lunch for gnocchi" meant just that. As we finished off bowl after bowl of the little potato dumplings, swathed in meat sauce and sprinkled with Parmesan cheese, we began to feel quite stuffed. Finally, there were no more. Imagine our horror when the plates were cleared, new ones put down, and out came roast chicken and rabbit, roast potatoes, and salad. We were expected to eat all this up as well, and then dessert and liqueurs! To refuse would have been rude.

While Mita still makes gnocchi for my brother whenever he's around, she long ago taught me how to do it myself. In Teverina, gnocchi is made rustically, without eggs and without pressing the characteristic little grooves into the dough. The secret to light gnocchi is restraint with the flour. The more flour you add, the tougher they become. Mita boils her potatoes in their jackets until they're just done, then quickly slips off the peels, rices the potatoes, mixes in the flour, and sets about rolling out the gnocchi, all in the blink of an eye. In lieu of boiling the potatoes and risking overcooking (which would leave them waterlogged and in need of too much flour), I bake them. You still have to work quickly, since the steam from the hot potato helps it bond with the flour to make a dough that comes together quickly without egg. Use tomato sauce or ragù to dress these gnocchi, or toss with plain melted butter and shaved white truffles.

2½ pounds large Yukon Gold potatoes

1¾–2 cups all-purpose flour, plus more for rolling

½ cup Slow-Cooked Tomato Sauce (page 140) or 1 cup Classic Central Italian Meat Ragù (page 168)

½ cup freshly grated Parmigiano-Reggiano cheese

Medium-coarse sea salt and coarsely ground black pepper

Heat oven to 425°F.

Prick potatoes with a fork and bake until tender, about 50 minutes. While potatoes are still hot, peel and push potatoes through a ricer into a bowl. Add 1¾ cups flour, stir, and transfer mixture to a flour-dusted work surface. Knead, adding remaining ¼ cup flour in tablespoonfuls if needed, just until dough comes together. Cover with a clean dish towel and let rest for 10 minutes.

Bring a large pot of generously salted water to a boil.

Pull off a fistful of dough, leaving the rest under towel. Dust work surface with flour again. Using the palm of your hand, roll dough into a 1-inch-diameter rope. Cut into ⅓-inch-wide pieces. Holding your hand flat with fingers together, briskly roll each gnocchi back and forth under your fingers to form a little dowel-shaped piece, then roll through a little flour to lightly coat and transfer to a lightly floured baking sheet, keeping gnocchi in a single layer; be careful not to crowd them, or they will stick to one another. Repeat with remaining dough.

Gently warm tomato sauce.

Using a wide sieve and working in batches, gently shake excess flour from gnocchi. Add to boiling water and cook, removing with a slotted spoon or skimmer as they rise to the surface, 3 to 5 minutes. Transfer to a bowl. Toss gnocchi gently with sauce and cheese. Sprinkle with salt and pepper to taste, and serve immediately.

CLASSIC TUSCAN EGGPLANT PARMESAN

SLOW-COOK RECIPE / MAKES 8 SERVINGS

This beautifully light central Italian version of eggplant Parmesan is best made in late summer, when you can find fresh-picked young eggplant, ideally from nearby farms. Older specimens suck up much more oil during the first part of the cooking process, making for a greasy dish. Though this is not a pasta dish, it is often eaten as the pasta course, and it makes a great main dish that tastes even better when reheated the next day.

NOTE: Fry your eggplant while the milk for the *besciamel* is steeping, then finish the *besciamel* after the eggplant is cooked, so that you can use the sauce as soon as it is ready (it will otherwise thicken as it sits).

1 28-ounce can whole peeled San Marzano tomatoes
 Extra-virgin olive oil for frying
6 pounds eggplant, sliced lengthwise into ½-inch-thick slices
 Fine sea salt
3½ cups Besciamel Sauce (page 181)
1 cup freshly grated Parmigiano-Reggiano cheese
¼ cup thinly sliced fresh basil leaves
1 tablespoon cold unsalted butter, cut into bits

Pass tomatoes and their juices through a food mill. Discard solids and set puree aside.

Heat 1 inch oil in a large skillet over medium-high heat until hot but not smoking. Slide pieces of eggplant into pan until you have a single layer, and brown on both sides, 3 to 4 minutes per side. Drain slices in a single layer on paper towels and sprinkle with salt. Repeat with remaining slices, adjusting heat as you go and adding more oil if necessary to brown, not burn, eggplant.

Heat oven to 350°F.

Place about ¼ cup *besciamel* and about ¼ cup tomato puree in bottom of a 9-by-13-inch baking dish and spread together into a thin even layer. Arrange one quarter of eggplant slices in a single layer over sauce, overlapping slightly if necessary. Cover eggplant slices with about ¾ cup *besciamel* and about ½ cup tomato puree. Spread together into an even layer and sprinkle with 2 tablespoons cheese and 1½ teaspoons basil. Repeat 2 more times, using ¾ cup *besciamel* and ½ cup tomato puree and sprinkling with the cheese and basil each time. Arrange remaining one quarter of eggplant slices on top. Spread remaining *besciamel* and remaining tomato puree together in an even layer over top layer of eggplant. Sprinkle with remaining cheese and basil and dot with butter.

Bake, uncovered, until bubbling and hot, about 40 minutes. Let stand for 10 minutes before cutting.

POLENTA WITH AROMATIC HERB BUTTER

SLOW-COOK RECIPE / MAKES 4 SERVINGS

This polenta is a great side for rich meaty dishes, such as Peppery Braised Short Ribs (page 286), Roasted Venison with Cider-Braised Leeks (page 322), wild boar loin, or any chicken dish.

Though the ingredient list for the butter is long, it's absolutely worth making. It can be made ahead and kept refrigerated or frozen until you are ready to use it. Don't worry if you don't have access to all of the herbs; just make sure there's a good variety. In addition to or in place of the herbs listed, you can use oregano, marjoram, winter or summer savory, tarragon, lemon balm, and/or lemon verbena. In Tuscany, I substitute wild nepitella, a sort of minty oregano that grows everywhere, for the mint. The only herb I wouldn't suggest using is rosemary, which would overwhelm the milder herbs.

        6 cups water
    1¹/₂ teaspoons medium-coarse sea salt
    1¹/₂ cups polenta
      ³/₄ cup Aromatic Herb Butter (recipe follows)
           Coarsely ground black pepper

Bring water and salt to a boil in a large saucepan. Whisk in polenta, reduce heat to low, and simmer, stirring often, until polenta is thick and creamy, about 20 minutes. Stir in ¹/₂ cup herb butter and cook until polenta is soft to the bite, about 3 minutes more.

Transfer polenta to a serving bowl or individual plates. Make a well in center, add remaining herb butter, and sprinkle with pepper. Serve warm.

AROMATIC HERB BUTTER

SLOW-COOK RECIPE / MAKES 1 1/4 CUPS

Freeze the extra herb butter and enjoy slathered on grilled steaks and fish, rubbed over the skin of a whole chicken before roasting, or tossed with hot rice or with steamed baby carrots or other steamed or sautéed vegetables.

1	pound (4 sticks) unsalted butter
20	fresh chives
15	fresh thyme sprigs
8	fresh flat-leaf parsley sprigs
6	fresh mint sprigs
4	fresh basil sprigs
3	fresh lovage sprigs
1	fresh sage sprig
8	juniper berries
1	fresh bay leaf or 3 dried
5	whole cloves
1 1/2	teaspoons wild fennel pollen (see page 15)
1	teaspoon coriander seeds
1/4	teaspoon black peppercorns
	Handful of fennel fronds

Put butter in a medium saucepan, with all remaining ingredients on top, and melt over low heat. Stir once with a wooden spoon to submerge herbs, and continue to cook at a very gentle simmer until herbs are wilted and butter has taken on a slightly greenish color, 15 to 20 minutes.

Remove from heat, cover, and let infuse at room temperature for 1 hour.

Strain butter through a sieve into a container with a lid, pressing on herbs to extract as much flavor as possible. Cover and refrigerate.

When butter has firmed, scrape off sediment that has risen to top, replace cover, and refrigerate or freeze until ready to use. It can be refrigerated for up to 1 week or frozen for up to 6 months.

FISH

In restaurants all over the Mediterranean, local fish is always on the menu. The waiter presents a small fresh-caught specimen for one or two people or a big one for four or six, trots back to the kitchen, and then soon returns with a beautifully cooked fish, which he fillets tableside. The preparation is remarkably simple: the fish is roasted, fried, or grilled and served with just a little olive oil, a squeeze of lemon juice, and a pinch of sea salt. What makes it taste so good is less the preparation and more that the fish is at most a day out of the ocean.

Living here on the East Coast, I am lucky to enjoy sweet Maine shrimp in January, shad roe in the spring, striped bass in June and July, local oysters and herring in the fall and winter months, and more. From the West Coast comes wild salmon in the summertime; from Portugal, in season, rich sardines and tender octopus. But in New York City and in many other cosmopolitan cities, some fish get star status in restaurants not for their taste but because they are familiar to diners. No matter that they may be farm-raised and flown in from a distance or on the brink of extinction. And all the while, exquisite and inexpensive wild fish, like porgy and tautog, from healthy local stocks are ignored. If you make an effort to learn about what's fresh and abundant in your area, you will end up with a good value and the most flavorful fish available.

If you don't live on a coast, access to fresh fish is more difficult but, these days, hardly impossible. More and more markets are making a commitment to sell high-quality sustainable seafood. There are also great companies that will ship fresh fish by next-day air (see Sources, page 357). Developing a relationship with the people behind the counter at the fish market or the fishermen at the farmers' market will give you access to loads of information about good fish—where it comes from, how it's caught, and what it tastes like. If you are lucky enough to live in a city with a Chinatown, that's another great place to find exquisitely fresh fish.

No matter where you shop, there are a few cardinal rules when purchasing fish. Fish (and fish shops, for that matter) should smell a bit sweetly of the sea; any ammoniated or other off odor means bad fish. Look for firm, bright-fleshed fish with shiny skin and a clean ocean scent, stored in clean ice. Some species' eyes cloud up instantly upon death, and others remain clear. Nonetheless, eyes should look alive, not sunken and dull. Never buy fish that appears damaged in any way.

Understanding seafood issues (wild versus farmed, for example) and purchasing fish from abundant stocks are as important as understanding how to buy fresh fish and are, in my opinion, a matter of taste in every sense of the word. Making sustainable choices with our purchasing dollars as chefs and consumers will ensure good seafood eating for a long time to come. On the West and East Coasts, farmers' markets often have seafood stalls. These small day-boat fishermen catch fish in a manner that is not harmful to the ocean's environment. You may not always recognize the names of all the fish they sell, but take a chance and try something new; you'll likely find a new favorite. As for farm-raised fish, its flavor is inferior to wild-caught.

Generally, in terms of preparation, fish can be grouped into what I like to think of as "flavor families." Italians talk about *pesce azzurro*, dark oily fish such as sardines, anchovies, mackerel, eel, and tuna. Then there are what I consider the meaty white contingent: black bass, striped bass, and snapper, all fairly interchangeable; the flaky white fish, such as cod, hake, haddock, and halibut; and delicate white fish like sole, flounder, and fluke.

Having recipes for different flavor families of fish rather than for individual fish gives you a lot of flexibility, letting whatever is freshest steer you when deciding what to cook. Oily fish are good with bright, bitter, crunchy, and acidic elements, such as pickled onions or shaved fennel, and they also do well with rich accompaniments like lentils or red wine sauce. White-fleshed fish, such as cod, halibut, and striped bass, lend themselves to lighter, salady types of things, though they can also take vegetables such as fresh peas or roasted beets.

When you cook the recipes in this chapter, or any fish recipe, you shouldn't feel constrained by the specific fish called for. Instead, seek out the absolute freshest fish you can find and match it to a compatible recipe. As a general rule, though, adjust the cooking time if you have a piece of fish that's a different thickness than the recipe calls for, with more time (by 1 to 3 minutes) for a thicker piece, less for a thinner one.

FISH

Cacciucco alla Livornese (Mediterranean Shellfish Stew) | 206

Roasted Scallops with "Snail Butter" and Mâche | 209

North African Spiced Shrimp | 212

Salmon with Sugar Snap Peas and Bacon | 213

Cold Poached Salmon with Greek Yogurt and Dill Sauce | 214

Salmon with Parsnip Puree and Citrus–Pea Sprout Salad | 218

Grilled Tuna with Tomatoes, Grilled Red Onion, and Arugula | 220

Seared Tuna in Porchettata | 222

Hake with Salsa Verde | 223

Grilled Mako Shark Skewers with Shaved Radish and Parsley Salad | 225

Seared Cod with Green Olive, Lemon, and Parsley Relish | 226

Broiled Cod with Red Wine Sauce and Roasted Vegetables | 228

Salt Cod Stewed with Chickpeas and Greens | 230

Monkfish with Olives, Potatoes, and Sun-Dried Tomatoes | 232

Halibut with Brussels Sprout Leaves, Black Olives, and Chili | 235

Skate with Blood Orange, Red Onion, and Bottarga Salad | 236

Bluefish and Summer Vegetables | 238

Grilled Mackerel with Kohlrabi Slaw | 240

CACCIUCCO ALLA LIVORNESE
(MEDITERRANEAN SHELLFISH STEW)

SLOW-COOK RECIPE / MAKES 8 SERVINGS

Cacciucco alla livornese is the Tuscan version of the fish stews found in port towns all around the Mediterranean. One winter day, my mother and I drove three hours from Teverina to the western coast of Tuscany to eat authentic *cacciucco*— the famed fish and shellfish stew of the Tuscan coast—as research for her cookbook *Flavors of Tuscany*. We ate a fabulous meal as the pale winter sunshine

disappeared, and we talked at great length with the chef-owner about the proper procedure for making the stew. He poached each fish separately in fish broth and then combined them to make a refined version. A few years later, Alberta Innocenti, a great Tuscan home cook, taught me this much simpler way of making *cacciucco*, which has equally tasty results.

While you can vary the fish and shellfish according to what's at hand, the octopus is a must. Its long, slow cooking gives the stew its deep, rich flavor base. Octopi come in many different sizes and so have varying cooking times; just keep cooking gently until you have tender and delicious octopus pieces, then you can quickly finish the dish with the remaining seafood.

By changing the spices and herbs, you can use this basic recipe to make any number of regional variations. Add a pinch of saffron and serve it with aïoli to give it a Provençal twist. More spice and cilantro give it a North African bent. Serve it over toasted bread as the French and the Tuscans do, or pair it with couscous as they do in Sicily.

FLAVOR TIP: In Italy, seafood cooks often add a wine cork to the stew while cooking octopus, in the belief that the cork helps to tenderize it. It's hard to say whether this is a myth or not, but I like to believe it works.

3	celery stalks, cut lengthwise into 3 or 4 pieces each
1	large bunch fresh flat-leaf parsley, leaves coarsely chopped, plus more chopped parsley for garnish
1	medium onion, quartered
1	small fennel bulb, stalks trimmed to a few inches, coarsely chopped
1	large carrot
5	garlic cloves
2	dried árbol chilies
¼	cup extra-virgin olive oil, plus more for drizzling
⅔	cup dry white wine
1	tablespoon tomato paste, preferably double-concentrate (see page 19)
3½	pounds octopus, cleaned and cut into 1-inch pieces, or whole baby octopus
⅔	cup water
2	teaspoons medium-coarse sea salt, plus more for serving
1½	pounds squid, cleaned and cut on the bias into ½-inch pieces, tentacles left whole

1 35-ounce can whole peeled San Marzano tomatoes, with their juices

1½ pounds cod or other mild white fish fillets, cut into 1-inch squares

1 pound medium shrimp, head-on if possible, peeled

24 littleneck clams, cockles, or Manila clams, scrubbed

1 pound mussels, scrubbed and debearded

8 large slices country bread, toasted

Coarsely ground black pepper

In a food processor, pulse celery, parsley leaves, onion, fennel, carrot, 4 garlic cloves, and chilies until finely chopped.

Heat oil in a large Dutch oven or other heavy pot over medium heat. Add chopped vegetables, stir, and cook until softened, about 7 minutes. Stir together wine and tomato paste to dissolve paste, add mixture to vegetables, and simmer until liquid has mostly evaporated.

Add octopus, water, and salt (and a cork, if you have one; see Tip); stir, reduce heat to medium-low, and simmer gently, stirring occasionally, until octopus is tender, about 1½ hours (or longer if necessary), or about ½ hour for baby octopus.

Add squid and continue gently simmering for 30 minutes.

Pass tomatoes with their juices through a food mill. Add tomato puree and cod to pot, increase heat to medium-high, and cook, stirring occasionally, until cod is cooked through, about 7 minutes. Add shrimp, clams, and mussels, stir, and continue cooking until shrimp are opaque and clams and mussels have opened, 3 to 4 minutes more. Remove from heat. Discard any mussels or clams that have not opened.

Cut remaining garlic clove in half lengthwise and rub toasted bread slices with cut sides; discard garlic. Place a slice of toast in bottom of each bowl. Ladle stew over toast, sprinkle with parsley and a pinch each of salt and pepper, and drizzle with oil. Serve immediately.

ROASTED SCALLOPS
WITH "SNAIL BUTTER" AND MÂCHE

QUICK-COOK RECIPE / MAKES 4 MAIN-COURSE SERVINGS; 6 SMALL PLATES

One of my earliest memories of living in Paris is entering the local bistro as a three-year-old, being greeted by the courtly waiter, and then being charmed by a dish that immediately caught my eye: escargots on display in a glass case. The pretty round shells sat face up and were stuffed with a pale green butter that made them oh so delicious. I don't think escargots have ever tasted as wonderful to me since, but I have found that the butter has many tasty applications beyond snails. It goes particularly well with rich seafood, such as scallops. Try it this way, or smear it over split lobster or shrimp and broil, roast, or cook in a wood oven, should you be so lucky to have one.

SNAIL BUTTER

- 1¼ cups loosely packed fresh flat-leaf parsley leaves
- 2 garlic cloves, coarsely chopped
- 5 tablespoons unsalted butter, at room temperature
  Grated zest of ½ lemon

SCALLOPS

- 4 ounces field-grown mâche, baby spinach, or watercress
- 2 pounds dry-packed medium scallops
  Medium-coarse sea salt and coarsely ground black pepper
- 1 tablespoon extra-virgin olive oil
  Juice of 1 lemon (about 2 tablespoons)
  Crusty bread, sliced and toasted

Heat oven to 350°F.

FOR SNAIL BUTTER: Finely chop parsley and garlic together. Place in a bowl, add butter and zest, and mash together with a fork until well combined.

Place mâche in a large bowl. Set aside.

FOR SCALLOPS: Generously season scallops with salt and pepper. Heat a large cast-iron pan over high heat until quite hot. Add oil and then scallops, slowly feeding them into pan, being careful not to crowd pan or lower the temperature of it; as scallops form a crusty brown sear on the bottom, 3 to 4 minutes, move them on top of each other and add more to the pan. When all scallops are browned on one side, remove pan from heat and dot scallops with snail butter.

Place skillet in oven for 5 minutes to melt butter and cook scallops through.

Transfer scallops and butter to bowl with mâche, add lemon juice, toss, and serve immediately, with crusty bread to sop up buttery juices.

NORTH AFRICAN SPICED SHRIMP

QUICK-COOK RECIPE / MAKES 4 TO 6 SERVINGS

The mix of spices in this easy shrimp rub is reminiscent of North Africa, though the Aleppo pepper actually hails from Syria and Turkey. Serve this simple dish with herbed rice (see page 260) or a green salad.

FLAVOR TIPS: If the best shrimp you can get are smaller or larger than those specified, buy them and adjust the cooking time accordingly.

Dried spices vary in quality, and even the best lose flavor over time. If you can't get good ground coriander, cumin, and other spices, purchase whole seeds and toast them in a heavy skillet over low heat, shaking the pan back and forth until fragrant, then grind in a spice grinder or coffee grinder.

1	tablespoon Aleppo pepper (see page 16) or 1–2 dried red chili peppers, crushed
2	teaspoons ground coriander
1	teaspoon ground cumin
1/2	teaspoon ground ginger
1/4	teaspoon ground turmeric
5	tablespoons extra-virgin olive oil, plus more if needed
2	pounds large shrimp, peeled
	Juice of 1 large lime (about 2 tablespoons)
	Medium-coarse sea salt

In a large bowl, mix together Aleppo pepper, coriander, cumin, ginger, and turmeric. Add 2 tablespoons oil and stir to combine. Add shrimp and toss to coat. Marinate in the refrigerator for 4 to 6 hours.

Heat 2 tablespoons oil in a large cast-iron or other heavy skillet over high heat. Add shrimp in batches, being careful not to overcrowd pan, and cook until browned and opaque throughout, about 2 minutes per side. Transfer cooked shrimp to a large bowl as you go, and add more oil to pan if necessary.

When all shrimp are cooked, toss with remaining tablespoon oil and lime juice, and season with salt to taste. Serve warm or at room temperature.

SALMON WITH SUGAR SNAP PEAS AND BACON

QUICK-COOK RECIPE / MAKES 4 TO 6 SERVINGS

Salmon and peas is an old New England combination, and one I play with, using fresh sugar snap peas in place of shell peas. You can substitute shell peas if you have a good source, but even at the farmers' market, the sugar snaps are often fresher. Render the bacon and cook the onion ahead of time, if you like, then just reheat and add the peas when you are ready to serve.

FLAVOR TIP: Broiling the fish skin side up turns the skin crisp and blistered, adding a crunchy, flavorful element.

- 1 2-pound wild salmon fillet with skin
  Medium-coarse sea salt and coarsely ground black pepper
- 2 tablespoons extra-virgin olive oil
- 3 slices thick-cut bacon
- 1/3 cup minced onion
- 1/2 cup water
- 1 pound sugar snap peas, trimmed
- 1 tablespoon unsalted butter
- 1/4 cup chopped fresh mint

Heat broiler. Line a small baking sheet with foil.

Season flesh side of salmon with salt and pepper and place skin side up on baking sheet. Brush skin side with oil and season lightly with salt and pepper. Set aside.

Place bacon in a large skillet and cook over low heat until fat is mostly rendered, about 10 minutes. Add onion, stir to combine, and cook until onion has softened, about 10 minutes. Add water, increase heat to high, and bring to a simmer; cook for 2 minutes. Add peas and 3/4 teaspoon salt and cook until peas are tender and water has evaporated, about 8 minutes. Add butter and mint and stir to combine. Remove from heat.

While peas are cooking, broil fish until skin is blackened and blistered and flesh is cooked through, about 10 minutes. Remove from oven.

With a knife or spatula, cut salmon into 4 to 6 pieces, and transfer to serving plates. Spoon warm peas and bacon over fish, and serve.

COLD POACHED SALMON
WITH GREEK YOGURT AND DILL SAUCE

SLOW-COOK RECIPE / MAKES 6 SERVINGS

Fennel, shallots, fresh herbs, lemon peel, and other aromatics combined with white wine and water make a poaching broth that infuses salmon with a delicate flavor. You can vary the aromatics based on what you have on hand: celery instead of fennel, scallion in place of shallots, and fresh basil, thyme, or dill instead of chervil or parsley—all work well. The key is to use some kind of fresh green herb, some sort of onion, and peppercorns.

Here a thick, rich yogurt sauce is used as a marinade for the poached fish and as a sauce when serving the salmon. If you don't have access to Greek yogurt (Fage is a common brand), simply drain whole-milk yogurt in cheesecloth for a few hours to thicken.

FLAVOR TIP: Buy wild-caught or organic salmon—the flavor difference alone is worth the extra cost. Look for a piece of fillet that is fairly uniform in thickness.

POACHING LIQUID

5 cups cold water

3 cups dry white wine

1 small fennel bulb, fronds and stalks coarsely chopped, bulb thinly sliced

1 medium onion, thinly sliced

2 large shallots, sliced

2 garlic cloves

2 leafy fresh chervil or flat-leaf parsley sprigs

Peel from 1 lemon

1 tablespoon good white wine vinegar

1 teaspoon coarse sea salt

1/4 teaspoon black peppercorns

1 2- to 2 1/2-pound wild salmon fillet, skinned and cut into 2 equal pieces

1   cup Greek yogurt (see headnote)

½   cup chopped fresh dill

¼   cup extra-virgin olive oil

1   tablespoon plus 1 teaspoon red wine vinegar

1   heaping tablespoon minced shallot

1   tablespoon warm water

½   teaspoon fine sea salt

FOR POACHING LIQUID AND SALMON: Combine all poaching liquid ingredients in a large wide saucepan or Dutch oven. Cover and bring just to a boil; immediately reduce heat to medium-low, add salmon, cover, and simmer for 5 minutes. Remove from heat and let sit, covered, for 15 minutes.

Uncover salmon and allow to cool to room temperature in broth, about 1 hour. When broth is cool, carefully transfer fish to a platter, using two large spoons or spatulas to keep it intact (discard broth).

FOR SAUCE: Whisk all ingredients together. Spread over salmon and refrigerate for at least 30 minutes or up to 8 hours before serving.

SALMON WITH PARSNIP
PUREE AND CITRUS—
PEA SPROUT SALAD
(PAGE 218)

SALMON WITH PARSNIP PUREE
AND CITRUS-PEA SPROUT SALAD

SLOW-COOK RECIPE / MAKES 4 SERVINGS

Most vegetable purees are made by boiling vegetables in water, then draining and pureeing them and adding fat, such as butter, cream, or crème fraîche. I prefer to steam the vegetables gently in a small amount of water and fat, slowly stewing them in their own juices, which makes for a lighter and more flavorful result. (The photograph is on the previous page.)

I use blood oranges here for their sweet-tart flavor, but tangerines or Meyer lemons can be substituted. If you can't get your hands on baby pea sprouts, substitute parsley leaves or chopped arugula.

FLAVOR TIP: You can use this puree technique for any kind or combination of root vegetables, such as parsley root and celery root or turnip and parsnip.

PARSNIP PUREE

1 tablespoon unsalted butter

1 tablespoon extra-virgin olive oil

1 small onion, coarsely chopped

½ cup water

Fine sea salt

1¾ pounds parsnips, peeled and cut into ½-inch pieces

SALAD

2 blood oranges (see headnote)

4 small radishes, grated or julienned on a mandoline

2 cups loosely packed baby pea sprouts (see headnote)

2 tablespoons extra-virgin olive oil

½ teaspoon Aleppo pepper (see page 16), piment d'Espelette (see page 16), or other crushed dried red chili pepper

Fine sea salt

4 6-ounce salmon fillets with skin

Fine sea salt and coarsely ground black pepper

¼ cup extra-virgin olive oil

FOR PUREE: Heat butter and oil in a medium saucepan over medium heat until butter is melted. Add onion, ¼ cup water, and a pinch of salt. Reduce heat to medium-low and cook, stirring occasionally, until onion is softened, about 5 minutes. Add parsnips, remaining ¼ cup water, and another pinch of salt. Cover, reduce heat to lowest setting, and gently steam until parsnips are very tender, 45 minutes to 1 hour.

Remove from heat and puree with an immersion or regular blender or pass through a food mill. Cover to keep warm.

FOR SALAD: Using a sharp paring knife, trim off tops and bottoms of oranges. Stand each orange on end and carefully cut peel and pith from flesh, following curve of fruit from top to bottom. Trim away any remaining pith. Cut each orange crosswise into thin slices.

Combine oranges, radishes, pea sprouts, oil, chili, and salt to taste in a medium bowl; toss together.

FOR SALMON: Pat fillets dry with paper towels. Generously season skin side with salt and pepper. Heat oil in a large cast-iron skillet over medium-high heat. Add fillets, skin side down, in a single layer (do this in batches if necessary) and cook, tilting pan and carefully spooning hot oil over top of fish, until skin is blistered and crisp, about 5 minutes. Turn and cook until fish is cooked through, 3 to 4 minutes more. Transfer to a plate.

Spoon parsnip puree onto plates and top with salmon. Top salmon with salad, drizzle salad juices over everything, and serve.

GRILLED TUNA WITH TOMATOES, GRILLED RED ONION, AND ARUGULA

QUICK-COOK RECIPE / MAKES 4 SERVINGS

In the summer, when the market is overflowing with fantastic heirloom tomatoes in every shape, size, and color, and fresh local tuna is fished off the coast of Long Island, I am inspired to make this dish. Truly fresh-caught tuna has a slight iridescent gloss and is meltingly tender and rich-tasting. Whether it's deep red bluefin or lighter-colored albacore, it should be prepared simply and served rare.

FLAVOR TIP: The richness of fatty fish like tuna goes well with bright, acidic elements, such as the tomatoes and lemon.

> 1¼ pounds heirloom tomatoes
> 3 tablespoons extra-virgin olive oil, plus more for fish
> Coarse sea salt
> 1 medium red onion, cut into ³/₈-inch-thick rings
> 4 6- to 8-ounce tuna steaks, about 1 inch thick
> Coarsely ground black pepper
> 1 bunch arugula, washed and torn
> Juice of 1 lemon (about 2 tablespoons)

Core tomatoes and slice into quarters or eighths, depending on size. Place in a large bowl and toss with 1 tablespoon oil and ¼ teaspoon salt.

Heat a grill pan over high heat. Grill onion until charred on both sides and softened, about 5 minutes per side. Remove from pan and set aside.

Season tuna steaks with salt and pepper and rub fish with 1 tablespoon oil. Grill for about 2 minutes per side for rare. Transfer to a cutting board and cut diagonally in half.

Drain juices from tomatoes and discard. Add onion, separating it into rings. Add arugula, remaining 2 tablespoons oil, lemon juice, and salt and pepper to taste. Toss well.

Arrange tuna on four plates. Pile salad in between and over pieces of fish. Sprinkle salad juices and some extra pepper around each plate, and serve immediately.

SEARED TUNA IN PORCHETTATA

QUICK-COOK RECIPE / MAKES 4 SERVINGS

Wild fennel pollen, with its resinous sage-and-pine-like flavors, makes a great dry rub. When mixed with hot chili, it contrasts well with the rich taste of sushi-grade tuna. Adding fennel pollen to a meat or fish dish is often referred to in Italy as *in porchettata*, meaning "in the style of pork," since wild fennel is so often combined with pork. This simple dish marries well with the creamy plainness of Slow-Cooked Cannellini Beans (page 42) or boiled fresh-dug potatoes drizzled with olive oil and sprinkled with sea salt.

- 1/4 cup plus 2 tablespoons wild fennel pollen (see page 15)
- 2 teaspoons Aleppo pepper (see page 16) or finely ground dried red chili pepper (ground in a spice mill)
- 1/2 teaspoon fine sea salt
- 4 6-ounce tuna steaks, about 1 inch thick
- 3 tablespoons extra-virgin olive oil, plus more for drizzling
- 1/2 lemon, cut into quarters

Combine fennel pollen, chili, and salt; spread on a plate. Lightly drizzle tuna with oil on both sides. Coat each piece with spice mixture, gently pressing so that spices adhere to fish.

Heat 3 tablespoons oil in a large cast-iron skillet over high heat. Add tuna and cook for about 2 minutes per side for rare. Serve with lemon.

HAKE WITH SALSA VERDE

QUICK-COOK RECIPE / MAKES 4 SERVINGS

Italian salsa verde is one of those great pick-me-up sauces that add bright-ness and zip to a dish. Although it's best known as a companion sauce for the Northern Italian classic boiled dinner known as *bollito misto*, it seems made for fish. I like to use hake. It's a delicious underappreciated fish, with a delicate, sweet flesh. That said, just about any fish is nice with salsa verde, so go with what's freshest.

SALSA VERDE

1/3	cup salt-packed capers
1	cup coarsely chopped fresh flat-leaf parsley
2	anchovy fillets
5	cornichons
	Finely grated zest of 1 lemon
1/2	teaspoon fine sea salt
1/2	cup extra-virgin olive oil
	Juice of 1 lemon (about 2 tablespoons)
2	tablespoons extra-virgin olive oil
4	6- to 8-ounce hake fillets (see headnote)

Heat broiler. Line a small baking pan with foil.

FOR SALSA VERDE: Soak capers in a bowl of cold water for 10 minutes, then rinse in 2 or 3 changes of water; drain well. Process capers, parsley, anchovy fillets, cornichons, lemon zest, and salt in a food processor to a slightly chunky puree. With machine running, slowly add oil and lemon juice.

Drizzle oil over hake and place fillets on baking pan. Broil until fish is flaky and opaque throughout, about 10 minutes.

Remove from oven and serve with salsa verde.

GRILLED MAKO SHARK SKEWERS
WITH SHAVED RADISH AND PARSLEY SALAD

QUICK-COOK RECIPE / MAKES 4 SERVINGS

Many shark varieties are overfished; mako is still quite plentiful and really tasty. Similar to swordfish in color, taste, and texture, it grills beautifully, and it marries well with citrus and strong spices. Pacific halibut, tuna, sea bass, and sturgeon are great substitutes, if necessary. Za'atar—a spice well worth seeking out—adds a delicious Middle Eastern touch, but the combination of grilled fish, radish, and parsley is lovely even without it.

FLAVOR TIP: Macerating shallots, or any onion, with a pinch of salt mellows and sweetens their sharp bite.

1½	pounds mako shark steaks, cut into 1½-by-1-inch pieces
1½	tablespoons za'atar (see page 15)
2	tablespoons plus 2 teaspoons extra-virgin olive oil
1	medium shallot, very thinly sliced
	Fine sea salt
8	ounces radishes (about 20 small to medium), sliced into very thin rounds
½	cup loosely packed fresh flat-leaf parsley leaves
1	tablespoon fresh lemon juice
	Coarsely ground black pepper

In a large bowl, toss together shark, za'atar, and 1 tablespoon plus 2 teaspoons oil. Cover and marinate at room temperature for 1 hour.

Build a hot fire in a charcoal grill.

Just before cooking shark, stir together shallot and ¼ teaspoon salt in a small bowl and let sit for 10 minutes. Add radishes, parsley, and lemon juice and toss to combine.

Season shark with salt and pepper and thread onto metal skewers. Grill until lightly charred on both sides and cooked through, about 3½ minutes per side.

Transfer skewers to a platter and immediately drizzle with remaining tablespoon oil. Serve with radish and parsley salad.

SEARED COD WITH GREEN OLIVE, LEMON, AND PARSLEY RELISH

QUICK-COOK RECIPE / MAKES 4 SERVINGS

The simple relish here can be varied in many ways. You can try arugula in place of parsley and oranges instead of lemon, or a mix of citrus. Add a pinch of crushed dried red chili pepper for some heat, if you like. Strong-flavored Picholine olives play off the acidity of the lemons and the bitterness of the parsley, but you can use any flavorful olive.

FLAVOR TIP: Spoon-basting, using fresh herbs and other aromatics and hot oil or butter, is a technique I often use to build flavor in a dish. The hot oil cooks the herbs and picks up the flavor, transferring it into the flesh of the fish.

- 2 lemons
- 1 cup loosely packed fresh flat-leaf parsley leaves
- 1 cup Picholine olives, pitted and coarsely chopped
- 1 large shallot, minced
  Fine sea salt
- 4 6- to 8-ounce skinless cod fillets, about 1 inch thick
  Coarsely ground black pepper
- 3 tablespoons extra-virgin olive oil
- 4 fresh thyme sprigs

Using a sharp paring knife or vegetable peeler, cut 4 wide slices of lemon peel, avoiding white pith; set aside. Then trim off tops and bottoms of lemons. Stand each lemon on end and carefully cut remaining peel and pith from flesh, following curve of fruit from top to bottom. Trim away any remaining pith. Working over a large bowl, cut each section away from membranes, cutting as close to membranes as you can, and dropping segments into bowl. Squeeze juices from membranes into bowl.

Add parsley, olives, shallot, and ⅛ teaspoon salt to lemons. Stir, and let sit for 30 minutes.

Season fish with salt and pepper. Heat oil in a large cast-iron skillet over medium-high heat. Place fish flesh side down in pan. Top each fillet with a slice of lemon peel and a sprig of thyme. Cook, carefully tilting pan and spooning hot oil over fish, until fish is opaque throughout and has a nice crust on the flesh side, 10 to 12 minutes.

Carefully transfer fish to plates, turning it flesh side up. Top with relish and serve.

BROILED COD WITH RED WINE SAUCE AND ROASTED VEGETABLES

QUICK-COOK RECIPE / MAKES 4 SERVINGS

The firm flesh of cod stands up to this robust sauce, and the dish looks dramatic—snowy white cod and deep purple red wine sauce. The sweetness of the carrots balances the acidity of the wine. If small carrots are not available, use medium skinny carrots cut into 3-inch lengths.

FLAVOR TIP: Reducing wine with onions enhances the wine's sweetness while counteracting its acidic nature. Adding a chili and cloves further deepens the flavor.

1	pound small new potatoes, cut in half
8	ounces small heirloom carrots (see headnote)
4	ounces cipollini, cut in half lengthwise, or pearl onions
4	tablespoons extra-virgin olive oil
	Medium-coarse sea salt and coarsely ground black pepper
1	cup dry red wine
1	medium onion, thinly sliced
1	medium dried red chili pepper
2	whole cloves
1	cup homemade chicken broth (page 108)
1	1½-pound cod fillet, about 1½ inches thick
1	tablespoon unsalted butter
2	tablespoons finely chopped fresh chives or flat-leaf parsley

Heat oven to 400°F.

Toss potatoes, carrots, and cipollini with 2 tablespoons oil and season well with salt and pepper. Spread vegetables on a baking sheet and roast, stirring once or twice, until golden and tender, about 35 minutes.

While vegetables are roasting, combine wine, sliced onion, chili, and cloves in a medium saucepan. Bring to a boil and cook until wine is reduced by half, about 10 minutes. Strain wine and discard solids.

Return wine to saucepan and add chicken broth. Bring to a boil and reduce by half again, to about ¾ cup. Remove from heat and set aside.

When vegetables are ready, remove from oven and cover loosely to keep warm. Increase oven heat to broil. Line a baking pan with foil.

Place cod, flesh side up, on prepared pan. Season liberally with salt and pepper and drizzle with remaining 2 tablespoons oil. Broil until opaque throughout, about 15 minutes.

When cod is close to ready, bring sauce back to a good simmer and whisk in butter.

Transfer cod to a large serving platter. Pile vegetables on top of and around fish, drizzle sauce on top, sprinkle with chives, and serve.

SALT COD STEWED WITH CHICKPEAS AND GREENS

SLOW-COOK RECIPE / MAKES 4 SERVINGS

Inzimino is a Tuscan stew with some sort of fish and greens (and occasionally chickpeas) that are cooked a very long time until they are silky. This dish probably goes back to at least medieval times. My version is rich and many-layered. The greens can vary—spinach, Swiss chard, or even turnip greens—but choose just one; the other flavors in the dish are complex enough as is.

FLAVOR TIP: Look for whole pieces of salt cod. The fish should be white, not yellowed or overly dry. Italians will tell you that the best flavor comes from salt cod with bones and skin, and I agree, but more often than not, I head for the skinless, boneless variation for ease. Soaking the cod and changing the water often is an essential step; generally I soak it until I can no longer taste salt when I put my tongue to the fish. The more frequently you change the water, the faster the cod will desalinate.

1³/₄ pounds salt cod

1 cup dried chickpeas

¹/₂ head garlic, plus 2 garlic cloves, peeled

1 leafy fresh sage, rosemary, or thyme sprig

¹/₂ teaspoon fine sea salt, plus more to taste

3 medium carrots, coarsely chopped

2 celery stalks, coarsely chopped

1 medium onion, coarsely chopped

1 medium dried red chili pepper

¹/₄ cup olive oil, plus more for drizzling

1 tablespoon tomato paste, preferably double-concentrate (see page 19)

1 cup water

2 bunches Swiss chard, stemmed and cut into 1-inch-wide ribbons

Sliced peasant bread, toasted and rubbed with a cut garlic clove (optional)

Place cod in a medium bowl, cover with water, and refrigerate, changing water 4 or 5 times per day, for 24 to 48 hours.

Meanwhile, rinse chickpeas. Place chickpeas, ½ head garlic, and herb in a large saucepan and cover with water by 3 inches. Soak for 8 hours, or overnight.

Place saucepan over medium-low heat and bring liquid to a simmer; this will take about an hour. Cook at a bare simmer until chickpeas are tender, about 1 hour more. Stir in salt. Set aside.

Drain cod and cut into 1-by-½-inch pieces; set aside. Process carrots, celery, onion, garlic cloves, and chili in a food processor until finely chopped.

Heat oil in a large Dutch oven or other heavy pot over medium-high heat. Add vegetable mixture and cook, stirring occasionally, until softened, about 4 minutes. Dissolve tomato paste in water, add to vegetables, and simmer until water evaporates, about 7 minutes.

Add chickpeas and their cooking liquid. Bring to a simmer, then add chard and cod. Cover, reduce heat, and cook at a gentle simmer, stirring occasionally, for 45 minutes.

Uncover pot and simmer for another 45 minutes, until flavorful and slightly thickened.

Season stew with salt if necessary. Serve with a drizzle of oil, with or without garlic toast.

MONKFISH WITH OLIVES, POTATOES, AND SUN-DRIED TOMATOES

QUICK-COOK RECIPE / MAKES 4 SERVINGS

The accompaniment for this fish is a wintertime take on caponata, the Sicilian dish of mixed summer vegetables, including eggplant and tomatoes, fried gently in olive oil and flavored with capers, herbs, and vinegar. I use potatoes instead of eggplant and sun-dried tomatoes in place of fresh. The firm texture and mild flavor of monkfish make it a good choice for this hearty dish.

FLAVOR TIP: I prefer loose-packed sun-dried tomatoes to those packed in oil. Their flavor is much more vibrant, and it's not compromised by the taste of the oil, which is often inferior. Loose-packed sun-dried tomatoes should have a nice orange-red color and a fairly soft texture, not be dark and brittle.

- ½ cup extra-virgin olive oil
- 1½ pounds Yukon Gold potatoes, peeled and cut into ¼-inch dice
- 2 tablespoons unsalted butter
- 4 garlic cloves, gently smashed and peeled
- 1 tablespoon chopped fresh thyme
  Fine sea salt
- ½ cup Gaeta olives, pitted
- ½ ounce sun-dried tomatoes (about 5), cut crosswise into thin strips (see Tip)
- 1 tablespoon salt-packed capers, rinsed several times and drained
- 1 cup dry white wine
- 1½ pounds monkfish fillet, cut into 4 pieces
  Coarsely ground black pepper
- ¼ cup chopped fresh flat-leaf parsley

Heat oven to 350°F.

Heat ¼ cup oil in a large deep ovenproof skillet over high heat. Add potatoes and cook, without stirring, until a nice crust forms on bottom, about 5 minutes. Stir and cook until close to tender, about 5 minutes more.

Add butter, garlic, thyme, and a pinch of salt and cook, stirring occasionally, for 5 minutes. Add olives, sun-dried tomatoes, and capers and cook for 1 minute more. Add wine, bring to a simmer, and remove from heat.

Season fish with salt and pepper. Heat remaining ¼ cup oil in a large skillet over high heat. Add fish (in batches, if necessary) and cook, undisturbed, for 1 minute, then tilt pan slightly and, using a large spoon, baste fish with hot oil. Cook until a golden crust forms on bottom of fish, about 5 minutes. Gently release fish with a spatula and transfer it, golden side up, to skillet with potato mixture.

Transfer skillet to oven and bake until fish is cooked through, 15 to 18 minutes. Top with parsley and serve.

HALIBUT WITH BRUSSELS SPROUT LEAVES, BLACK OLIVES, AND CHILI

QUICK-COOK RECIPE / MAKES 4 SERVINGS

Halibut is a meaty white fish with a lovely texture that can take on aggressive pairings. White wine softens the intensity of the olives and smooths out the strong taste of the cabbage. Since Atlantic halibut stocks have been largely depleted, I look for wild-caught halibut from Pacific waters.

FLAVOR TIP: Separating the Brussels sprouts into leaves instead of using them halved or whole yields a more delicate texture and sweeter flavor.

1	pound Brussels sprouts
4	6- to 8-ounce halibut fillets, about 1 inch thick
	Fine sea salt and coarsely ground black pepper
1/4	cup extra-virgin olive oil, plus more for drizzling
2	garlic cloves, smashed and peeled
20	Moroccan or oil-cured black olives, pitted
1	dried red chili pepper, coarsely chopped
1/2	cup dry white wine
1	tablespoon unsalted butter

Heat broiler.

Cut stem from each Brussels sprout and separate sprouts into leaves. Thinly slice cores of sprouts.

Line a small baking pan with foil. Season fish with salt and pepper and drizzle lightly with oil. Place on baking pan and broil until opaque throughout, about 10 minutes.

While fish is cooking, heat 1/4 cup oil in a large deep skillet over high heat. Add garlic and, stirring constantly, cook until lightly golden, about 30 seconds. Add Brussels sprouts, olives, and chili; stir to combine. Add wine, bring to a boil, and cook, stirring occasionally, until wine evaporates. Stir in butter and cook until incorporated. Remove from heat.

Serve halibut hot, with Brussels sprouts.

SKATE WITH BLOOD ORANGE, RED ONION, AND BOTTARGA SALAD

QUICK-COOK RECIPE / MAKES 4 SERVINGS

In Sicily this classic winter salad is served on its own, which you can certainly do, but I like it best on top of seared fish, so you experience a great play of fresh and preserved fish flavors. If you happen to have a heavy oval stainless steel fish skillet, this is a great recipe to use it for, but any heavy skillet will do.

FLAVOR TIP: Adding the parsley to the hot butter before adding the lemon juice fries the herb, intensifying its flavor.

4	blood oranges
1	small red onion, cut into very thin rings
3/4	cup loosely packed fresh flat-leaf parsley leaves, plus 3 tablespoons finely chopped parsley
1	small fresh hot red chili pepper, thinly sliced
	Fleur de sel or other medium-coarse sea salt
3	tablespoons extra-virgin olive oil
4	pieces boneless, skinless skate wing (about 2 pounds)
	Coarsely ground black pepper
2–4	tablespoons vegetable oil
2	tablespoons unsalted butter
1	tablespoon fresh lemon juice
1/2	ounce *bottarga di muggine* or *bottarga di tonno* (see page 11), any wax and thin skin removed

Using a paring knife, cut peel and pith from oranges, then cut flesh crosswise into very thin slices; remove seeds. Place slices in a large bowl, sprinkle with onion, whole parsley leaves, chili, and a pinch or two of salt, and drizzle with olive oil. Toss gently just to combine. Set aside.

Season skate with salt and pepper. Heat a large cast-iron skillet over high heat until good and hot. Add 2 tablespoons vegetable oil and 2 fish pieces and sear, without moving fish, occasionally tilting pan and spooning hot oil over top, until nicely crusty and brown on bottom, about 4 minutes. Transfer to a warm serving platter or warm plates and repeat with remaining pieces, adding up to 2 tablespoons more vegetable oil to pan only if needed.

Drain oil from pan and return pan to low heat. Add butter. When it begins to foam, about 30 seconds, add chopped parsley and swirl pan until parsley is fried and butter is browned, about 20 seconds. Remove from heat, add lemon juice, and swirl to combine, then immediately drizzle over fish.

Pile orange salad over top of fish. Using a rasp or fine grater, grate bottarga evenly over fish and salad. Serve immediately.

BLUEFISH AND SUMMER VEGETABLES

QUICK-COOK RECIPE / MAKES 4 SERVINGS

For this dish, you need a strong oily fish to stand up to the pungent flavors of the chopped garlic and parsley, which cooks only slightly in the residual heat of the pan-roasted baby eggplant.

1¼ pounds cranberry beans in the pod, shelled

½ cup finely chopped fresh flat-leaf parsley

1 garlic clove, minced

4 tablespoons extra-virgin olive oil, plus more for drizzling

8 ounces baby Japanese eggplant, cut in half lengthwise and flesh side scored in a diamond pattern

½ pint grape tomatoes or local cherry tomatoes

½ cup water

Fine sea salt

1½ pounds bluefish or mackerel fillets, ¾ to 1 inch thick

Coarsely ground black pepper

Bring a medium saucepan of water to a boil. Add beans, cover, and cook until tender, about 10 minutes. Drain.

Stir together parsley and garlic.

Heat 2 tablespoons oil in a large cast-iron skillet over medium-high heat. Add eggplant cut side down, in batches if necessary, and cook, turning once, until golden on both sides and somewhat collapsed, 2 to 3 minutes per side. Remove to a plate, cut side up, and sprinkle with all but 2 tablespoons of parsley mixture.

Heat broiler.

Heat remaining 2 tablespoons oil in a large heavy saucepan over medium-high heat. Add tomatoes and cook until they begin to burst, about 2 minutes. Add remaining parsley mixture, beans, water, and a pinch of salt. Cook, stirring occasionally, until tomatoes start to collapse and sauce comes together, about 12 minutes.

While sauce is cooking, line a baking pan with foil and lay fish on it in a single layer, skin side up. Drizzle with oil, season with salt and pepper, and broil until cooked through, about 10 minutes.

Spoon bean sauce onto plates, top with fish and eggplant, drizzle with a little more oil, and sprinkle with salt. Serve warm.

GRILLED MACKEREL WITH KOHLRABI SLAW

QUICK-COOK RECIPE / MAKES 4 SERVINGS

Mackerel is a healthful and delicious but underappreciated fish. When shopping for it, look for bright clear eyes, iridescent skin, and a clean, nonfishy smell. Its strong rich flavor perfectly balances this citrusy cabbage-like slaw. Use as much chili as you like.

12	ounces trimmed kohlrabi, julienned or grated
6	medium radishes, julienned or thinly sliced
5	celery stalks from the heart, thinly sliced on the bias
¼	cup fresh lime juice
1¾	teaspoons fine sea salt
1–2	teaspoons minced fresh red chili pepper
3	tablespoons extra-virgin olive oil, plus more for fish
1½	pounds mackerel or bluefish fillets

Preheat a grill if grilling outdoors.

Place kohlrabi, radishes, celery, lime juice, salt, and chili in a large bowl. Stir together and let sit until vegetables begin to wilt, about 5 minutes. Add oil and stir to combine.

Meanwhile, heat a grill pan, if using, over high heat. Rub a little oil into flesh side of fish. Grill fish skin side down for 5 minutes. Turn and cook for 3 minutes more.

Transfer fish to plates, top with slaw, spoon some slaw juices over, and serve immediately.

CHICKEN AND OTHER BACKYARD LIVESTOCK

Chicken, rabbits, guinea hens, ducks, and squab show up regularly on the Mediterranean table, since anyone can raise them on a small parcel of land. The preparations are simple: stewed, braised, or roasted, cooked to well done. In Tuscany, wild game birds frequently find their way into pasta sauces, an excellent way to make a small amount of precious meat feed many people.

In Italy I grew up eating honest-to-goodness farm chicken—the kind that ran around in the dirt, pecking worms out of the ground, eating grass and dried corn to its heart's content, and living in fear of the fox. When I came back to America as a young adult and began shopping for myself, I found it peculiar to buy chicken in the supermarket, wrapped up in plastic, the breastbone buried in unusually plumped-up flesh. American chicken was a woeful disappointment in both taste and texture. Thankfully, tasty chicken is now easier to find.

The meat of backyard chickens is firmer than that of commercial poultry. Though the fowl are a bit scrawny in comparison, with big protruding breastbones, the meat has an incredibly rich and very chickeny flavor that comes through best in simple dishes. Mita, our Tuscan neighbor, most often hacks them into eight or ten pieces, douses them with olive oil, sprinkles them with rosemary, garlic, and sea salt, and roasts them in a wood oven until crispy and well done. She sometimes batters and fries them in extra-virgin olive oil and occasionally cooks them in a stew with cockscombs and chicken necks.

To approximate the flavor of those chickens here in the United States, I look for organic, pasture-raised local chickens. "Pasture-raised," or "grass-fed," refers to livestock raised on a nutrient-rich, low-fat diet of fresh grass in the warm months and stored grasses (hay and grass silage) in the wintertime. The chickens raised this way lead a relatively stress-free life, spending much of their time outside clucking and pecking away at the grass, and eating on their own natural schedules, all of which significantly reduces the need for antibiotics. Their waste enriches the soil they graze on—a closed-loop system and another natural and healthy process—instead of contaminating rivers, streams, and groundwater. Their meat and eggs taste worlds better than those of commercial birds, and the eggs are also higher in vitamins and omega-3 fatty acids. Duck, guinea hen, and rabbit have even richer flavor. Dark and rich, duck pairs well with strong spices, citrus, and honey. The breasts, quick-cooked in a skillet, are terrific with grains and greens. Duck's high fat content makes it perfect for roasting whole: score the skin and roast it on a rack or a bed of vegetables so that the fat melts into the pan and the bird comes out of the oven moist but with a fabulously crispy skin.

Lighter in flavor than duck but stronger than chicken, guinea hen is not as readily available as duck, but it's well worth seeking out. The meat lends itself to stronger, bolder flavor combinations and accompaniments, such as barley and dandelion greens.

The flavor profile of rabbit is similar to that of poultry. Mild, meaty, and lean, it is delicious braised or roasted. Rabbit can be intimidating, since it's often sold whole. Just whack it into portion-sized pieces with a good strong cleaver (or ask the butcher to do this).

Pasture-raised poultry and other meats are not often found at the supermarket, but times will change. They are widely available, however, via mail order (see Sources, page 357), through Community Supported Agriculture groups (CSAs), and at farmers' markets. Buying from sources like this, even via phone or Internet, allows you to "know your farmer"—which is the best way to ensure that what you eat was raised right.

CHICKEN AND OTHER BACKYARD LIVESTOCK

Roast Chicken with Sage, Garlic, and Lemon Peel | 246

Za'atar Chicken | 248

Roast Chicken with Oyster-Sage Stuffing | 250

Bacon-and-Herb-Rubbed Salt-Baked Chicken | 253

Roast Chicken with Farro Salad with Preserved Lemon | 254

Chicken Salad with Tarragon, Toasted Pine Nuts, and Golden Raisins | 256

Roast Chicken with Braised Red Peppers and Onion | 258

Braised Chicken Hash with Wild Mushrooms and Herbed Rice | 260

Chicken with Escarole, Apples, and Potatoes | 263

Duck Breast with Chanterelles, Chestnuts, and Pearl Onions | 265

Honey-and-Chili-Roasted Duck with Fennel and Farro | 268

Oven-Roasted Guinea Hen Breasts with Barley and Dandelion Greens | 270

Braised Rabbit with Lemon and Rosemary | 272

Roasted Rabbit with Shaved Celery and Fried Bread Salad | 274

ROAST CHICKEN WITH SAGE, GARLIC, AND LEMON PEEL

SLOW-COOK RECIPE / MAKES 4 SERVINGS

Rubbing butter mixed with chopped fresh garlic and whatever herbs or spices you like—here sage and lemon zest—under the skin of a chicken allows the flavor to permeate the meat, making for a simple, well-seasoned bird that is moist and rich in both texture and taste.

FLAVOR TIP: Letting chicken rest for 10 minutes after cooking ensures that the juices are reabsorbed into the meat. Carve too soon, and the juices end up on the cutting board instead.

1	4-pound chicken
1	lemon
22	large fresh sage leaves
3	garlic cloves
6	tablespoons (¾ stick) unsalted butter, at room temperature
	Fine sea salt
2	teaspoons extra-virgin olive oil
	Coarsely ground black pepper
2	small unpeeled onions, quartered
8	leafy fresh flat-leaf parsley sprigs
2	medium carrots, cut into 1-inch pieces
	Fleur de sel or other medium-coarse sea salt (optional)

Heat oven to 425°F.

Rinse chicken under cold water and pat dry with paper towels. Tuck wings under back. Using a sharp paring knife or vegetable peeler, carefully cut peel from lemon in vertical strips, avoiding bitter white pith. Finely chop lemon peel, sage, and garlic together; place in a bowl, add butter and 1 teaspoon salt, and stir well with a fork to combine. Cut lemon into quarters.

Using your fingers and a small sharp knife, carefully loosen skin of chicken from flesh of breasts and thighs. Slip butter mixture between skin and flesh, spreading it over breasts and thighs. Rub skin with oil and season generously with salt and pepper. Salt and pepper cavity of bird, then stuff it with 4 onion quarters, parsley sprigs, and lemon quarters. Tie legs together with kitchen twine.

Put remaining onion quarters and carrot pieces in a roasting pan and place chicken, breast side up, on top. Roast for 15 minutes, then reduce oven temperature to 350°F and continue roasting until juices run clear and leg joint moves easily, or an instant-read thermometer inserted into thickest part of thigh reads 165°F, 1 to 1¼ hours more.

Remove chicken from oven, sprinkle with a little fleur de sel, if desired, and let rest for 10 minutes before serving.

ZA'ATAR CHICKEN

SLOW-COOK RECIPE / MAKES 4 SERVINGS

Za'atar is a Middle Eastern spice mixture made of dried wild thyme, sesame seeds, sumac (the deliciously tart ground dried berries of the sumac plant), and salt. In Lebanon it's often sprinkled over bread or chicken. It's a condiment I always have on hand, and it's really pretty good on almost everything, including fish and vegetables. Here I mix the seasoning with butter and stuff it under the skin of the bird. If you don't have za'atar, try the same method with other good-quality dried herb mixes.

- 1 4-pound chicken
- 3 tablespoons unsalted butter, at room temperature
- 4 garlic cloves, finely chopped
- 2 tablespoons za'atar (see page 15)
- 1 lemon
- 1 tablespoon extra-virgin olive oil
- Fine sea salt and coarsely ground black pepper
- ½ small onion
- 4 fresh thyme sprigs
- Fleur de sel or other medium-coarse sea salt (optional)

Heat oven to 425°F.

Rinse chicken under cold water and pat dry with paper towels. Tuck wings under back. Using a fork, mix together butter, garlic, and za'atar. With a sharp paring knife or vegetable peeler, cut a 2-inch strip of peel from lemon, avoiding bitter white pith.

Using your fingers and a small sharp knife, carefully loosen skin of chicken from flesh of breasts and thighs. Slip butter mixture between skin and flesh of chicken, spreading it over breasts and thighs. Rub skin with oil and season generously with salt and pepper. Salt and pepper cavity of bird, then stuff it with lemon peel, onion, and thyme sprigs. Tie legs of bird together with kitchen twine.

Place chicken, breast side up, on a rack in a roasting pan. Roast for 15 minutes, then reduce oven temperature to 350°F and continue roasting, basting with pan juices every 20 minutes, until juices run clear and leg joint moves easily, or an instant-read thermometer inserted into thickest part of thigh reads 165°F, 1 to 1¼ hours more.

Remove from oven, sprinkle with a little fleur de sel, if desired, and let rest for 10 minutes before serving.

ROAST CHICKEN WITH OYSTER-SAGE STUFFING

SLOW-COOK RECIPE / MAKES 4 SERVINGS

I love the way oysters so effortlessly turn a humble chicken into a magnificent-ly luxurious dish. Oyster and chicken may seem a strange combination, but it really works. Seasoning the outside of the bird with fennel pollen complements the sage in the stuffing, though it is still delicious without.

1	4-pound chicken
	Fine sea salt and coarsely ground black pepper
12	large oysters, scrubbed
2½	tablespoons unsalted butter, at room temperature
9	¼-inch-thick slices brioche or Italian bread, crusts removed
9	large fresh sage leaves, finely chopped
2	teaspoons extra-virgin olive oil
1½	tablespoons wild fennel pollen (optional; see page 15)
2	cups dry white wine
	Fleur de sel or other medium-coarse sea salt (optional)
2	tablespoons chopped fresh flat-leaf parsley

Heat oven to 425°F.

Rinse chicken under cold water and pat dry with paper towels. Tuck wings under back. Generously season cavity of bird with salt and pepper.

Shuck oysters over a bowl, reserving juices. Using 1½ tablespoons butter, spread butter on one side of each bread slice and sprinkle slices with sage. Top each slice with 1 oyster, roll up, and stuff into cavity of bird. Add remaining 3 oysters, and tie legs of bird together with kitchen twine. Rub outside of bird with oil, sprinkle evenly with fennel pollen, if using, and season generously with salt and pepper.

Place chicken, breast side up, on a rack in a roasting pan. Roast for 15 minutes. Pour 1 cup wine and reserved oyster juices over chicken, reduce heat to 350°F, and con-tinue to roast, basting every 15 minutes, until juices run clear and leg joint moves easily, or an instant-read thermometer inserted into thickest part of thigh reads 165°F, 1¼ to 1½ hours more.

Remove pan from oven, sprinkle chicken with a little fleur de sel, if desired, and transfer to a cutting board to rest.

Pour off and reserve pan juices. Place roasting pan over high heat, add remaining 1 cup wine, and bring to a simmer, scraping up browned bits. Transfer liquid to a medium saucepan, bring to a boil, and cook until liquid is reduced to about 3 tablespoons. Whisk in reserved pan juices, remaining tablespoon butter, and parsley.

Serve chicken with sauce and stuffing.

BACON-AND-HERB-RUBBED
SALT-BAKED CHICKEN

SLOW-COOK RECIPE / MAKES 4 SERVINGS

A thick salt crust seals in the juices of the chicken while it cooks, and the bacon-herb rub both acts as a barrier to the salt and bastes the meat. The result is a very tender, very tasty bird.

FLAVOR TIP: The chicken is cooked breast side down here, as gravity helps make it even moister, drawing down the juices so they are absorbed into the meat.

8	ounces sliced bacon, coarsely chopped
4	garlic cloves, peeled
15	large fresh sage leaves
6	fresh rosemary sprigs, leaves only
2	dried árbol chilies
5	large egg whites
4	pounds (7 cups) fine sea salt
1	4-pound chicken

Heat oven to 400°F.

Process bacon to a puree in a food processor. Transfer to a bowl. Puree garlic, herbs, and chilies together in processor; add to bacon and mix well.

In a large bowl, whisk egg whites until frothy. Add salt and stir to combine.

Line a 9-by-13-inch baking dish with foil, leaving a 2- to 3-inch overhang on the two long sides. Place one third of salt mixture in baking dish and press it into a nice flat bed for chicken. Pat one third of bacon mixture over breast of chicken and place chicken, breast side down, on salt bed. Cover chicken with rest of bacon mixture. Use remaining salt mixture to form a complete shell around chicken.

Bake for 2 hours. Remove from oven and allow chicken to rest for 10 minutes.

Break salt crust and remove. Remove skin, pull off meat in pieces, and serve.

ROAST CHICKEN WITH FARRO SALAD WITH PRESERVED LEMON

QUICK-COOK RECIPE / MAKES 4 SERVINGS

This is a summer lunch dish I like to throw together when I have leftover roast chicken. Za'atar Chicken (page 248) is especially good to use here, since its Middle Eastern flavors go well with the preserved lemon, but you can use any roast chicken. The warmth of the cooked farro—a nutty-flavored whole grain—and the chicken helps the preserved lemon release its heady flavor, infusing the whole dish, while the celery heart offers a clean, grassy flavor and a crunchy texture.

FLAVOR TIP: Preserved lemon, a common Moroccan ingredient, has a salty, lightly pickled flavor that is more complex than regular lemon. Look for it in ethnic and specialty markets (see Sources, page 357).

- 1 cup farro (see page 13)
- Heart from 1 bunch celery, about 5 stalks
- ³⁄₄ cup loosely packed fresh flat-leaf parsley leaves
- Peel of ¹⁄₂ preserved lemon, thinly sliced (see Tip), or finely grated zest of 1 lemon
- ¹⁄₄ cup plus 2 tablespoons extra-virgin olive oil
- 2 small red onions, cut into eighths
- 2 cups large shreds or chunks white or dark meat from a roast chicken (see headnote), with crispy skin if you like, warmed in a low oven
- 2 tablespoons fresh lemon juice, or more to taste
- Medium-coarse sea salt and coarsely ground black pepper

Bring a medium saucepan of salted water to a boil. Add farro and cook until it is just tender but still has a bite, 12 to 15 minutes. Drain (do not rinse).

While farro is cooking, thinly slice celery on a mandoline or with a sharp knife. Place in a large bowl and toss with parsley leaves, lemon zest, and ¹⁄₄ cup oil.

Add warm farro to celery mixture and toss to combine.

Heat remaining 2 tablespoons oil in a large skillet over medium-high heat. Add onions and cook, turning with tongs, until browned on all sides, about 5 minutes. Add to farro mixture.

Add chicken and lemon juice; toss to combine. Season with salt and pepper and additional lemon juice if needed. Serve warm or at room temperature.

CHICKEN SALAD WITH TARRAGON, TOASTED PINE NUTS, AND GOLDEN RAISINS

QUICK-COOK RECIPE / MAKES 4 SERVINGS

I first learned a version of this salad in the province of Siena in Tuscany, where it was made from goose that was poached and then marinated with herbs and pine nuts in the local fruity, peppery oil. It's a dish that is unabashedly about the love of olive oil, so don't be shocked by the quantity used. Serve it with fresh-baked bread and simple salad greens.

FLAVOR TIP: Make this salad a few hours before serving if possible, and let it marinate at room temperature, which will allow the flavors to meld together more. If you choose to refrigerate it overnight or have refrigerated leftovers, be sure to bring it to room temperature before serving.

POACHED CHICKEN

- 2 carrots, coarsely chopped
- 2 celery stalks, coarsely chopped
- 1 medium unpeeled onion, cut into eighths
- 3 unpeeled garlic cloves
- 1/2 lemon, sliced in half
- 6 fresh flat-leaf parsley sprigs
- 3 fresh thyme sprigs
- 1 tablespoon black peppercorns
- 1 teaspoon fine sea salt
- 1 cup dry white wine
- 1/4 cup red wine vinegar
- 3 1/2 – 4 pounds bone-in chicken breasts (with skin)

- 1/2 cup golden raisins
- 1/2 cup pine nuts
- 3 scallions, thinly sliced on the bias

$^1/_4$ cup chopped fresh tarragon

$^1/_4$ cup chopped fresh chervil or flat-leaf parsley

3 tablespoons chopped fresh chives

$^3/_4$ cup extra-virgin olive oil

1 tablespoon mild white wine vinegar, such as Vin Santo (see page 7)

1 teaspoon medium-coarse sea salt

Coarsely ground black pepper

FOR POACHED CHICKEN: Put carrots, celery, onion, garlic, lemon, parsley, thyme, peppercorns, salt, wine, and vinegar in a large pot. Add 8 cups water and bring to a boil.

Add chicken, cover, reduce to a gentle simmer, and simmer until cooked through, about 30 minutes. Remove chicken from liquid and let cool; discard poaching liquid.

Pull meat off bone, discarding bones and skin. Shred chicken into pieces.

Soak raisins in warm water for 15 minutes; drain.

While raisins are soaking, toast pine nuts in a skillet over medium heat, tossing constantly, until lightly golden. Transfer to a plate.

Combine chicken, raisins, pine nuts, scallions, tarragon, chervil, chives, oil, vinegar, and salt in a large bowl and toss well. Season with pepper. Let sit at room temperature (see Tip), if desired, or serve immediately.

ROAST CHICKEN
WITH BRAISED RED PEPPERS AND ONION

SLOW-COOK RECIPE / MAKES 4 SERVINGS

These braised red peppers are a take on *peperonata,* the classic Tuscan dish of braised peppers and onions most often served as a side or a crostini topping. Slow-cooking the peppers results in a tender texture and lush sweetness that marries well with the chicken.

- 4 large red bell peppers
- 4 plum tomatoes
- 3 tablespoons extra-virgin olive oil
- 1 large onion, thinly sliced
- Fine sea salt
- 4 garlic cloves, smashed, 2 peeled, 2 with peel left on
- 1/2 cup water
- 1 4-pound chicken, cut into 8 pieces
- Coarsely ground black pepper
- 1 tablespoon unsalted butter
- 2 teaspoons chopped fresh rosemary

Char peppers over a gas burner set on high or a hot charcoal fire, turning frequently, until skins are blackened and blistered on all sides. Transfer to a bowl and seal tightly with plastic wrap; let sit for 15 minutes.

While peppers are resting, bring a large saucepan of salted water to a boil. Fill a large bowl with ice and water. Add tomatoes to boiling water and blanch for 45 seconds, then shock in ice water and drain immediately. Peel, seed, and coarsely chop tomatoes. Set aside.

Rub skins off peppers and remove and discard cores and seeds. Slice peppers lengthwise into 1½-inch-wide strips. Place in a bowl and set aside.

Heat 2 tablespoons oil in a small heavy saucepan over medium-high heat. Add onion and a pinch of salt. Cook, stirring frequently, until onion has softened, about 5 minutes. Add 2 peeled garlic cloves and cook, stirring occasionally, for 2 minutes more. Add peppers, with any juices, and water. Reduce heat to low, stir, cover, and cook for 40 minutes.

Add tomatoes and cook, uncovered, until sauce has thickened and peppers are falling-apart tender, about 1 hour more.

Meanwhile, heat oven to 450°F.

Season chicken with salt and pepper.

Heat remaining tablespoon oil and butter in a large ovenproof skillet over medium-high heat until butter is melted. Add chicken, skin side down, and cook until browned, about 10 minutes. Turn chicken pieces skin side up, top with remaining unpeeled garlic cloves, and sprinkle chicken with rosemary.

Place skillet in oven and roast until chicken is cooked through, about 20 minutes. Serve hot with sauce.

BRAISED CHICKEN HASH
WITH WILD MUSHROOMS AND HERBED RICE

SLOW-COOK RECIPE / MAKES 4 SERVINGS

Braising chicken legs in red wine makes for a robust wintry hash. Though I wasn't always a fan of dark meat—an admitted gastronomic crime—this rich braise made a convert of me. Serve it over the herbed rice or warm polenta with sautéed bitter greens.

FLAVOR TIP: Substitute white wine, and you will get a more delicate version, similar to the Braised Guinea Hen Ragù (page 172).

CHICKEN

2¹⁄₂–3 pounds whole chicken legs (with thighs and skin)

Coarse sea salt and coarsely ground black pepper

¹⁄₄ cup extra-virgin olive oil

2 small onions, cut into ¹⁄₂-inch pieces

2 medium carrots, cut into ¹⁄₂-inch pieces

2 celery stalks, cut into ¹⁄₂-inch pieces

1 small fennel bulb, trimmed and cut into ¹⁄₂-inch pieces

3 garlic cloves, smashed and peeled

1 cup dry red wine

1 cup water

2 bay leaves

HERBED RICE

1 tablespoon unsalted butter

1 onion, minced

1 cup jasmine rice

1¹⁄₂ cups water

1 cup mixed chopped fresh herbs, such as basil, tarragon, savory, mint, cilantro, and/or chives

2–3 teaspoons extra-virgin olive oil

Fine sea salt and coarsely ground black pepper

MUSHROOMS

2 tablespoons unsalted butter

2 tablespoons extra-virgin olive oil

12 ounces oyster, black trumpet, or chanterelle mushrooms, trimmed, large ones cut in half

1/3 cup chopped fresh flat-leaf parsley

1 garlic clove, thinly sliced

Heat oven to 300°F.

FOR CHICKEN: Season chicken with salt and pepper. Heat oil in a large Dutch oven or other heavy ovenproof pot over medium-high heat. Add chicken skin side down and cook until browned on both sides, about 10 minutes. Transfer to a bowl and set aside. Add onions, carrots, celery, fennel, and garlic to pot and cook, stirring occasionally, until lightly browned, about 8 minutes. Using a slotted spoon, transfer vegetables to bowl with chicken. Drain fat from pan.

Return pot to stove over medium-high heat and add browned chicken, vegetables, wine, water, and bay leaves and bring to a simmer over medium-high heat. Cover, transfer to oven, and cook until chicken is falling off bones, about 40 minutes. Remove chicken from oven and let cool slightly.

Remove bay leaves from chicken and discard. Remove chicken pieces and pull off meat, discarding skin and bones. Return meat to pot with vegetables; set aside.

FOR HERBED RICE: While chicken is cooking, melt butter in a medium saucepan over medium heat. Add onion, stir, and cook, stirring, until softened, about 7 minutes. Add rice and water; cook as directed on package until just tender and most of liquid is absorbed. Remove rice from heat, stir in herbs and oil, and season generously with salt and pepper. Cover to keep warm.

FOR MUSHROOMS: Heat butter and oil in a large saucepan over medium-high heat until butter is melted. Add mushrooms and cook, stirring once, for 2 minutes. Add parsley and garlic and cook for 1 minute more to soften. Transfer to pot with chicken and vegetables.

Heat hash over medium heat for a few minutes, stirring once or twice to mix. Season with salt and pepper to taste and serve hot over rice.

CHICKEN WITH ESCAROLE, APPLES, AND POTATOES

QUICK-COOK RECIPE / MAKES 4 SERVINGS

Using one skillet to accomplish several steps, you build flavor in the pan as you cook. Use an interesting variety of fresh-dug potatoes from the farmers' market, if available. Fingerlings are one of my favorites; you can also try tiny purple potatoes or red-skinned ones.

FLAVOR TIP: Smashing boiled whole small potatoes, rather than cutting up large ones, and frying them in butter gives you lots of crispy brown edges and fluffy, tender centers.

12 ounces small new potatoes

4 8-ounce boneless chicken breasts with skin

Fine sea salt and coarsely ground black pepper

3 tablespoons extra-virgin olive oil

5 tablespoons unsalted butter

2 semi-tart apples, such as Empire or Macoun, peeled, cored, and cut into eighths

1 garlic clove, smashed and peeled

1 pound escarole, leaves torn

1/2 cup dry white wine

Heat oven to 250°F.

Bring a large saucepan of salted water to a boil. Add potatoes and cook until tender, about 7 minutes. Drain and place on a plate in a single layer to cool.

When potatoes are just cool enough to handle, flatten each one slightly by gently pressing on it with the side of a chef's knife. Set aside.

Season chicken with salt and pepper. Heat oil in a large skillet over medium-high heat. Add chicken, skin side down, in batches if necessary, and cook until skin is golden, 5 to 7 minutes. Turn and cook until underside is lightly golden, about 3 minutes. Transfer to a baking pan, cover with foil, and place in oven.

Drain oil from skillet, return to medium-high heat, and add 2 tablespoons butter. Add only as many apples as will fit in a single layer and cook, turning apples as they brown, until golden on all sides, 3 to 4 minutes. Transfer to a plate. Repeat with any remaining apples.

Add 2 more tablespoons butter to skillet. Add only as many potatoes as will fit in a single layer, sprinkle with salt and pepper, and cook over medium-high heat, turning once, until potatoes are warmed through and golden, about 2 minutes per side. Transfer to a plate. Repeat with any remaining potatoes.

Add garlic and as much escarole as you can comfortably fit into skillet, increase heat to high, and cook, stirring, until escarole starts to wilt and you can add more, about 1 minute. Add remaining escarole and cook until just wilted, about 1 minute more. Add wine and cook until escarole is tender and wine is slightly reduced. Add apples and cook until warmed through, about 2 minutes. Remove from heat.

Remove chicken from oven and pour any juices from pan into skillet with escarole and apples. Stir to combine.

Divide potatoes among four plates, then add chicken and escarole mixture, leaving juices in skillet. Return skillet to high heat, bring juices to a boil, and boil for 1 minute. Whisk in remaining tablespoon butter. Season sauce with salt and pepper, pour over chicken, and serve.

DUCK BREAST WITH CHANTERELLES, CHESTNUTS, AND PEARL ONIONS

QUICK-COOK RECIPE / MAKES 4 SERVINGS

Chanterelles come into season in both the early summer and the fall. Deliciously meaty, these bright yellow fungi are among the most flavorful and distinct-tasting mushrooms of all. When I find them, I build a whole meal around them, often using rich and tender duck breast. Make sure you have all of your ingredients prepped ahead of time, as things come together quickly when you're wrapping up this dish, and you'll want to have everything in place.

FLAVOR TIP: Cooking the duck breasts over low heat for 40 minutes renders all the fat from them and makes the skin deliciously crispy.

- 2 1-pound boneless duck breasts, with skin
  Fine sea salt and coarsely ground black pepper
- 8 ounces pearl onions or small cipollini
- 2 tablespoons extra-virgin olive oil
- 2 tablespoons unsalted butter
- 8 ounces chanterelles or oyster mushrooms, trimmed, large ones cut in half
- ½ cup frozen peeled chestnuts (see Sources, page 357), thawed
- 1 garlic clove, thinly sliced
- ¼ cup water
- ¼ cup chopped fresh flat-leaf parsley

Heat oven to 400°F.

Score duck skin in a crosshatch pattern with a small sharp knife, and season duck all over with salt and pepper. Place duck, skin side down, in a cast-iron skillet and cook over low heat until fat is rendered and skin is golden and crispy, about 40 minutes.

While duck is cooking, place onions in a small baking dish, drizzle with oil, and season with salt and pepper. Roast until golden, about 30 minutes. Remove from oven.

When duck skin is golden and fat has rendered, strain and reserve fat. Return pan to high heat, return duck breasts to pan, flesh side down, and cook for 3 minutes for medium-rare. Transfer breasts to a cutting board and let rest for 10 minutes.

While duck is resting, return skillet to heat. Add butter and 1 tablespoon reserved duck fat and heat over high heat. Add mushrooms and 2 pinches salt; cook, stirring and coating mushrooms with fat, for 2 minutes. Add chestnuts, stir, and cook for 1 minute more. Add garlic, stir, and cook for 2 minutes more to soften. Add water and roasted onions and simmer until onions are heated through and flavors have blended, about 2 minutes more. Remove from heat, add parsley, and season with salt and pepper to taste.

Slice duck and add juices to mushroom mixture. Arrange duck on plates, spoon mushroom mixture over, and serve.

HONEY-AND-CHILI-ROASTED DUCK WITH FENNEL AND FARRO

SLOW-COOK RECIPE / MAKES 4 SERVINGS

Slow-roasting duck and finishing it with orange juice and honey make for a beautifully lacquered skin and exquisitely tender flesh. Accenting the sweet ingredients with the heat of ground chili is Moroccan in style.

FLAVOR TIP: Scoring the skin of the duck breast allows the fat to slowly melt away as it cooks, basting and flavoring the meat and leaving the skin crispy.

DUCK

- 2 celery stalks, cut crosswise into 4 pieces each
- 2 carrots, cut into 2-inch pieces
- 1 medium unpeeled onion, quartered
- 1 leek, trimmed, cut crosswise in half and rinsed
- 4 unpeeled garlic cloves
- 6 large fresh thyme sprigs
- 6 large fresh sage sprigs
- 2/3 cup fresh orange juice (from about 3 juice oranges)
- 2 tablespoons chestnut honey (see page 20)
- 1 5-pound duck
- 1/2 teaspoon piment d'Espelette (see page 16) or other crushed dried red chili pepper

  Fine sea salt and coarsely ground black pepper

FARRO

- 1/4 cup extra-virgin olive oil
- 2 medium fennel bulbs, trimmed, quartered, and cored
- 1 serrano chili
- 1 1/2 cups farro (see page 13)
- 1 tablespoon fresh thyme leaves

1³/₄ cups homemade chicken broth (page 108)

1 cup fresh orange juice (from about 4 juice oranges)

Fine sea salt

Heat oven to 300°F.

FOR DUCK: Place celery, carrots, onion, leek, garlic, thyme, and sage in a 9-by-13-inch baking dish. Whisk orange juice and honey together; set aside.

With the tip of a sharp knife, score skin over duck breasts in a crosshatch pattern. Season duck all over with chili, salt, and pepper, and place on top of vegetable mixture, breast side up. Roast for 1 hour.

Baste duck with fat and juices from pan, and continue roasting for another 1 hour and 15 minutes.

Baste duck with one third of orange juice mixture and continue to cook, basting with orange juice mixture 2 more times, until skin is golden and crispy and duck is cooked through, about 45 minutes more. Remove duck from oven and let rest for 15 minutes before carving.

FOR FARRO: While duck is cooking, heat oil in a large Dutch oven or other heavy pot over medium-high heat. Add fennel cut side down, add chili, and cook, turning occasionally, until fennel is browned on all sides, 8 to 10 minutes.

Add farro and thyme; stir. Add broth, orange juice, and a good pinch of salt. Cover, reduce heat, and simmer gently until farro is tender but still firm, about 25 minutes. Uncover and cook until liquid has mostly evaporated, 5 to 10 minutes more.

Remove farro from heat. Mash chili pepper with a fork and stir to combine with farro. Season with additional salt if necessary. Cover to keep warm.

Carve duck and serve with farro.

OVEN-ROASTED GUINEA HEN BREASTS WITH BARLEY AND DANDELION GREENS

QUICK-COOK RECIPE / MAKES 4 SERVINGS

Guinea hen goes well with bitter dandelion greens and earthy barley, which is prepared like risotto here. You'll likely have to buy the birds whole, but you can save the legs and thighs for Braised Guinea Hen Ragù (page 172). A good butcher will cut the bird into parts for you if you need him to. You can substitute chicken breasts; the cooking time will probably be longer.

¼ cup plus 2 tablespoons extra-virgin olive oil

2 tablespoons unsalted butter

1 small onion, finely chopped

1 garlic clove, minced

Medium-coarse sea salt

1 cup barley

3 cups Rich Chicken Broth (page 108), heated until hot

4 boneless guinea hen breasts with skin (see Sources, page 357)

Coarsely ground black pepper

8 ounces dandelion greens or chicory

Heat oven to 375°F.

Heat 2 tablespoons oil and 1 tablespoon butter in a medium saucepan over medium-high heat until butter is melted. Add onion, garlic, and a pinch of salt. Cook, stirring, until onion is translucent, about 4 minutes.

Add barley and stir to coat. Add 1 cup hot chicken broth and simmer, stirring, until broth is almost absorbed. Continue cooking, adding broth by ½-cupfuls, until barley is tender, 15 to 20 minutes. Remove from heat.

While barley is cooking, season guinea hen with salt and pepper. Heat remaining ¼ cup oil in a large ovenproof skillet over medium-high heat. Add guinea hen and brown on both sides, about 8 minutes. Drain oil from skillet, turn breasts skin side up if necessary, and dot with remaining tablespoon butter.

Transfer to oven and bake until just cooked through, about 10 minutes. Remove from oven.

Add dandelion greens to cooked barley and stir over medium-low heat to wilt greens and heat barley through. Season with salt and pepper, and serve with guinea hen.

BRAISED RABBIT WITH
LEMON AND ROSEMARY

SLOW-COOK RECIPE / MAKES 6 TO 8 SERVINGS

The strips of lemon peel are a wonderful part of this Tuscan-inspired dish. Their bitterness is transformed into a tender, jam-like citrusy element that can and should be eaten with every bite. This recipe can be cut in half if you want to serve four; use only the liquid you need to just cover the rabbit pieces, no more. Serve with polenta, rice (herbed, page 260, or plain), or smashed boiled or roasted potatoes.

FLAVOR TIP: To get the deepest flavor from this braise, you'll want a nice brown crust on the rabbit pieces before you add your liquid. Brown them in a Dutch oven (I favor the enameled cast-iron type) or other heavy pot over high heat, don't crowd the pot, and don't move the pieces around too much while they brown. Otherwise you end up with steamed rabbit, which is much less tasty.

2	lemons
2	2 1/2-pound rabbits
	Medium-coarse sea salt and coarsely ground black pepper
1/4	cup plus 2 tablespoons extra-virgin olive oil
4	garlic cloves, smashed and peeled
8	fresh rosemary sprigs, snipped in half crosswise
2	cups dry white wine
1	cup water

Heat oven to 350°F.

With a sharp paring knife or vegetable peeler, cut peel from lemons in wide vertical strips, avoiding bitter white pith. Set aside.

Cut each rabbit in half lengthwise, then crosswise into 8 roughly equal pieces. Season rabbit pieces with salt and pepper. Heat 1/4 cup oil in a large Dutch oven or other heavy pot over high heat. Add 3 or 4 rabbit pieces and brown well on all sides, 4 to 6 minutes per side. Transfer to a bowl and repeat with remaining pieces.

Reduce heat to low. Add remaining 2 tablespoons oil, garlic, lemon peel, and rosemary; cook, stirring occasionally, until garlic is golden, about 2 minutes. Add wine, bring to a simmer, and scrape up any browned bits from bottom of pot. Add rabbit pieces and juices, placing largest, meatiest pieces on bottom and rest on top.

Add water, bring to a simmer, cover, and braise in oven until rabbit is tender, about 1 hour and 20 minutes.

Transfer rabbit to a platter and place pot over high heat. Bring juices to a simmer and reduce to about 1 cup, about 25 minutes.

Pour hot juices, along with garlic, rosemary, and lemon peel, over rabbit pieces and serve.

ROASTED RABBIT WITH SHAVED CELERY AND FRIED BREAD SALAD

QUICK-COOK RECIPE / MAKES 4 SERVINGS

I love celery, especially the hearts and leaves. The heart, the inner three to five stalks, brings great texture and flavor to all sorts of salads, without the stringiness or bitterness of the outer ribs (these do their job best in stocks and braises and, of course, *soffritto*—the requisite base of sautéed diced vegetables of Italian ragùs and stews). In this warm salad, herbed roasted rabbit is topped with a cool, crunchy celery and bread salad. Use good-sized herb sprigs, or add a couple more if yours are small.

3 large fresh rosemary sprigs, leaves only

3 large fresh savory sprigs, leaves only

3 leafy fresh sage sprigs, leaves only

4 garlic cloves

1 2³/₄- to 3-pound rabbit

5 tablespoons extra-virgin olive oil, plus more for frying

4 ounces country bread, cut into ¹/₂-inch cubes (about 2 cups)

1 celery heart, and as many celery leaves as you want

1 tablespoon good red wine vinegar, such as Volpaia

Fine sea salt and coarsely ground black pepper

Finely chop herbs together with garlic. Cut rabbit in half lengthwise, then crosswise into 8 pieces. Toss with herb mixture and 2 tablespoons oil in a bowl, then transfer to a baking dish, scraping oil and herb mixture over top. Let marinate at room temperature for 30 minutes or in the refrigerator for as long as overnight. If marinating overnight, bring rabbit to room temperature before roasting.

Heat oven to 450°F.

Roast rabbit until golden and cooked through, 40 to 45 minutes.

When rabbit is close to being done, heat ¹/₂ inch oil in a medium skillet over high heat until a bread cube dropped in turns golden. Remove test cube, add remaining cubes,

and fry, stirring with a slotted spoon, until golden, about 30 seconds. Drain on paper towels.

Thinly slice celery heart and toss with celery leaves, remaining 3 tablespoons oil, vinegar, and salt and pepper to taste. Add bread cubes and toss to combine. Serve rabbit warm, topped with salad.

BEEF, VEAL, PORK, LAMB, AND VENISON

When I shop for meat, I first consider how the animal was raised. No doubt about it, labels are often confusing, and many times the people behind the supermarket meat counter have a surprising lack of knowledge about the meat they sell. Farmers' markets, sourcing collaboratives, like CSAs (Community Supported Agriculture groups), and mail-order sources (see page 357) are the best channels for purchasing meat.

A quick 101: cattle, dairy cows, goats, bison, and sheep are ruminants, or grass eaters. When fed grain and raised in confinement, as they are on industrial farms, not only are they prone to serious illness (which in turn requires heavy dosing of antibiotics) but the nutritional value and the taste of their meat are significantly compromised. Meat from grain-fed animals has more fat and cholesterol, as well as more chemicals (since grains are often laden with pesticides), than that of their grass-fed or organic counterparts. It also has fewer vitamins, omega-3 fatty acids, and other important nutrients. Organic and grass-fed meats look, smell, and taste better than conventional commercial meat, and they are produced in a more environmentally sound manner.

The people who sell meat at my farmers' market raise the animals and frequently slaughter them themselves. Generally the prime cuts are too expensive for everyday use, so I tend to buy the less pricey shoulder or stewing meats, reserving prized cuts for special occasions. I also eat in the Mediterranean style, consuming smaller portions of meat than the typical American and not eating meat at every meal.

When you start dealing with small farmers and meat purveyors, you may find some variability in their products. Some chickens will have more flavor than others; one order of pork chops might be more tender than another. I liken it to the shapes and colors of heirloom tomatoes—some differ in color from tomato to tomato; some seasons are better than others.

Different types of cuts demand different cooking techniques to bring out the best in them. Tougher cuts, such as shoulder, shank, and ribs, are best for slow, low, moist-heat cooking methods like stewing and braising and in ragùs. The emphatic flavor of these cuts holds up through the long cooking time, which renders the meat exquisitely soft and spoon-tender. For long braises and stews, I season the meat aggressively and build complexity of flavor with agents like anchovies, vinegar, and aromatic herbs and vegetables.

More tender prime cuts, such as tenderloins and chops, benefit from a lighter hand with seasoning and quick high-heat cooking. Good sea salt and coarsely ground pepper, extra-virgin olive oil, and maybe a little squeeze of lemon juice are often all that's needed, letting the flavor of the meat itself shine through.

BEEF, VEAL, PORK, LAMB, AND VENISON

Grilled Skirt Steak with
Cucumber and Avocado Salad | 281

Bistecca Chianina | 284

Peppery Braised Short Ribs | 286

Braised Oxtail | 289

Veal Saltimbocca | 290

Roasted Veal Chops with Winter
Vegetables and Anchovy Butter | 292

Free-Range Veal Shoulder with
Baby Carrots and Mustard
Greens | 295

Calf's Liver with Brown Butter,
Sage, and Wilted Dandelion
Greens | 297

continued

Grilled Lamb Brochettes
with Shaved Onion Salad | 300

Crisp Fried Lamb Chops with Lemon
and Rosemary | 303

Pan-Roasted Lamb Chops with
Capers, Olives, Onions, and Smashed
Potatoes | 304

Roasted Rack of Lamb with Minty
Bulgur Salad | 306

Roasted Leg of Lamb with Black
Olives | 309

Braised Lamb Shoulder with Green
Tomatoes and Concord Grapes | 310

Winter Lamb Stew with Turnips,
Carrots, and Celery Root | 312

Baked Pork Chops with Peaches | 314

Skillet-Cooked Pork Chops with
Morels and Lentils | 316

Slow-Roasted Pork Shoulder | 318

Braised Pork Loin with Prunes | 321

Roasted Venison with
Cider-Braised Leeks | 322

GRILLED SKIRT STEAK WITH CUCUMBER AND AVOCADO SALAD

QUICK-COOK RECIPE / MAKES 4 SERVINGS

The fresh tastes of this dish make for great summer eating. The richness of the avocado contrasts well with the meaty beefiness of the skirt steak and the crisp, refreshing crunch of the cucumber. Topping the warm steak slices with the salad both softens the cucumber just a bit and draws the flavor and aroma from the avocado and basil leaves.

FLAVOR TIP: Skirt steak tends to be thin and not uniform in its thickness, two reasons you'll want to pay attention to the meat while it's on the fire. Cooked to medium-rare, the cut is wonderfully tender and flavorful. Overcooked, it becomes dull-tasting and tough. Follow the cooking times below, and let the meat rest before slicing it. You can always throw thicker pieces back on the grill if necessary.

- 2 pounds skirt steak
  Fine sea salt and coarsely ground black pepper
- 1 large avocado, pitted, peeled, and diced (1/2 inch)
- 1 large cucumber, peeled, halved lengthwise, and sliced into half-moons
- 1/2 cup packed fresh basil leaves
- 3 tablespoons extra-virgin olive oil
- 3 tablespoons fresh lemon juice

Bring steaks to room temperature. Meanwhile, build a hot fire in a charcoal grill. Mix together a small bowl of salt and pepper.

Lay steak on grill and cook on one side, moving it once or twice so it sears evenly, for 2 minutes. Turn, season cooked side with salt and pepper, and cook, moving it once or twice, an additional 2 minutes for medium-rare. Transfer to a cutting board, seasoned side down, season second side, and let rest for 5 minutes.

While steak is resting, combine avocado, cucumber, basil leaves, oil, and lemon juice. Season to taste with salt and pepper.

Slice steak against the grain and serve topped with salad.

BISTECCA CHIANINA
(PAGE 284)

BISTECCA CHIANINA

QUICK-COOK RECIPE / MAKES 2 TO 3 SERVINGS

The Florentines call this simple dish *bistecca Fiorentina*, but many Tuscan and Umbrian purists assert that it is more aptly named *Chianina* for the majestic giant white cattle originally raised by the Etruscans as work animals in the Val di Chiana—the valley that lies between the hill town of Cortona and the rolling hills of Siena. Chianina is a special breed of cow whose genetic makeup, diet, young slaughter age (older than veal, but not by much), and extended hanging time produce pale rose-colored lean meat that is low in cholesterol yet extremely rich in flavor and beautifully uniform in texture—in fact, unique. *Bistecca Chianina* is most often and ideally a T-bone steak, cut at least 1½ inches thick (and up to 3 inches) and cooked over hot wood coals until the outside is nicely seared but the center is still rare. If your steak is thinner than 2 inches, cook it for less time than indicated. It should be eaten with nothing more than a drizzle of olive oil and perhaps a squeeze of lemon.

True Chianina is not yet available in America. However, you can grill a magnificent thick-cut American T-bone or porterhouse steak in the same manner and have a really great meal. I find that grass-fed, versus grain-fed, beef most closely approximates the flavor of Chianina. Whichever you choose, you'll need to order the meat from a specialty butcher or your local farmer. As simple as this recipe is, the result depends on the quality of the ingredients—good extra-virgin olive oil, sea salt, and the beef—and vigilant attention to the cooking technique. (The photograph is on the previous page.)

FLAVOR TIP: Note that the meat is not seasoned until it has cooked. This is an Italian technique that helps produce a drier sear than presalting the beef, and it makes the contrast between the salty, crisp outside and the tender rare unsalted interior all the more pronounced. This goes against the advice of every American and French chef I've ever met, but I truly believe it produces a superior result.

1   2½- to 3-pound T-bone or porterhouse steak, at least 2 inches thick

Medium-coarse sea salt, such as fleur de sel, and coarsely ground black pepper

1–2   tablespoons extra-virgin olive oil

1   lemon, cut into wedges

Bring steak to room temperature.

Build a large fire in a charcoal grill and let it burn down to a medium-high to high-heat fire (be sure to wait until flames have died down completely or you will burn the outside of your meat).

Mix together a small bowl of salt and pepper. Score fat on edges of steak.

Lay steak on grill and cook, shifting steak every 30 seconds to get an even char on one side, for about 7 minutes. Turn steak, season cooked side, and cook, moving it every 30 seconds to get a thick, even crust on second side, 5 to 7 more minutes for medium-rare to rare. (Cook longer for a thicker piece of meat.) Transfer steak to a cutting board, seasoned side down, season second side, and let rest for 10 minutes.

Slice steak and serve at once, drizzled with olive oil and lemon juice.

PEPPERY BRAISED SHORT RIBS

SLOW-COOK RECIPE / MAKES 4 TO 6 SERVINGS

In Pontassieve, the suburb of Florence where this dish originated, it's known as *peposo di Brunelleschi*, referring to the Renaissance architect who designed and built Florence's beloved Duomo. Stories abound as to how the dish got its name—some say the tile workers negotiated a deal with the great architect whereby they worked long hours in exchange for a daily ration of the dish. But I think it's safe to assume that they slow-cooked the meal for themselves while firing their wares in nearby kilns.

I first tasted the dish at the legendary Tuscan butcher Dario's, in Panzano in Chianti, where he had prepared it with the more classic beef shin, serving it with Tuscan bread and slightly acidic local Chianti. Here, the braising technique and the red wine and aromatics draw out the richness and tenderness from short ribs, an economical and readily available cut of beef. The peppery spice cuts both the fat of the meat and the richness of the wine. It's great with Polenta with Aromatic Herb Butter (page 199), couscous, or any root vegetable puree.

FLAVOR TIP: You can use this basic marinade for all red meats and game (lamb shank, beef shin, boar, beef rump, oxtail, and more). The purpose of all marinades is twofold: to enhance flavor and increase tenderness. The acid in the marinade (in this case, wine) breaks down the tough fibers of the meat and mellows any gamy flavor. Herbs, spices, and other ingredients further enhance the flavor. You can add or substitute one or a combination of other flavor enhancers to this basic marinade, such as fresh thyme or savory, orange peel, coriander seeds, or fennel seeds or fronds. I give a wide time range for marinating this meat; the longer you leave the meat in the marinade, the stronger and more pronounced the flavor.

 10 unpeeled garlic cloves

  1 medium carrot, coarsely chopped

  1 celery stalk, coarsely chopped

  1 small onion, coarsely chopped

  3 bay leaves

  2 fresh rosemary sprigs

  1 fresh sage sprig

 1/4 cup black peppercorns, tied in a square of cheesecloth

 10 juniper berries

  4 whole cloves

  1 750-ml bottle Chianti or other dry red wine

  6 1-pound beef short ribs

     Medium-coarse sea salt and coarsely ground black pepper

  2 tablespoons extra-virgin olive oil

 1/2 cup dry red wine

  2 heads garlic, broken into cloves but not peeled

     About 3 cups water

FOR MARINADE: Combine garlic, carrot, celery, onion, herbs, and spices in a large bowl. Add wine, then add ribs, cover, and marinate, refrigerated, for 24 to 48 hours.

Heat oven to 275°F.

Remove ribs from marinade. Remove peppercorns from cheesecloth and set aside; discard remaining marinade. Season ribs generously with salt and pepper.

Heat oil in a large Dutch oven or other heavy ovenproof pot over high heat. Brown short ribs in batches until quite crispy and well browned on both sides, about 5 minutes per side. Remove ribs from pot and set aside. Drain fat from pot and discard.

Return pot to high heat, add wine, and stir, scraping up browned bits, for about 1 minute. Remove from heat.

Return short ribs to pot, along with garlic cloves and peppercorns. Add enough water to almost cover ribs, cover pot, place in oven, and cook for 1½ hours.

Reduce oven temperature to 200°F and continue cooking until meat is meltingly tender and falling off bones, about 3 hours more. Remove from oven.

Remove ribs from liquid and set aside. Strain liquid, pressing on garlic cloves to extract as much flavor as possible. Skim fat from liquid, return liquid to pot, and add ribs. Bring to a gentle simmer. Add 2 teaspoons pepper, stir to combine, and serve.

BRAISED OXTAIL

SLOW-COOK RECIPE / MAKES 4 SERVINGS

Oxtail, when cooked slowly and gently to break down its tough fibers, is possibly the most flavorful and tender cut of beef. This hearty braise is delicious with a side of mashed or roasted potatoes, but you can also pull the meat from the bones and toss it (and its delectable sauce) with pasta.

- 3 pounds 1-inch-pieces meaty oxtails (have your butcher cut them up)
  Fine sea salt and coarsely ground black pepper
- 1/4 cup extra-virgin olive oil
- 4 carrots, coarsely chopped
- 4 celery stalks, coarsely chopped
- 1 large onion, coarsely chopped
- 1 750-ml bottle Chianti or other dry red wine
- 2 fresh savory, rosemary, or thyme sprigs
- 1 bay leaf
  About 2 cups water
- 2 pints grape, teardrop, or cherry tomatoes

Heat oven to 325°F.

Toss oxtails with 2 teaspoons salt and a generous amount of pepper. Heat oil in a large Dutch oven or other heavy ovenproof pot with a lid over high heat. In batches, brown oxtails well on one side, about 6 to 8 minutes, then turn and cook on other side just until lightly browned, 1 to 2 minutes. Transfer to a plate.

Add carrots, celery, onion, and 1/4 teaspoon salt to pot; stir to coat vegetables with oil. Cook, stirring frequently, until vegetables are softened and browned, about 15 minutes; reduce heat if vegetables begin to burn.

Drain vegetables in a colander, discard oil, and return vegetables to pot. Add oxtails, wine, savory, and bay leaf. Add enough water to come just to the top of meat. Cover, place in oven, and cook for 1½ hours.

Uncover, scatter tomatoes over braise, return to oven, and cook, uncovered, until meat is extremely tender and tomatoes are browned and collapsed, 1 to 1½ hours more. Gently mix and serve.

VEAL SALTIMBOCCA

QUICK-COOK RECIPE / MAKES 4 SERVINGS

This dish has long been a staple of Roman trattorias and home cooks alike, beloved for its flavor, ease, and simplicity. The Romans argue over whether the prosciutto and sage should be sandwiched between the meat or placed around it and fried until crisp, which is the way I like it best. The prosciutto seasons the whole dish, so you shouldn't need to add salt.

1½ pounds veal cutlets

4 ounces thinly sliced prosciutto

1 bunch fresh sage

All-purpose flour for dredging

2–3 tablespoons extra-virgin olive oil

2 tablespoons unsalted butter

Coarsely ground black pepper

½ cup dry white wine

Special equipment: toothpicks

Lay veal cutlets on a cutting board; top each with 1 to 2 slices prosciutto, distributing prosciutto evenly. Place 2 sage leaves on top of prosciutto at either end of each cutlet. Using toothpicks, pin sage leaves and prosciutto to cutlets. Dredge bare side of cutlets in flour.

Heat 2 tablespoons oil and 1 tablespoon butter in a large skillet over medium-high heat until butter is melted. Add cutlets in batches, if necessary, prosciutto side down, sprinkle with pepper, and cook until browned, about 2 minutes. Turn and cook until second side is browned, about 2 minutes more, adding additional oil if necessary. Transfer veal to a platter.

Add wine to pan and scrape up browned bits. Add any juices from plate with veal and simmer until liquid reduces and starts to thicken, about 4 minutes. Add remaining tablespoon butter and stir until melted, then pour sauce over veal and serve.

ROASTED VEAL CHOPS WITH WINTER VEGETABLES AND ANCHOVY BUTTER

SLOW-COOK RECIPE / MAKES 4 SERVINGS

Great veal chops don't need much fuss. Roasting or grilling them to medium or medium-rare, then sprinkling them with salt and pepper, and drizzling with olive oil, brings out the delicate taste of the meat. Anchovy butter's subtle saltiness is a great match for the sweetness of the meat, and it's the best "sauce" for veal I've found.

If you can't find baby carrots and turnips, cut larger ones in half and then into ½-inch pieces. Switch the vegetables for this dish according to the season. In the summer, I like to use green beans or fresh-dug new potatoes.

FLAVOR TIPS: Cipollini onions have a distinctly sweet flavor. Their flat shape makes them nice for pan- or oven-roasting. Look for them at farmers' markets and specialty shops.

If you have thinner chops, be sure to reduce the cooking time.

ANCHOVY BUTTER

4 anchovy fillets

1 garlic clove, coarsely chopped

4 tablespoons (½ stick) unsalted butter, at room temperature

1 tablespoon fresh lemon juice

Coarsely ground black pepper

12 ounces mixed heirloom baby carrots, trimmed and scrubbed (see headnote)

8 ounces baby turnips, peeled and cut in half

4–5 tablespoons extra-virgin olive oil

Medium-coarse sea salt and coarsely ground black pepper

1 tablespoon unsalted butter

12 ounces cipollini or pearl onions (see Tips)

1 cup water

4 free-range veal rib chops (about 10 ounces each), 1½ inches thick (see Tips)

2 tablespoons chopped fresh flat-leaf parsley

Heat oven to 400°F.

FOR ANCHOVY BUTTER: Finely chop anchovy fillets and garlic together to make a fine paste. Transfer to a small bowl and mix in butter and lemon juice; season generously with pepper. Set aside in a cool part of kitchen or refrigerate until ready to use.

FOR VEGETABLES AND VEAL: Toss carrots and turnips with 2 tablespoons oil. Spread on a baking sheet, season with salt and pepper, and roast until golden and tender, 15 to 20 minutes.

Meanwhile, heat 1 tablespoon oil and butter in a large deep heavy skillet with a lid or large Dutch oven over medium heat until butter is melted. Add onions, in a single layer, with a pinch of salt and cook until browned on both sides, about 5 minutes per side. Add water, reduce heat to low, cover, and cook for 10 minutes. Uncover, turn onions over, and increase heat to medium-high. Cook until onions are glazed and liquid has almost completely evaporated. Remove from heat.

When carrots and turnips are ready, remove from oven, add to onions, and stir gently to combine; set aside.

Reduce oven temperature to 300°F.

Season veal chops liberally with salt and pepper. Heat 1 tablespoon oil in a large skillet over medium-high heat. Add 2 veal chops and cook until well browned, about 4 minutes per side; transfer to a shallow baking pan. Repeat with remaining chops; add more oil if necessary. When all 4 chops are browned, place in oven and cook for 8 to 10 minutes for medium-rare, or a few minutes less if you have thinner chops.

Remove chops from oven and let rest. Gently warm vegetables over medium-low heat for a few minutes, then toss with anchovy butter and parsley.

Serve chops topped with vegetables.

FREE-RANGE VEAL SHOULDER
WITH BABY CARROTS AND MUSTARD GREENS

SLOW-COOK RECIPE / MAKES 6 SERVINGS

This is a simple roast, so be sure to shop well. The bitterness of the mustard greens plays off the sweetness of the roast carrots and the clean, plain taste of the meat. For variation, try turnip tops, radish leaves, or broccoli raab in place of the mustard greens, and sweet root vegetables, like parsnips or rutabaga, with or instead of the carrots.

Free-range veal is pinker than traditional veal, as the animals are raised on a combination diet of mother's milk and grasses.

NOTE: Use carrots that are about ⅓ inch in diameter and 3 to 5 inches long, as opposed to tiny ones, which will overcook in this recipe. If baby carrots are unavailable, use skinny medium-sized carrots, and cut them in half on the bias.

1	3-pound free-range veal shoulder roast
	Fine sea salt and coarsely ground black pepper
1¼	pounds mixed heirloom baby carrots (20–25; see Note), tops trimmed to ½ inch, scrubbed
½	cup extra-virgin olive oil
⅔	cup dry white wine
10	large fresh thyme sprigs
3	garlic cloves, smashed and peeled
1½	pounds mustard greens, stemmed and coarsely chopped
¼	cup water

Heat oven to 450°F.

Season veal with salt and pepper and place in a 9-by-13-inch baking dish. Scatter carrots around meat. Drizzle ¼ cup oil over veal and carrots and sprinkle carrots with salt. Roast for 35 minutes.

Pour wine over roast and scatter thyme around. Roast until an instant-read thermometer inserted into thickest part of meat reads 135°F, for medium-rare, about 25 minutes. Remove from oven and allow meat to rest while you cook greens.

Heat remaining ¼ cup oil and garlic in a large skillet over medium-high heat, stirring occasionally, until garlic is golden, about 3 minutes. Add greens (in batches if necessary) and ¼ teaspoon salt; stir. Add water and cook, stirring, until greens start to wilt, about 2 minutes. Remove from heat and continue stirring occasionally until greens are fully wilted, about 2 minutes more. Adjust seasoning if necessary.

Slice veal and serve with greens and carrots, drizzling resting juices over top.

CALF'S LIVER WITH BROWN BUTTER, SAGE, AND WILTED DANDELION GREENS

QUICK-COOK RECIPE / MAKES 4 SERVINGS

Liver is at its most flavorful when cooked to medium, nicely browned on the outside and still slightly pink in the center. The bitter dandelion greens complement the richness of the meat beautifully. And liver is filled with nutrients and antioxidants. If your childhood memories are not good, give it a second chance with this recipe.

NOTE: Since liver is a filter organ, it holds on to toxins, which is why I insist on buying only antibiotic- and hormone-free liver of any type—calf, rabbit, pork, or chicken.

4	$1/2$-inch-thick pieces calf's liver, preferably organic (about $1^1/2$ pounds)
$3/4$	cup all-purpose flour
	Medium-coarse sea salt and coarsely ground black pepper
3	tablespoons extra-virgin olive oil
1	tablespoon unsalted butter
4	fresh sage leaves
2	garlic cloves, smashed and peeled
1	large bunch dandelion greens, roughly chopped, rinsed but not dried
$1/2$	lemon
4	thick slices ciabatta bread or Tuscan loaf, grilled or toasted

Heat oven to 350°F.

Dredge liver with flour, shaking off excess, and season with salt and pepper. Heat 2 tablespoons oil in a large cast-iron or other heavy skillet over medium-high heat until hot. Add liver in 2 batches and cook, turning once, until browned but still pink inside, about 2 minutes per side. As pieces brown, lay them in a baking dish in a single layer.

Place liver in oven and cook until medium, about 5 minutes. Remove from oven.

While liver is in oven, melt butter in same skillet over medium heat. As it begins to foam, add sage leaves and cook until crisp, about 2 minutes. Set aside.

Heat remaining tablespoon oil and garlic in a large skillet over medium heat, stirring occasionally, until garlic is lightly browned, about 5 minutes. Add dandelion greens with water clinging to them and cook, using tongs to turn greens, until thoroughly wilted but still bright green, about 5 minutes. Remove from heat, squeeze lemon over top, and season with salt and pepper. Divide liver among plates and drizzle with cooking juices. Serve greens over liver. Top with fried sage and serve with toasted bread.

GRILLED LAMB BROCHETTES
WITH SHAVED ONION SALAD

QUICK-COOK RECIPE / MAKES 8 SMALL-PLATE SERVINGS;
4 TO 6 MAIN-COURSE SERVINGS

Among my favorite street foods are the highly spiced marinated grilled brochettes of all sorts that are found all over North Africa and the Middle East. The meat is often stuffed into pita bread and served with a little finely chopped salad or pickles.

1½	tablespoons coriander seeds
1	tablespoon cumin seeds
	Grated zest of 1 navel orange
1	¾-inch piece fresh ginger, peeled and finely grated
2	garlic cloves, minced
¼	teaspoon Aleppo pepper (see page 16) or other crushed dried red chili pepper, plus more for salad
¼	cup extra-virgin olive oil
2½	pounds boneless lamb leg, trimmed of excess fat and cut into 1-by-2-inch cubes
½	small onion, thinly shaved on a mandoline or vegetable slicer
1¼	teaspoons coarse sea salt
	Fine sea salt and coarsely ground black pepper
2	tablespoons fresh lime juice

Toast coriander and cumin seeds together in a small skillet over medium heat, shaking pan frequently, until spices are fragrant, 2 to 3 minutes. Remove from heat and let cool slightly.

Grind toasted spices in a spice grinder or coffee grinder and transfer to a large bowl. Add orange zest, ginger, garlic, and Aleppo pepper; stir to combine. Whisk in oil. Add lamb and toss to coat. Marinate in the refrigerator for 3 hours.

Thread marinated lamb onto metal skewers and bring to room temperature. Build a moderately hot fire in a charcoal grill.

Toss onion with coarse salt in a small bowl. Let sit for 10 minutes.

While the onion macerates, season lamb generously with salt and pepper. Place on grill and cook, turning every couple of minutes, until all sides are browned and lamb is cooked through, about 8 minutes. Transfer to a serving platter.

Add lime juice and a good pinch of Aleppo pepper to onion; toss to combine. Serve lamb warm, with onion salad on the side.

CRISP FRIED LAMB CHOPS
WITH LEMON AND ROSEMARY

QUICK-COOK RECIPE / MAKES 4 SERVINGS

Cooks in olive oil–producing countries love to deep-fry foods in extra-virgin olive oil (including sweets). Olive oil adds a lusciousness that you don't get from other oil. This same batter and technique can be used for all sorts of meats: chicken, or rabbit, or pieces of tender beef or pork.

FLAVOR TIP: Resist the urge to move the chops while they are frying—you want to keep the golden crust intact.

    1   cup all-purpose flour
    1/2 teaspoon baking powder
    1 1/2 cups club soda
         About 3 cups extra-virgin olive oil for deep-frying
    8   lamb rib chops (about 1 1/2 pounds), pounded to 1/8 inch thick
         Medium-coarse sea salt and coarsely ground black pepper
    6   fresh rosemary sprigs
    5   garlic cloves, gently smashed and peeled
    2   lemons, cut into wedges

In a large bowl, whisk together flour and baking powder. Whisk in club soda. Let batter rest for 10 minutes.

Fill a large deep skillet with oil and heat over medium-high heat to 360° to 365°F (use two skillets if you like). Lightly season 2 lamb chops with salt and pepper, coat with batter, and quickly and carefully lay chops in hot oil. Cook until first side is golden, 2 to 3 minutes. Carefully turn and cook until other side is golden, 3 to 4 minutes more (reduce heat if chops are browning too quickly). Transfer fried chops to paper towels to drain, and immediately sprinkle with salt and pepper. Repeat with remaining chops, adding rosemary and garlic to hot oil 1 minute before last chops are done. Remove pan from heat.

Crumble fried rosemary on top of chops, squeeze juice of a few lemon wedges over top, and serve with fried garlic and remaining lemon wedges.

PAN-ROASTED LAMB CHOPS WITH CAPERS, OLIVES, ONIONS, AND SMASHED POTATOES

SLOW-COOK RECIPE / MAKES 4 SERVINGS

This onion-olive-caper sauce marries well with the lamb and is also particularly tasty mixed with the potatoes. Sprinkling hot just-cooked potatoes—be they mashed, smashed, or whatever—with freshly grated lemon zest turns ordinary tubers into a memorable side dish.

7	tablespoons extra-virgin olive oil
4	tablespoons (½ stick) unsalted butter
1½	pounds small to medium cipollini onions or pearl onions
	Fine sea salt
½	cup pitted arbequina olives
2	tablespoons salt-packed capers, rinsed several times and drained
2½	cups water, plus more if needed
1	tablespoon honey
2	pounds German Butterball potatoes or small new potatoes
4	garlic cloves, smashed and peeled
2	tablespoons chopped fresh thyme or rosemary leaves
2	tablespoons chopped fresh marjoram leaves or 4 sage leaves, chopped
	Coarsely ground black pepper
2¼	pounds lamb rib chops (8–12 chops)
	Finely grated zest of 1 lemon

Heat 2 tablespoons oil and 2 tablespoons butter in a wide heavy pot over medium-low heat until butter is melted. Add onions and a pinch of salt. Cook until browned on both sides (turning once or twice if cipollini; stirring occasionally if pearl onions), about 20 minutes. Transfer onions to a plate and pour off fat from pan.

Return pan to medium-low heat, add olives and capers, and cook for 1 minute, stirring and scraping up browned bits. Return onions to pan, add water, and bring to a simmer. Reduce heat to low and cook at a very gentle simmer, adding more water if necessary to keep about ½ inch liquid in pan, until onions are meltingly tender and liquid has reduced to about 1½ tablespoons, about 40 minutes. Remove from heat, add honey, and stir to combine. Set aside.

While onions are braising, heat oven to 400°F.

Bring a pot of abundantly salted water to a boil. Add potatoes and cook until tender enough to smash gently, about 15 minutes. Drain and let cool, then gently flatten each potato with the side of a chef's knife.

Arrange potatoes in a single layer in a shallow roasting pan and sprinkle with 3 tablespoons oil. Scatter garlic cloves and herbs over potatoes, and season with a couple pinches each salt and pepper. Dot with remaining 2 tablespoons butter. Roast until golden, about 25 minutes.

About 5 minutes before potatoes are done, heat remaining 2 tablespoons oil in a large cast-iron or other heavy skillet over high heat. Season lamb with salt and pepper and brown well, 2 to 3 minutes per side. Remove from heat.

Drizzle 1 tablespoon fat from skillet over potatoes in roasting pan. Arrange lamb chops over potatoes, then scatter onions over lamb, scraping all sauce from onion pan. Return to oven until onions are heated through and flavors are blended, about 10 minutes.

Remove pan from oven, scatter lemon zest over everything, sprinkle with salt, and serve.

ROASTED RACK OF LAMB
WITH MINTY BULGUR SALAD

QUICK-COOK RECIPE / MAKES 4 SERVINGS

A quick roast using high heat results in a moist, succulent rack of lamb with a good contrast of crisp edges to tender meat. The minty bulgur is both a play on the classic lamb and mint combination and a spin on tabouli, my favorite Lebanese salad. If your cucumbers have thick waxy skin, peel them; otherwise, leave them unpeeled.

1	cup fine bulgur
1/2	cup plus 1 tablespoon fresh lemon juice (from 3–4 large lemons)
2	garlic cloves
3	fresh sage sprigs, leaves only
3	fresh rosemary sprigs, leaves only
2	leafy fresh thyme sprigs, leaves only
1	teaspoon fine sea salt
	Coarsely ground black pepper
2	1½- to 1¾-pound lamb racks (8 ribs each)
¾	cup extra-virgin olive oil
2	medium cucumbers, cut lengthwise in half and sliced very thin
1	cup coarsely chopped fresh mint
3	scallions, thinly sliced on the bias

Heat oven to 450°F.

Combine bulgur and lemon juice in a medium bowl and let bulgur soak for 35 minutes.

While bulgur is soaking, finely chop garlic, sage, rosemary, and thyme together. Mix with ½ teaspoon salt and a generous amount of pepper.

Score fat side of lamb racks. Rub each with 1 tablespoon oil and half of herb mixture. Stand racks up, facing each other, with fat side out, in a roasting pan and lean

them together, bones crossing. Roast until temperature registers 130° to 135°F on an instant-read thermometer for medium-rare, about 30 minutes. Remove lamb from oven, transfer to a cutting board, and let rest for 10 minutes.

Add cucumbers, mint, scallions, remaining ½ teaspoon salt, and remaining ½ cup plus 2 tablespoons oil to bulgur, and toss to combine.

Slice lamb racks into ribs and serve warm with bulgur salad.

ROASTED LEG OF LAMB WITH BLACK OLIVES

SLOW-COOK RECIPE / MAKES 6 SERVINGS

Americans and the English tend to associate mint with lamb, but having grown up in the Mediterranean, I usually think of the more assertive black olives, rosemary, and garlic, which are traditionally used there to flavor this gamy meat. Serve with Polenta with Aromatic Herb Butter (page 199).

FLAVOR TIP: Chopping the herbs, garlic, and olives together allows the aromatic oils of all the ingredients to blend, making for a deeply flavored and more amalgamated paste than if chopped separately and then mixed together.

- 1/4 cup pitted Gaeta olives
- 2 garlic cloves
- 3 large fresh rosemary sprigs, leaves only
- 2 large fresh oregano sprigs, leaves only
- 1 3½- to 4-pound butterflied leg of lamb
    Medium-coarse salt and coarsely ground black pepper
- 2 tablespoons extra-virgin olive oil

Heat oven to 375°F.

Finely chop olives, garlic, rosemary, and oregano together.

Using a sharp paring knife, make 10 small slits, about ½ inch deep, all over outside of lamb, and insert some herb mixture into each one. Spread leftover herb mixture over inside of leg, roll up, and tie with kitchen twine. Season with salt and pepper.

Heat oil in a large cast-iron or other heavy ovenproof skillet. Add lamb and cook until seared on all sides, about 4 minutes per side. Place in oven and roast until temperature registers 155°F on an instant-read thermometer for medium, about 1 hour.

Remove lamb from oven and let rest for 10 minutes before slicing.

BRAISED LAMB SHOULDER
WITH GREEN TOMATOES AND
CONCORD GRAPES

SLOW-COOK RECIPE / MAKES 4 SERVINGS

This dish is traditionally made in the Italian countryside with sweet ripening wine grapes and acidic green tomatoes as the summer wanes. The sweetness of the grapes boosts the flavor of the season's last tomatoes, no longer sun-ripened and worthy of eating raw. Here in America, where wine grapes are less frequently available, I use our intensely aromatic native Concord grapes—purple-black beauties with an intense sweet, slightly tangy, almost floral taste. Though they are not often sold in supermarkets, you can find Concord grapes at farmers' markets or at a pick-your-own farm.

Serve the braised lamb over couscous or rice.

1½ cups Concord grapes (see headnote)
2¼ pounds boneless lamb shoulder, cut into 1½-inch cubes
Fine sea salt and coarsely ground black pepper
¼ cup extra-virgin olive oil
4 medium green tomatoes
4 garlic cloves
¾ cup dry white wine

Heat oven to 350°F.

Using a skewer or toothpick, puncture each grape and push out and discard seeds.

Toss lamb with 2 teaspoons salt and several turns of the pepper mill. Heat oil in a large Dutch oven or other heavy ovenproof pot over high heat. Add lamb in batches in a single layer, without crowding, and brown well on at least one side. As the pieces brown, push them to side of pot and add more pieces, until all lamb is well browned. Using tongs, transfer meat to a bowl.

Pour off all but 3 to 4 tablespoons oil from pot, then return pot to high heat and add whole green tomatoes and garlic. Cook, turning frequently, until tomatoes and garlic cloves are lightly browned, about 3 minutes.

Return lamb to pot, along with grapes and wine. Cover, place in oven, and cook until lamb is tender, about 1 hour. Make sure each diner gets a whole tomato and a garlic clove along with a hearty serving of meat and sauce.

WINTER LAMB STEW WITH TURNIPS, CARROTS, AND CELERY ROOT

SLOW-COOK RECIPE / MAKES 6 SERVINGS

This dish is based on the French spring classic *navarin d'agneau*, in which young turnips, peas, asparagus, tender potatoes, and lamb are stewed together so the flavors blend, yet they retain some of their individuality. In the wintertime, I like to pair the turnips with other winter vegetables. Although both the anchovy and the vinegar will go unnoticed in the final tasting of the dish, they play an important role in building complexity.

Lamb shoulder works well here, because the fat helps to tenderize the meat and keep it moist over the long, slow cooking; boneless leg of lamb is also good.

3	pounds boneless lamb shoulder, excess fat trimmed, cut into 1½-inch pieces
	Medium-coarse sea salt and coarsely ground black pepper
4½	tablespoons extra-virgin olive oil, plus more if needed
6	medium carrots, cut into ½-inch slices
1	pound medium turnips, cut into quarters, or into sixths if large
1	large celery root, peeled and cut into ½-inch cubes
2	large leeks, trimmed, sliced into ¾-inch rounds, and rinsed well
2	garlic cloves, smashed and peeled
2	anchovy fillets
3	cups water
¼	cup mild red wine vinegar
2	tablespoons chopped fresh tarragon

Season lamb generously with salt and pepper. Heat 1½ tablespoons oil in a large Dutch oven or other heavy pot over medium-high heat. Add lamb in batches in a single layer, without crowding, and cook until well browned and a crust forms on first side, about 7 minutes. Lightly brown on remaining sides, using a slotted spoon or tongs to remove browned pieces as you go, transferring them to a large plate. Set lamb aside.

Add remaining 3 tablespoons oil to pot and heat over medium-high heat until hot. Add one quarter of carrots, turnips, and celery root, lightly season with salt and pepper, and cook, stirring frequently, until vegetables are golden, about 5 minutes. With a slotted spoon, transfer vegetables to a second plate. Repeat, adding more oil if necessary, until all vegetables are browned. Brown leeks and garlic, adding more oil if necessary, and transfer to plate with vegetables.

Drain all but 1 tablespoon fat from pot and reduce to medium heat. Add anchovies and cook, stirring, until dissolved, about 1 minute. Add lamb, vegetables, water, and vinegar; bring to a gentle simmer, cover, and cook for 1 hour and 15 minutes.

Remove cover and continue cooking for 20 minutes more. Stir in tarragon and cook until lamb is spoon-tender, about 20 minutes more.

Season with salt and pepper, and serve.

BAKED PORK CHOPS WITH PEACHES

QUICK-COOK RECIPE / MAKES 4 SERVINGS

Pork and fruit is a classic combination and one with many variations. Americans love to pair the meat with apples, and the French like it with prunes; juicy summer-ripened peaches are another tasty match. As the chops pan-sear here, they are flavored with thyme and garlic. Peaches, cooked in the same pan with wine, create a delicious sauce.

Served with a simple salad, this makes a great summer meal.

NOTE: Scoring the fat around each chop with a knife will prevent the chops from twisting and cooking unevenly.

4   8- to 10-ounce pork chops, 1½ inches thick

   Medium-coarse sea salt and coarsely ground black pepper

1   tablespoon extra-virgin olive oil

4   garlic cloves, gently smashed and peeled

4   fresh thyme sprigs

4   tablespoons (½ stick) unsalted butter

2   large peaches, peeled with a sharp paring knife, pitted, and quartered

¼   cup water

2   tablespoons dry white wine

Heat oven to 300°F.

Score the fat on the edges of each pork chop in 2 or 3 places, and season with salt and pepper.

Heat oil in a large heavy skillet over medium-high heat. Add 2 pork chops and cook until browned on both sides, about 3 minutes per side. Place half of garlic and thyme on top of chops and add 1 tablespoon butter to pan. Using a large spoon to baste chops with melted butter, cook for 3 minutes more. Transfer pork chops and contents of pan to a baking dish and repeat with remaining 2 chops, garlic, thyme, and another tablespoon of butter.

Transfer chops to oven and cook to medium (the meat should still be pink inside), about 15 minutes.

Meanwhile, wipe fat from skillet. Add 1 tablespoon butter, peaches cut side down, and a pinch of salt and cook over medium-high heat until peaches are browned on cut side, about 5 minutes.

Drain fat from pan, add water and wine, and bring to a boil over medium-high heat. Cook until liquid is reduced to about 2 tablespoons. Remove from heat.

When pork is ready, transfer chops to a platter, discarding thyme and garlic, and pour any juices from pan over peaches. Reheat peaches and sauce over medium-high heat, then add remaining tablespoon butter and swirl to incorporate.

Spoon peaches and sauce over pork chops and serve.

SKILLET-COOKED PORK CHOPS WITH MORELS AND LENTILS

QUICK-COOK RECIPE / MAKES 4 SERVINGS

My mother is always shocked to hear me say it, since I hated them so vehemently as a child, but I love lentils. They are great in a salad or as an accompaniment to pork or fish, or just plain by themselves with lots of chopped fresh parsley and olive oil. When morels are in season, I like to sauté them, as here, with a little cream—a rich garnish that is perfect with the other flavors of this dish.

FLAVOR TIP: Morels have a wonderful unique taste, but you can try other exotic mushrooms, such as chanterelle, oyster, or porcini.

LENTILS

- 1 carrot, coarsely chopped
- 1 celery stalk, coarsely chopped
- 1 small onion, coarsely chopped
- 2 tablespoons extra-virgin olive oil
- 1½ cups small Italian, French, or Spanish dried lentils (see page 13), rinsed and picked over
- 2½ cups water
- ½ cup Chianti or other dry red wine
- 1 teaspoon medium-coarse sea salt

PORK CHOPS

- 4 8- to 10-ounce pork chops, 1½ inches thick
  Medium-coarse sea salt and coarsely ground black pepper
- ¼ cup extra-virgin olive oil
- 3 tablespoons unsalted butter
- 3 garlic cloves, gently smashed and peeled
- 8 ounces morel mushrooms, trimmed (see Tip)
- ¼ cup dry red wine
- 2 tablespoons heavy cream
- ¼ cup chopped fresh flat-leaf parsley

FOR LENTILS: Finely chop carrot, celery, and onion together. Heat oil in a medium sauce-pan over medium-high heat. Add vegetable mixture, reduce heat to medium, and cook, stirring occasionally, until vegetables are tender, about 7 minutes.

Add lentils and stir to combine. Add water and wine, bring to a bare simmer, and cook, uncovered, until lentils are tender, about 45 minutes. Add salt and stir well to combine. Remove from heat.

FOR PORK CHOPS: While lentils are cooking, score fat on each pork chop in 2 or 3 places, and season with salt and pepper. Heat oil in a large skillet over medium-high heat. Add 2 pork chops and cook until well browned, about 10 minutes; turn and cook until medium (the meat will still have some pink inside), about 2 minutes more. Transfer to a plate. Repeat with remaining 2 chops.

Pour fat from pan, return pan to medium-high heat, and add butter. Cook until butter is melted. Add garlic and cook until lightly golden, about 15 seconds. Add morels and cook, stirring, for 8 minutes, until tender. Add wine, cream, juices from resting pork chops, and a pinch or two each of salt and pepper. Bring to a boil and cook until liquid is reduced and thickened, about 4 minutes. Add parsley, stir to combine, and remove from heat.

Spoon sauce over pork chops and serve with lentils.

SLOW-ROASTED PORK SHOULDER

SLOW-COOK RECIPE / MAKES 6 SERVINGS

One of the pillars of Tuscan cooking is *arrosto morto* (literally, "dead roast"), a pork roast, or sometimes veal, heavily seasoned with herbs and garlic and cooked slowly at low heat until incredibly tender. In Teverina, we cooked our traditional Thanksgiving pork loin this way on a spit roast in front of the wood fire.

Pork shoulder, a highly flavorful and somewhat fatty cut, is perfect for the same kind of slow cooking in a low oven. Your patience will reward you with a house full of exceptional pork aromas and tender meat with crisped-up, sweet, fatty skin.

FLAVOR TIP: Using white wine for basting creates a delicate sauce for this dish; red wine gives it a gamier flavor. I choose the wine based on what mood I'm in, or whatever I have kicking around the house.

20	fresh sage leaves
3	fresh thyme sprigs, leaves only
3	fresh rosemary sprigs, leaves only
2	garlic cloves, coarsely chopped
2	tablespoons wild fennel pollen (see page 15)
1¹/₂	teaspoons medium-coarse sea salt
1¹/₂	teaspoons coarsely ground black pepper
1	3³/₄- to 4-pound boneless pork shoulder (with skin, not tied)
2	tablespoons extra-virgin olive oil
¹/₂	cup dry white or red wine

Heat oven to 250°F.

Finely chop sage, thyme, rosemary, and garlic together (you can do this by pulsing in a food processor or by hand). Place mixture in a small bowl, add fennel pollen, salt, and pepper, and stir together well.

With a sharp knife, score pork skin in a crosshatch diamond pattern, making ⅛-inch-deep cuts 1 inch apart. With a paring knife, make about 10 incisions (about ½ inch deep) all over the pork and stuff with one third of herb mixture. Tie pork into a compact roast with kitchen twine, brush oil over skin, and rub all over with remaining herb mixture.

Set pork skin side up in a roasting pan. Roast for 2 hours.

Pour wine over pork and baste with wine and accumulated juices. Continue roasting, basting once every half hour, until skin is well browned and meat is spoon-tender, 2½ to 3 hours more.

Remove from oven and let meat rest for 15 minutes before slicing and serving.

BRAISED PORK LOIN WITH PRUNES

SLOW-COOK RECIPE / MAKES 6 SERVINGS

Pork loin with prunes is a French tradition. Using both fresh and dried ginger deepens the flavor of the dish.

- 12 pitted prunes
- 1 2-inch piece fresh ginger, peeled and coarsely chopped
- 5 garlic cloves, peeled
- 1 3-pound pork loin roast
  - Medium-coarse sea salt and coarsely ground black pepper
- 1/4 cup extra-virgin olive oil
- 6 fresh thyme sprigs
- 1 cup port
- 1 tablespoon ground ginger
- 1 cup homemade chicken broth (page 108)

Heat oven to 350°F.

Chop together 3 prunes, fresh ginger, and 1 garlic clove. With a paring knife, make 6 slits in top of pork loin and 6 slits in bottom; push prune mixture into slits. Season pork all over with salt and pepper.

Heat oil in a large Dutch oven or other heavy ovenproof pot over medium-high heat. Add pork and cook, turning occasionally, until browned on all sides, about 12 minutes. Transfer pork to a plate, and pour off all but about 1 teaspoon oil from pot. Scrape out any burnt bits, return pork to pot, and place over medium heat. Add remaining 4 garlic cloves and cook, stirring, until garlic has browned a bit, 3 to 4 minutes. Remove from heat.

Sprinkle remaining 9 prunes and thyme sprigs around pork, and pour port over. Sprinkle ground ginger over top of loin, then pour broth over. Cover, place in oven, and cook until an instant-read thermometer inserted diagonally at least 2 inches into meat registers 150°F, about 1 hour. Transfer pork loin to a cutting board and let rest for 10 to 15 minutes.

While loin is resting, bring cooking liquid to a low boil and cook until reduced to about 1 cup, about 15 minutes.

Slice loin, spoon sauce over slices, and serve.

ROASTED VENISON WITH CIDER-BRAISED LEEKS

SLOW-COOK RECIPE / MAKES 6 SERVINGS

I love the flavor of venison—the funkier the better. The red wine tempers some of the wild flavor while also adding richness. The lean, tonic intensity of the venison is tempered by the creamy lushness of the sweet cider-braised leeks.

FLAVOR TIP: Venison is very low in fat and is thus best cooked rare to medium-rare; if cooked beyond, it will be dry. An instant-read thermometer will help you cook it to the right temperature.

VENISON MARINADE

- 1 carrot, cut into 1-inch pieces
- 1 celery stalk, cut into 1-inch pieces
- 1 medium onion, quartered
- 3 garlic cloves, gently smashed and peeled
- 1 shallot, quartered
- 2 fresh rosemary sprigs
- 8 juniper berries
- 2 bay leaves
- 1 tablespoon black peppercorns
- 1 750-ml bottle Chianti or other dry red wine
- 1 3- to 4-pound venison rack, split into 2 racks, tough membranes removed

LEEKS

- 6 medium leeks, trimmed and cut lengthwise in half
  Fine sea salt and coarsely ground black pepper
- 2 tablespoons unsalted butter
- 2 tablespoons extra-virgin olive oil, plus more for venison
- ¼ cup plus 2 tablespoons apple cider
- ¼ cup plus 2 tablespoons dry white wine
- ½ cup heavy cream

FOR VENISON MARINADE: Combine carrot, celery, onion, garlic, shallot, rosemary, juniper berries, bay leaves, peppercorns, and red wine in a large bowl or nonreactive pot. Add venison, cover, and marinate in the refrigerator for at least 12 hours, or overnight.

Put an oven rack in center position, with no racks above it, and heat oven to 425°F.

FOR LEEKS: Rinse leeks well, fanning them as you do to get out all dirt between layers, and pat dry with paper towels. Season leeks with salt and pepper.

Heat butter and oil in a large ovenproof skillet over medium-high heat until butter is melted. Add half of leeks, cut side down, and cook, turning once, until well browned on both sides, about 15 minutes; reduce heat if necessary. Transfer to a plate and cook remaining leeks. Remove pan from heat. Return remaining leeks to pan, cut side up.

Whisk cider and wine together and pour over leeks. Cover pan tightly with foil and place in oven. Cook until leeks are tender, about 25 minutes.

FOR VENISON: Meanwhile, drain venison (discard marinade), and pat dry. Rub venison with oil and season generously with salt and pepper. Stand racks up, facing each other with fat side out, in a roasting pan and lean them together, bones crossing. Place venison in oven and roast until an instant-read thermometer registers 125°F for rare, about 23 minutes. Remove venison from oven and let rest on stovetop cooling.

Remove foil from leeks, add cream, and stir well. Raise oven temperature to 450°F, return leeks to oven, and cook until cream is thickened and bubbling, about 15 minutes. Remove from oven.

Cut venison into individual chops and serve with warm leeks and sauce.

SWEETS AND CORDIALS

Whether enjoyed as a jolt in the morning, as an afternoon pick-me-up with coffee, or as the final course of a special feast, sweets in the Mediterranean are not as saccharine as American desserts. A bowl of small local strawberries, tossed with a little sugar and a splash of Prosecco, or a crème caramel flavored with coffee and cardamom exemplifies the Mediterranean approach in which sweet ingredients are counterbalanced so they don't clobber the palate.

Salt also plays an important role, simultaneously enhancing and offsetting sweetness. In cookies and cakes, salt heightens flavors that would be a bit flat without it. In other desserts, like my lemon-and-chili-infused chocolate ganache tart, a light crunch of medium-coarse sea salt adds a pleasing textural element. If you've enjoyed a chocolate-dipped pretzel or potato chip, or a caramel flavored with fleur de sel, you already know that combination.

Along with salt, some other savory ingredients drive my dessert repertoire. Used to make pound cake, olive oil produces a lusher result than butter. The cake doesn't taste of olive oil per se, but the oil delivers a light but moist result, wonderfully different from butter. And herbs like fresh thyme and bay leaves bring flavor to cookies—and to *rosolio*, a Southern Italian cordial that's a nice alternative to dessert and easy to make at home.

SWEETS AND CORDIALS

Strawberries
with Prosecco | 327

Summer Fruit with Lemon,
Sugar, and Mint | 328

Pecorino and Pears with
Chestnut Honey | 329

Plum Sorbetto | 330

Chestnut Honey and
Walnut Semifreddo | 332

Lemon Gelato | 334

Panna Cotta with
Pomegranate Molasses | 335

Orange Panna Cotta with
Orange Marmalade | 337

Jasmine Tea Panna Cotta
with Shaved Dark
Chocolate | 338

continued

Coffee Cardamom
Crème Caramel | 339

Montebianco | 342

Semolina Bread Pudding with
Concord Grapes | 344

Tuscan Biscotti with Lemon,
Pine Nuts, and Thyme | 346

Lemon Olive Oil Cake | 348

Spicy Lemon–Chocolate
Ganache Tart | 350

Plum Galette | 352

    Favorite Tart Dough | 353

Fragolino | 354

Fresh Bay Leaf Rosolio | 356

STRAWBERRIES WITH PROSECCO

QUICK-COOK RECIPE / MAKES 4 SERVINGS

Strawberries pair well with effervescent Prosecco, the sparkling wine made from a variety of white grapes grown in the Conegliano and Valdobbiadene regions north of Venice. Since you use only a touch, get a nice bottle and plan on drinking the rest before, with, or after the meal. Adjust the sugar if needed, based on the sweetness of your berries. You can also try this recipe with a dry rosé.

- 1 quart local strawberries, hulled, cut in half or into quarters, depending on size
- 1 teaspoon sugar
- 1/4 cup Prosecco

Place berries in a bowl and sprinkle with sugar. Add Prosecco, stir together, and divide among bowls, pouring berry juices over top.

SUMMER FRUIT WITH LEMON, SUGAR, AND MINT

QUICK-COOK RECIPE / MAKES 4 SERVINGS

In this simple Italian classic, lemon juice draws out the flavors of the various fruits, while the sugar boosts the sweetness of the fruit and counteracts the acidity of the lemon. You can use this technique with just one of the fruits, choosing any of those below, or with melon. Sugar plums, which are small and almond-shaped, with purple-green skin and green flesh, are one of the few plum varieties whose skin is not bitter, but any type will do.

3	medium peaches, peeled with a sharp paring knife, pitted, and sliced
	Juice of 1 lemon (about 2 tablespoons)
6–8	small sugar plums, pitted and cut into quarters or eighths (see headnote)
½	pint raspberries
½	pint blueberries, preferably wild
1½	teaspoons sugar
8–10	fresh peppermint, spearmint, or any other mint leaves, torn if large, plus a few sprigs for garnish

Toss peaches and lemon juice together in a large serving bowl. Add plums, raspberries, blueberries, sugar, and mint; toss to combine. Top with herb sprigs and serve.

PECORINO AND PEARS WITH CHESTNUT HONEY

QUICK-COOK RECIPE / MAKES 4 SERVINGS

When I first served this to my father, he declared it "the original dessert," saying it epitomized the land of milk and honey. It is common these days to find the combination of well-aged pecorino with chestnut honey in Italian trattorias, but I like it even better with pears. Serve this on plates or simply put each ingredient out on the table and let your guests help themselves.

4   medium Bosc or other ripe pears

4   ounces aged Pecorino Toscano cheese (see page 18),
     broken into rough 1/2-inch pieces

     Chestnut honey for drizzling (see page 20)

Cut pears in half and core; cut into medium-thick slices. Divide slices among four plates. Divide cheese among plates, drizzle honey over pears and cheese, and serve.

PLUM SORBETTO

QUICK-COOK RECIPE / MAKES 4 CUPS

When fruit is wonderfully abundant and you want a simple homemade dessert, sorbet is perfect. Here the plum skins add both texture and beautiful specks of color. Add more sugar if you like a sweeter sorbet or if your fruit is not very sweet. I use this same recipe for blackberries (leaving the seeds in).

NOTE: If you like a very smooth sorbet or are planning to keep it more than a day or two, add an egg white during the last few minutes of churning. It will help emulsify and stabilize the sorbet.

- ¾ cup sugar
- ½ cup water
- 1½ pounds ripe plums (preferably local), pitted
- 1½ tablespoons fresh lemon juice

Combine sugar and water in a small saucepan and bring to a boil, stirring until sugar dissolves; cook at a low boil for 1 minute. Remove from heat and let syrup cool slightly.

Puree plums in a food processor until smooth. Stir together cooled syrup, plum puree, and lemon juice in a bowl until combined. Refrigerate until well chilled, about 3 hours.

Churn chilled mixture in an ice cream maker according to the manufacturer's instructions. Serve, or pack into a container and freeze.

CHESTNUT HONEY AND WALNUT SEMIFREDDO

SLOW-COOK RECIPE / MAKES 6 SERVINGS

Semifreddo is a classic Italian frozen dessert—neither gelato nor mousse, but somewhere in between the two. Walnuts toasted in butter and lightly salted add a pleasing flavor and textural contrast to a dessert that is traditionally very smooth.

FLAVOR TIP: The unique and assertive flavor of chestnut honey makes this dish. The honey's slightly bitter qualities cut the sweetness of the dessert and lend a sophisticated note.

- ½ tablespoon unsalted butter
- ½ cup coarsely chopped walnuts
- ¼ teaspoon fine sea salt
- 2 large eggs, separated
- 1 large egg yolk
- 3 tablespoons chestnut honey (see page 20)
- 2 tablespoons sugar
- 2 tablespoons water
- 1 cup heavy cream

Line an 8½-by-4½-by-2½-inch loaf pan with plastic wrap, leaving an overhang on all sides.

Melt butter in a small saucepan over low heat. Add walnuts and ⅛ teaspoon salt and stir to combine. Cook, stirring frequently, until nuts are fragrant and lightly golden, about 6 minutes. Remove from heat and set aside.

Fill a large bowl with ice water. In a medium metal bowl set over a saucepan of barely simmering water, briskly whisk together yolks, honey, sugar, water, and remaining ⅛ teaspoon salt until mixture is pale and thick, about 8 minutes. Place bowl in ice bath and whisk mixture just until cool, about 1 minute. Set aside.

In a clean bowl, beat egg whites to stiff peaks with an electric mixer. In another bowl, beat cream to soft peaks. Whisk one third of whites into yolk mixture, then gently but thoroughly fold in remaining whites and cream.

Spoon half of mixture into loaf pan; sprinkle with nuts. Spoon remaining mixture over nuts and smooth with a spatula. Fold overhanging plastic wrap over semifreddo, cover pan with plastic wrap, and freeze until firm, at least 3 hours, or up to 3 days.

To serve, chill six plates in refrigerator or freezer. Unfold plastic wrap covering semifreddo and turn out onto a cutting board. Peel off plastic wrap lining. Cut semifreddo into slabs, transfer to chilled plates, and serve immediately.

LEMON GELATO

QUICK-COOK RECIPE / MAKES 4 CUPS

This beautifully light and thoroughly lemony gelato reminds me of hot days at the end of the school year in Rome, when I'd plan my walk home based on how many gelato shops I needed to visit to keep myself refreshed in the intense heat that reflected off the ancient amber-colored walls of the city.

Good lemon gelato should taste vibrant and offer a perfect balance between sweet and tangy. This remarkably simple recipe gives you just that. Don't be alarmed by the milk curdling in the lemon juice; it will come together in the freezing of the gelato and you'll get a lush, creamy, very citrusy result. For variation, try fresh lime or blood orange juice in place of lemon.

FLAVOR TIP: Squeeze your lemons just before using to get the freshest taste from the juice.

- 1 cup sugar
- ¾ cup fresh lemon juice (from 5 or 6 lemons)
- ½ cup cold water
- 1 cup whole milk
- 2 large egg whites
- Pinch of fine sea salt

Whisk together sugar, lemon juice, and water in a medium bowl until sugar dissolves. Add milk and whisk to combine (it will curdle; this is okay).

In another bowl, whisk egg whites and salt until whites hold soft peaks. Fold egg whites into lemon juice mixture.

Churn mixture in an ice cream maker according to the manufacturer's instructions. Serve, or pack into a container and freeze.

PANNA COTTA WITH POMEGRANATE MOLASSES

SLOW-COOK RECIPE / MAKES 4 TO 6 SERVINGS

Dense sweet-tart pomegranate molasses, a Middle Eastern pantry staple, cuts the richness of the cream in this luscious panna cotta.

- 2 cups heavy cream
- 1¼ teaspoons unflavored gelatin
- ¼ cup sugar
- ½ vanilla bean, split lengthwise
- 3 large egg whites
- Pomegranate molasses for drizzling (see page 20)

Combine ¼ cup cream with gelatin in a medium bowl and let gelatin soften.

Combine remaining 1¾ cups cream, sugar, and vanilla bean in a medium saucepan, bring to a low boil, and boil for 3 minutes. Remove from heat and fish out vanilla bean. Scrape seeds from bean and add to cream; stir to combine. Discard bean.

Add hot cream mixture to gelatin mixture and whisk until gelatin is totally dissolved. Set bowl over an ice bath and stir until cooled to room temperature.

Beat egg whites to stiff peaks. Gently whisk half of whites into cream mixture, then fold in remaining whites. Transfer mixture to individual ramekins or dessert cups. Refrigerate until set, about 3 hours. Top with a drizzle of pomegranate molasses and serve.

PANNA COTTA

Panna cotta (literally, "cooked cream") is a Piemontese custard made without eggs. The cream is infused with aromatics and paired with matching sauces. Two things distinguish my basic panna cotta, a variation on my mother's recipe, published in her *Flavors of Tuscany*. It has a lighter, looser, creamier texture, due to a minimum of gelatin, and a lively, frothy top. Serve it from nice ramekins or dessert cups, as it won't hold its shape if turned out onto a plate.

If you can get good heavy cream from an organic local dairy, the results will be superior.

ORANGE PANNA COTTA
WITH ORANGE MARMALADE

SLOW-COOK RECIPE / MAKES 4 TO 6 SERVINGS

The cream for this panna cotta is deliciously infused with orange peel. The delicate flavor is then amplified with a bittersweet orange marmalade topping.

2	cups heavy cream
1¼	teaspoons unflavored gelatin
¼	cup sugar
	Finely grated zest of 1 orange
½	vanilla bean, split lengthwise
3	large egg whites
	Bitter orange marmalade

Combine ¼ cup cream with gelatin in a medium bowl and let gelatin soften.

Combine remaining 1¾ cups cream, sugar, orange zest and vanilla bean in a medium saucepan, bring to a low boil, and boil for 3 minutes. Remove saucepan from heat and remove vanilla bean. Scrape seeds from bean and add to cream; stir to combine. Discard vanilla bean.

Pour hot cream through a fine-mesh strainer into bowl with gelatin mixture; discard zest. Whisk until gelatin is totally dissolved. Set bowl over an ice bath and stir until cooled to room temperature.

Beat egg whites to stiff peaks. Gently whisk half of whites into cream mixture, then fold in remaining whites. Transfer mixture to individual ramekins or dessert cups. Refrigerate until set, about 3 hours.

To serve, top each panna cotta with a dollop of marmalade.

JASMINE TEA PANNA COTTA
WITH SHAVED DARK CHOCOLATE

SLOW-COOK RECIPE / MAKES 4 TO 6 SERVINGS

This is a play on the sweet English "cuppa," strong brewed tea with lots of sugar and milk. The dark chocolate shavings contrast with the creamy sweetness of the panna cotta and add a bitter flavor note that is especially nice with the pleasantly astringent note of the green tea.

2 cups heavy cream

1¼ teaspoons unflavored gelatin

¼ cup sugar

½ vanilla bean, split lengthwise

6 good-quality jasmine green tea bags

3 large egg whites

Good semisweet or bittersweet chocolate (at least 62% cacao)

Combine ¼ cup cream with gelatin in a medium bowl and let gelatin soften.

Combine remaining 1¾ cups cream, sugar, and vanilla bean in a medium saucepan, bring to a low boil, and boil for 3 minutes. Remove saucepan from heat and remove vanilla bean. Scrape seeds from bean, add to cream, and stir to combine; discard vanilla bean. Add tea bags, cover, and let steep for 4 minutes.

Remove tea bags, squeezing them over cream mixture before discarding. Add hot cream mixture to bowl with gelatin and whisk until gelatin is totally dissolved. Set bowl over an ice bath and stir until cream is cooled to room temperature.

Beat egg whites to stiff peaks. Gently whisk half of whites into cream mixture, then fold in remaining whites. Transfer mixture to individual ramekins or dessert cups. Refrigerate until set, about 3 hours.

To serve, shave chocolate over each panna cotta, using a vegetable peeler.

COFFEE CARDAMOM CRÈME CARAMEL

SLOW-COOK RECIPE / MAKES 6 SERVINGS

In Beirut, sweet dense coffee perfumed with cardamom is the beverage of choice for the men sitting around the coffeehouses playing backgammon and smoking their hookahs. Crème caramel, the French bistro staple, is perfectly suited to mixing with the flavors of the Old Colony.

CARAMEL

½ cup superfine sugar

¼ cup water

CUSTARD

1 heaping tablespoon green cardamom pods

1½ cups heavy cream

½ cup whole milk

3 tablespoons sugar

1 tablespoon instant coffee granules

1 large egg

3 large egg yolks

Pinch of fine sea salt

Special equipment: six ½-cup ramekins

Heat oven to 300°F. Set ramekins in a 9-by-13-inch baking dish.

FOR CARAMEL: Heat sugar and water in a small saucepan over low heat, stirring until sugar dissolves, 2 to 3 minutes. Increase heat to medium-high and, without stirring, boil sugar mixture until it becomes a golden brown caramel, about 6 minutes, gently swirling once it starts to color. Remove from heat. Working quickly, distribute caramel evenly among ramekins, gently turning each ramekin to coat bottom.

FOR CUSTARD: Toast cardamom pods in a small skillet over medium-low heat until lightly golden and fragrant, about 5 minutes. Remove from heat and crack pods, using a mortar and pestle.

Combine cracked cardamom pods, cream, milk, and sugar in a medium saucepan and bring just to a boil. Remove from heat, add coffee, and whisk to dissolve coffee. Let steep, uncovered, for 10 minutes.

Strain cream mixture into a bowl and discard cardamom pods.

Lightly beat egg and egg yolks together in a medium bowl. Gradually add ¼ cup cream mixture to eggs and whisk to combine. Add remaining cream mixture and salt, whisking to combine.

Distribute custard evenly among ramekins. Add enough hot water to baking dish to come halfway up ramekins. Cover baking dish with foil and make a few slits in foil with the tip of a paring knife. Bake until custard is set, about 55 minutes.

Remove custards from water bath and let cool completely, then chill until very cold, at least 4 hours, or up to 2 days.

Serve from ramekins or unmold onto plates.

MONTEBIANCO

SLOW-COOK RECIPE / MAKES 6 SERVINGS

Monte Bianco (Mont Blanc) is the highest peak in the European Alps, straddling France and Italy, and it is also the namesake of this classic Italian dessert: its pile of chestnut puree is said to resemble the beige of the mountain, and the slightly boozy whipped cream, the snowcap on its towering crest. Here it's all heaped atop a sweet crisp meringue and sprinkled with shavings of bittersweet chocolate. Though it does not often show up in many recipes for this dessert, to me the meringue base is an important textural component. When we lived in Rome, this was a favorite seasonal winter sweet and required eating on New Year's Eve.

MERINGUES

- 2 large egg whites
- 1/8 teaspoon salt
- 1/2 cup sugar

CHESTNUT PUREE

- 2 cups (about 10 1/2 ounces) frozen peeled chestnuts, thawed (see Sources)
- 3/4 cup plus 5 tablespoons heavy cream
- 5 tablespoons water
- 1 teaspoon sugar
- 1/4 teaspoon fine sea salt

TOPPING

- 1 cup heavy cream
- 1 tablespoon plus 1 teaspoon sugar
- 1 tablespoon Armagnac, cognac, or other brandy, or to taste

Bittersweet chocolate (at least 70% cacao)

FOR MERINGUES: Heat oven to 175°F with a rack in center. Line a baking sheet with parchment paper.

With an electric mixer, beat egg whites with salt at high speed until they just hold stiff peaks. With machine running, slowly add sugar, then continue to beat until whites hold stiff, glossy peaks, 1 to 2 minutes more.

Using a large soupspoon, scoop out 7 equal mounds of meringue and place them at least 3 inches apart on baking sheet (you are making an extra meringue in case one breaks). Using the back of a clean spoon dipped into cold water, flatten meringues into about 3½-inch-wide disks.

Bake meringues until dry but still white, about 1½ hours. Let cool in turned-off oven (with door closed) for 1 hour.

Transfer pan to a rack to cool completely.

When they are cooled, carefully lift meringues from parchment, peeling back parchment to release. Meringues can be made 1 week ahead and stored in an airtight container.

FOR CHESTNUT PUREE: In a medium heavy saucepan, bring chestnuts, ¾ cup cream, water, sugar, and salt to a bare simmer over low heat; cook until chestnuts are tender and liquid has mostly been absorbed, about 50 minutes.

Transfer chestnut mixture to a food processor, add remaining 5 tablespoons cream, and puree until smooth. Let cool. Chestnut puree can be made 1 day in advance and refrigerated; bring to room temperature before using.

FOR TOPPING: Whip cream with sugar until stiff. Fold in Armagnac. Chill until ready to serve.

To serve, push chestnut puree through a ricer over meringues, distributing it evenly. Do the same with whipped cream to create a mound of whipped cream strands. With a cheese grater or sharp knife, shave chocolate over tops. Serve immediately.

SEMOLINA BREAD PUDDING
WITH CONCORD GRAPES

SLOW-COOK RECIPE / MAKES 8 TO 10 SERVINGS

During the wine harvest in Tuscany, every bakery and pastry shop fills its shelves with *schiacciata con l'uva*, a delicious flatbread baked with intensely flavored, seedy local wine grapes and dusted with confectioners' sugar. I took the classic Tuscan flavor combination and adapted it to bread pudding. I use our New England Concord grapes, which have a deep flavor and perfumed aroma, but feel free to substitute any wine grape (table grapes are too sweet).

1½	pounds Concord grapes (see headnote)
12	ounces semolina bread with crusts, cut into 1-inch cubes
3	cups heavy cream
2	cups whole milk
1	vanilla bean, split, or 1½ teaspoons vanilla extract
4	large eggs
3	large egg yolks
1	cup sugar
½	teaspoon fine sea salt
⅛	teaspoon freshly grated nutmeg
1	tablespoon unsalted butter, at room temperature, for baking dish
1	tablespoon honey, preferably chestnut

Using a skewer or toothpick, puncture each grape and push out and discard seeds.

Place bread in a large bowl. Heat cream, milk, and vanilla bean, if using (add vanilla extract later), in a medium saucepan over medium-high heat until just simmering. Remove from heat.

Whisk eggs, yolks, sugar, salt, vanilla extract (if using), and nutmeg in a medium bowl. Discard vanilla bean and whisk cream mixture into eggs in a slow, steady stream. Pour over bread cubes, stir to combine, and let sit at room temperature, stirring occasionally, for 30 minutes.

Put oven rack in center position and heat oven to 350°F. Butter a 9-by-13-inch baking dish.

Fold grapes into bread mixture. Transfer to baking dish and bake, rotating dish once, until golden and set, 40 to 45 minutes.

Remove pudding from oven, drizzle with honey, and let cool slightly before serving.

TUSCAN BISCOTTI
WITH LEMON, PINE NUTS, AND THYME

SLOW-COOK RECIPE / MAKES 20 COOKIES

In Italy, what we in America call biscotti are known as *cantucci di prato*. Significantly smaller in size than the American version, they are traditionally flavored with almonds and orange zest. I have replaced these with pine nuts and lemon zest; the thyme is an added twist. Substitutions and flavor combinations can be many. You can try all sorts of different nuts, such as pistachios, hazelnuts, almonds, pecans, or walnuts; other citrus zest; or fresh herbs, even rosemary or savory.

2$\frac{1}{2}$	cups unbleached all-purpose flour
$\frac{3}{4}$	cup pine nuts
$\frac{1}{2}$	teaspoon baking powder
$\frac{1}{2}$	teaspoon baking soda
	Finely grated zest of 3 lemons
1	tablespoon fresh thyme leaves, coarsely chopped
	Pinch of fine sea salt
$\frac{3}{4}$	cup sugar
4	large eggs
1	large egg yolk
7	tablespoons unsalted butter, melted

Whisk together flour, nuts, baking powder, baking soda, zest, thyme, and salt in a large bowl.

With an electric mixer, beat sugar, 3 eggs, and yolk in a large bowl on high speed until mixture is thick and pale, about 5 minutes. Fold flour mixture into egg mixture. Fold in butter. Turn dough out onto a clean work surface and knead once or twice, until it comes together. Wrap tightly in plastic wrap and chill until firm, 30 to 45 minutes.

Put oven rack in center position and heat oven to 350°F. Line a baking sheet with parchment paper.

Divide chilled dough into 2 equal pieces. Form each into a log about 8 inches long and 2 inches wide. Place 1 inch apart on baking sheet. Press each log gently to flatten slightly. Lightly beat remaining egg and brush over logs to glaze.

Bake until golden and slightly firm to the touch, about 20 minutes, rotating pan once. Remove from oven, and reduce oven temperature to 300°F. Allow logs to cool slightly, 10 to 15 minutes.

Cut logs into 1-inch-thick slices on a slight bias. Arrange cookies on baking sheet in a single layer. Return to oven and bake until cookies are dry and crisp, about 15 minutes more. Let cool on racks, then store in an airtight container for up to 2 weeks.

LEMON OLIVE OIL CAKE

SLOW-COOK RECIPE / MAKES 10 SERVINGS

Versions of this simple cake are made all over Italy, to be eaten at breakfast with coffee or tea. Similar to pound cake, it differs mainly in that the fat used is olive oil instead of butter, which, surprisingly, results in a cake with an even richer and more unctuous character. Yogurt adds a subtle tang. Use your best extra-virgin olive oil here.

FLAVOR TIP: Whether you are baking or making a sauce or salad dressing, capture the flavorful oil that lies just beneath the peel of a lemon, lime, or orange by zesting the citrus directly into the bowl with the other ingredients.

1½ cups unbleached all-purpose flour
½ teaspoon baking powder
½ teaspoon baking soda
¼ teaspoon fine sea salt
3 large eggs
1 cup sugar
¾ cup plain whole-milk yogurt
Finely grated zest of 3 lemons
¾ cup extra-virgin olive oil

Put oven rack in center position and heat oven to 325°F. Lightly oil a 9-inch springform pan.

Whisk together flour, baking powder, baking soda, and salt in a medium bowl.

With an electric mixer, beat eggs and sugar in a large bowl on high speed for 5 minutes, or until pale and thick. Add yogurt and zest; beat to combine. With mixer on medium speed, add oil in a quick, steady stream. Reduce speed to low and gradually add flour mixture just until blended. Whisk batter by hand to make sure that all ingredients are incorporated.

Pour batter into pan. Bake, rotating pan once, until cake is golden, center springs back to the touch, and edges pull away from pan, 40 to 45 minutes. Let cool in pan for a minute or two on rack, then release from pan and let cool completely on rack before slicing.

SPICY LEMON-CHOCOLATE GANACHE TART

SLOW-COOK RECIPE / MAKES 8 SERVINGS

This recipe shows how easy it is to infuse a classic with new flavor elements. The hint of lemon seems to draw out the natural fruitiness of the chocolate, and spicy chilies counteract the chocolate's sweetness. The sea salt sprinkled over the top of the finished tart lends crunch and brings all of the flavors to a point on the tip of the tongue. This is one of my favorite and most complexly flavored desserts. A little slice goes a long way.

FLAVOR TIP: Chilies, like many dried pantry staples, vary greatly in flavor. Some may be very spicy, others less so; age is also a factor—older chilies are often less spicy. If you find the tart is not spicy enough, increase the chili (by one to start) the next time you make it.

1	cup plus 2 tablespoons heavy cream
1	lemon
2	dried árbol chilies
1/2	recipe Favorite Tart Dough (page 353; make full recipe and freeze rest for another time)
9	ounces good semisweet chocolate (at least 62% cacao), chopped
	Fleur de sel or other medium-coarse sea salt

Put cream in a small saucepan. Using a sharp knife or vegetable peeler, cut two 1-inch-wide lengthwise strips of peel from lemon; set lemon aside. Add to cream. Crumble chilies into cream (seeds and all). Bring mixture to a boil over high heat; stir and remove from heat. Cover and set aside to steep.

On a lightly floured surface, roll out dough to an 11-inch circle. Fit into an 8-inch fluted tart pan with a removable bottom. Fold edges of dough under around rim to form a double-thick edge and, using a paring knife, decoratively score edge. Lightly prick bottom all over with a fork. Refrigerate for at least 30 minutes.

Put oven rack in center position and heat oven to 475°F.

Remove tart shell from refrigerator and line with parchment paper. Weight with dried beans or pie weights. Bake for 15 minutes. Reduce heat to 250°F and continue baking until edges of crust are lightly golden, about 10 minutes. Remove weights and parchment paper and continue baking until bottom of crust appears dry, 10 to 15 minutes more. Let cool on a wire rack.

Gently melt chocolate in a double boiler; remove from heat. Pour cream mixture through a fine-mesh strainer over chocolate, pressing down on chilies and lemon peel to extract the most flavor; discard chilies and peel. Whisk cream and chocolate together, then zest remaining lemon over mixture and whisk to combine.

Pour chocolate mixture into tart shell. Chill in the refrigerator until set, about 1 hour. Sprinkle tart with about 1 teaspoon sea salt just before serving.

PLUM GALETTE

SLOW-COOK RECIPE / MAKES 10 SERVINGS

Italian prune plums are one of my favorite fruits for tarts because they are not overly sweet. I also like to use peaches or buttery sautéed apples, sometimes tossed with fresh rosemary or thyme. I encourage you to try an array of different fruits or combinations. Enjoy the tart with crème fraîche or vanilla ice cream, or by itself.

Favorite Tart Dough (recipe follows)
1¾ pounds prune plums, halved and pitted
3 tablespoons sugar
1 tablespoon fresh lemon juice
1 large egg
2 tablespoons heavy cream

On a lightly floured surface, roll out dough to an approximately 14-inch round, about ⅛ inch thick. Transfer to a large parchment-lined baking sheet. Prick dough all over with a fork and chill in the refrigerator while you prepare fruit.

Heat oven to 450°F. Put rack in center.

Put plums, 2 tablespoons sugar, and lemon juice in a bowl and toss to combine. Let stand, stirring occasionally, until plums are juicy, about 20 minutes.

Lightly beat egg and cream together and brush mixture over tart dough. Removing plums from bowl with a slotted spoon, arrange them in concentric circles, skin side up, on dough, overlapping them slightly and leaving a 3-inch border all around. Tuck any extra plums in between. Fold border of dough over fruit mixture, overlapping dough where necessary and pressing any folds together gently so they adhere.

Brush edges of dough with egg mixture and sprinkle fruit and dough with remaining tablespoon sugar. Bake for 20 minutes. Reduce heat to 375°F, rotate pan, and continue baking until juices are bubbling and slightly thickened, about 30 minutes more.

Let cool on a rack before serving.

FAVORITE TART DOUGH

MAKES ENOUGH FOR ONE 8-INCH GALETTE OR TWO 8-INCH TARTS

This flaky tart dough is akin to a rough puff pastry. Though it does not achieve the airy heights of true puff pastry, the layers of butter and flour create a similar texture. I often make a double batch and freeze half or save the scraps and fold them over grated Parmigiano-Reggiano cheese and black pepper to make fabulous party twists.

It's important that your surroundings are not too warm—the cooler the better—and that you have a good-sized space to work on. The dough starts out very loose on the board: trust it. As you add the water, you'll see that it comes together quite nicely. The amount of water you will need may vary with the humidity of your environment, so add it little by little.

NOTE: Though the dough will keep in the refrigerator for up to 1 week, the longer you store it, the less lift it will have. If you must make it further ahead, better to keep it frozen.

- 2¼ cups plus 2 tablespoons unbleached all-purpose flour
- ¼ teaspoon fine sea salt
- ½ pound (2 sticks) unsalted butter, cut into ½-inch cubes and chilled
- 8–10 tablespoons ice water

Whisk together flour and salt in a large bowl. Add butter and toss to coat with flour mixture. One by one, add 6 tablespoons ice water, stirring after each addition.

Transfer mixture to a clean work surface (it will be very loose) and mound in a pile. With a rolling pin, roll dough in a back-and-forth motion into a circle about ¼ inch thick. Sprinkle with 1 tablespoon ice water, fold mixture over itself, turn 90 degrees, and roll again. Add 1 tablespoon more water, fold, turn, and roll again, scraping dough off rolling pin with a butter knife or bench scraper. Repeat process 1 or 2 more times, until dough just comes together, being careful not to overwork it. Wrap and chill in the refrigerator for at least 2 hours, or overnight, before using. The dough can be frozen, wrapped in plastic, for up to 2 months.

FRAGOLINO

SLOW-COOK RECIPE / MAKES 3 CUPS; 6 TO 8 SERVINGS

Use the best local fruit you can find for this delicious strawberry cordial. For a peach version, use ¾ pound ripe peaches (about 4), cut in half, with the pits left in. They give a faint bitter almond flavor.

- 1 500-ml bottle vodka
- 1 pint strawberries, hulled
- 1¼ cups sugar
- 1 cup plus 2 tablespoons water

Combine vodka and strawberries in a covered container and place in a cool, dark spot in your pantry for 3 weeks.

Bring sugar and water to a simmer in a small saucepan over medium-high heat, stirring to dissolve sugar. Reduce heat and simmer for 1 minute. Remove from heat and let sugar syrup cool.

Stir cooled sugar syrup into vodka mixture; return to spot in pantry for 2 more weeks.

Strain *fragolino* into a container with lid (discard fruit) and refrigerate. Serve chilled.

MAKING CORDIALS

In the south of Italy, the easy homemade cordial *rosolio* is found in every home. The most common is *limoncello*, made with the aromatic peel of the big lemons that grow everywhere in the hills running down to the Mediterranean Sea. I have been served mandarin *rosolio* and strawberry, called *fragolino*, as well, and, once, a whole range of cordials made with spices such as cinnamon and cloves, which gave me the idea to make a version using fresh bay leaves (page 356). Very ripe and aromatic fruit is the key to the best flavor. As the fruit macerates in the vodka, it will transfer both flavor and aroma to the alcohol. The simple syrup cuts the harshness of the alcohol and preserves the fruit flavor.

FRESH BAY LEAF ROSOLIO

SLOW-COOK RECIPE / MAKES 3 CUPS; 6 TO 8 SERVINGS

The herbaceous quality and flavor of this *rosolio* make a delicious digestif. Look for fresh bay leaves in specialty food shops, or order them online.

1   500-ml bottle vodka

1   fresh bay sprig with 12 leaves

1¼   cups sugar

1   cup plus 2 tablespoons water

Combine vodka and bay sprig in a covered container and place in a cool, dark spot in your pantry for 3 weeks.

Bring sugar and water to a simmer in a small saucepan over medium-high heat, stirring to dissolve sugar. Reduce heat and simmer for 1 minute. Remove from heat and let sugar syrup cool.

Stir cooled sugar syrup into vodka mixture; return to spot in pantry for 2 more weeks.

Strain *rosolio* into a container with a lid and refrigerate (discard bay sprig). Serve chilled.

SOURCES

BOTTARGA

Order bottarga from www.chefshop.com or from Buon Italia (75 Ninth Avenue, New York, NY 10011; 212-633-9090; www.buonitalia.com).

CAPERS

Salt-cured capers are available at www.gustiamo.com. For Les Moulins Mahjoub capers, visit www.therogerscollection.com.

CHEESE

In New York City, Di Palo (206 Grand Street, New York, NY 10013; 212-226-1033) has the finest selection of Italian cheeses as well as the freshest Italian extra-virgin olive oils. The ambience is more like an old-fashioned Italian dry goods shop than a modern food emporium. Di Palo has been going strong for five generations; originally a *latticini*, or cheesemaker, Di Palo makes great cow's-milk mozzarella and ricotta. A website and a mail-order business are coming soon.

Buon Italia (75 Ninth Avenue, New York, NY 10011; 212-633-9090; www.buonitalia.com) carries excellent cheeses.

Formaggio Kitchen (two locations: 244 Huron Avenue, Cambridge, MA 02138; 888-212-3224; 120 Essex Street, Essex Street Market, New York, NY 10002; 212-982-8200; www.formaggiokitchen.com) is a great cheese shop with an extensive mail-order business.

CHESTNUT HONEY

Look for chestnut honey in specialty shops and fine grocery stores, or order from Zingerman's (620 Phoenix Drive, Ann Arbor, MI 48108; 888-636-8162; www.zingermans.com).

CHESTNUTS

Frozen peeled chestnuts can be found online and at Buon Italia (75 Ninth Avenue, New York, NY 10011; 212-633-9090; www.buonitalia.com).

FISH

Browne Trading Company (Merrill's Wharf, 260 Commercial Street, Portland, ME 04101; 800-944-7848; www.browne-trading.com) and Wild Edibles (Grand Central Market in Grand Central Station, Lexington Avenue at 43rd Street, New York, NY 10017; 212-687-4255; www.wildedibles.com) ship excellent fresh imported and domestic fish, including octopus, salt cod, and Maine shrimp.

GRAINS, BEANS AND LEGUMES

For Colfiorito lentils, go to www.gustiamo.com.

For Castelluccio lentils, farro, and dried chickpeas, visit or call Buon Italia (75 Ninth Avenue, New York, NY 10011; 212-633-9090; www.buonitalia.com) or Di Palo (206 Grand Street, New York, NY 10013; 212-226-1033).

For Spanish lentils, visit Despaña (408 Broome Street, New York, NY 10013; 212-219-5050; www.despanabrandfoods.com), a fantastic shop for Spanish foods, including grains, cheeses, meats, and spices.

La Tienda (3601 La Grange Parkway, Toano, VA 23168; 800-710-4304; www.latienda.com), another terrific resource for Spanish foods, has an extensive catalog and website.

For rice beans and an extensive selection of other dried beans, grains (including farro), and legumes, visit Kalustyan's (123 Lexington Avenue, New York, NY 10016; 212-685-3451; www.kalustyans.com).

GUINEA HEN

D'Artagnan (800-327-8246; www.dartagnan.com) will ship whole guinea hen, or breasts or legs.

OLIVE OIL

Il Buco restaurant (47 Bond Street, New York, NY 10012; 212-533-1932; www.ilbuco.com) sells fine Umbrian olive oil, as well as terrific sea salts and a variety of other hand picked Italian products.

An informative website, www.gustiamo.com is dedicated to bringing the finest artisanal Italian products to America. It carries a great selection of fine estate-bottled extra-virgin olive oils from Italy and more.

For Spanish, French, and other Mediterranean olive oils, including Italian, visit Zingerman's shop or website (620 Phoenix Drive, Ann Arbor, MI 48108; 888-636-8162; www.zingermans.com).

For Spanish olive oils and a vast array of other Spanish products, visit Despaña (408 Broome Street, New York, NY 10013; 212-219-5050; www.despanabrandfoods.com).

PASTA

DRIED PASTAS

For Latini pasta, www.gustiamo.com has the widest selection of shapes and sizes.

An extensive line of Pasta Setaro can be found at Buon Italia (75 Ninth Avenue, New York, NY 10011; 212-633-9090; www.buonitalia.com).

Benedetto Cavalieri pasta from Puglia is available at Williams-Sonoma shops.

Rustichella d'Abruzzo is available at The Pasta Shop at Rockridge Market Hall (5655 College Avenue, Oakland, CA 94618; 888-952-4005; www.markethallfoods.com) and at many Whole Foods Markets.

FRESH PASTAS

Look for fresh pasta locally. In New York City, Raffetto's (144 West Houston Street, New York, NY 10012; 212-777-1261) sells good fresh pasta and more. It does not mail-order, but the shop is worth a visit.

PRESERVED LEMONS

Preserved lemons can be found at Kalustyan's (123 Lexington Avenue, New York, NY 10016; 212-685-3451; www.kalustyans.com).

PROSCIUTTO, GUANCIALE, PANCETTA, AND SALAMI

Prosciutto di Parma and di San Daniele are available at most gourmet markets. Di Palo (206 Grand Street, New York, NY 10013; 212-226-1033) has some of the most carefully selected prosciutto I have seen.

Fantastic true Italian-style guanciale and pancetta, as well as high-quality imported prosciutto, can be mail-ordered at La Quercia (www.laquercia.us).

For great Italian-type salami, look for Paul Bertolli's Fra'Mani products at specialty grocers or order from www.framani.com.

Terrific cured meats can also be found at Seattle's Salumi Artisan Cured Meats (309 Third Avenue South, Seattle, WA 98104; 206-621-8772; www.salumicuredmeats.com).

SEA SALT

Isle of Motzia fiore di sale is imported exclusively by Il Buco restaurant (47 Bond Street, New York, NY 10012; 212-533-1932; www.ilbuco.com).

Boutique Sicilian sea salt is available at www.gustiamo.com.

SPICES AND CHILIES

The finest selection of spices I know is at Kalustyan's (123 Lexington Avenue, New York, NY 10016; 212-685-3451; www.kalustyans.com), which carries Aleppo pepper as well as a host of other dried red chili peppers, piment d'Espelette, sumac, za'atar, and wonderfully aromatic peppercorns. When in New York City, be sure to visit the shop for spices, grains, and much more.

Wild fennel pollen can be found at Il Buco restaurant (47 Bond Street, New York, NY 10012; 212-533-1932; www.ilbuco.com) and Zingerman's (620 Phoenix Drive, Ann Arbor, MI 48108; 888-636-8162; www.zingermans.com).

Look for premium Spanish goods at www.spanishtable.com, www.latienda.com, and www.zingermans.com.

The Rogers Collection sells the full line of Les Moulins Mahjoub products, including harissa, online at www.therogerscollection.com. You can also call 207-828-2000 for information about where Les Moulins Mahjoub products, as well as many fine olive oils, are sold in your area.

VINEGARS

For Vin Santo vinegar, visit or call Di Palo (206 Grand Street, New York, NY 10013; 212-226-1033). I especially like Agretto di Vino Santo di Montevertine; the importer, Doral International (718-224-7413) will ship to consumers.

For Volpaia vinegars, order from The Pasta Shop at Rockridge Market Hall (5655 College Avenue, Oakland, CA 94618; 888-952-4005; www.markethallfoods.com).

For fine sherry vinegar, go to or order from Despaña (408 Broome Street, New York, NY 10013; 212-219-5050; www.despanabrandfoods.com).

For Forum Cabernet Sauvignon red wine vinegar, go to or order from Salumeria Italiana (151 Richmond Street, Boston, MA 02109; 800-400-5916; www.salumeriaitaliana.com).

INDEX

Page references in *italic* refer to illustrations.

accompaniments, *see* side dishes; small plates
acids, 7–9
Aleppo pepper, 16
almond(s)
    Fried, Green Beans with Shaved Onion, Parmigiano-Reggiano and, *89*, 89–90
    Gazpacho, White, 104, *105*
    Spaghetti with Lemon Sole, Capers, Parsley and, 160–61, *161*
anchovy(ies), 11, 202
    Butter, 293–94
    Dressing, Hot, Warm Escarole Salad with, 77–78
    Maccheroni with White Beans, Mustard Greens and, 156, *157*
    Salsa Verde, 223
    Vinaigrette, Crisp Bitter Greens with, 76
Anderson, Burton, 183
appetizers, *see* small plates
apple(s)
    Chicken with Escarole, Potatoes and, *262*, 263–64
    Cider-Braised Leeks, 322–23
    Turnip, and Jerusalem Artichoke Soup, 113
árbol chilies, dried, 16
Arborio rice, 13, 183
Aromatic Herb Butter, 199–200
arrosto morto, 318
arugula
    Beet, and Cucumber Salad with Yogurt Dressing, 91
    Flank Steak Salad with Farro, Fresh Horseradish and, 98–99

Panzanella di Farro (Tuscan-Style Tomato Salad with Farro), 86, *87*
    Spicy, Smoked Trout Salad with Grapefruit and, 94, *95*
    Tomatoes, and Grilled Red Onion, 220, *221*
asparagus
    with Olive Oil and Queso Iberico, 36
    Pan-Roasted, with Bacon, *32–33*, 34–35
Avalle, Alberto, 64, 79
Avocado and Cucumber Salad, 281

bacon, 12
    -and-Herb-Rubbed Salt-Baked Chicken, *252*, 253
    Long Pasta with Red Cabbage, Walnuts, Rosemary and, 150–52, *151*
    Pan-Roasted Asparagus with, *32–33*, 34–35
    Pasta Carbonara, 159
    and Ramp Risotto, 192–93
    Salmon with Sugar Snap Peas and, 213
Baldo rice, 13, 183
balsamic vinegar, 8
barley
    and Dandelion Greens, 270–71
    Tabouli with Many Grains, 46–47
basting
    spoon-basting with herbs and hot oil or butter, 226
    with wine, 318
battuto, 100

bay leaf, 15
    Fresh, *Rosolio*, 356
bean(s), 358
    Cannellini, Slow-Cooked, 42
    cranberry, in Bluefish and Summer Vegetables, 238–39
    dried, 13
    Fava, Raw, Salad with Pecorino, 80–81, *81*
    Fresh Summer, Simmered in Tomato Sauce, 43
    Rice, and Sweet Pumpkin Soup with Crème Fraîche and Crispy Seeds, *114*, 114–16
    white, in *Ribollita* (Tuscan-Style Vegetable and Bread Soup), 118–20
    White, Soup with Ramps, 124–25
    see also chickpea(s)
Becchina, Gian Franco, 162
beef, 277–89
    Bistecca Chianina, *282–83*, 284–85
    Flank Steak Salad with Farro, Arugula, and Fresh Horseradish, 98–99
    Meat Ragù, Classic Central Italian, 168–69
    Oxtail, Braised, 289
    Short Ribs, Peppery Braised, 286–88, *287*
    Skirt Steak, Grilled, with Cucumber and Avocado Salad, 281
    see also veal
beet(s)
    Arugula, and Cucumber Salad with Yogurt Dressing, 91

beet(s) (cont.)
  Pan-Roasted Brussels Sprouts, Turnips and, with Warm Farro, 61–62
  Roasted, Orange and Mint Leaf Salad with, 92, 93
Bertolli, Paul, 12, 359
Besciamel Sauce, 181–82
Biscotti with Lemon, Pine Nuts, and Thyme, Tuscan, 346–47, 347
Bistecca Chianina, 282–83, 284–85
Bitter Greens, Crisp, with Anchovy Vinaigrette, 76
black bass, 202
Blackberry Sorbetto, 330
blood orange(s), 8
  Citrus–Pea Sprout Salad, 216–17, 218–19
  and Mint Leaf Salad with Roasted Beets, 92, 93
  Red Onion, and Bottarga Salad, 236–37
blueberries, in Summer Fruit with Lemon, Sugar, and Mint, 328
bluefish
  Grilled, with Kohlrabi Slaw, 240
  and Summer Vegetables, 238–39
Boar, Wild, Ragù, Tuscan, 176–77
bottarga, 11, 357
  Blood Orange, and Red Onion Salad, 236–37
  Celery, and Cherry Tomato Salad, 79
  Pasta with, 162–63
bread
  Brioche and Roasted Corn Pudding, 58–59
  Crostini, Chicken Liver, 67–68
  crumbs, in Fried Eggplant Balls, 60
  Crumbs, Toasted Seasoned, 155
  Fried, and Shaved Celery Salad, 274–76, 275
  Pita, Lebanese Salad with (Fattouche), 88
  Pudding, Semolina, with Concord Grapes, 344–45
  and Vegetable Soup, Tuscan-Style (Ribollita), 118–20
Brioche and Roasted Corn Pudding, 58–59
broths
  chicken, homemade vs. store-bought, 13
  Chicken, Rich, 108–9
  defatting, 109

Parmesan, with Pea Shoots, 117
for risotto, 183
Shrimp, 186
for soups, 101
Browne Trading Company, 358
Brussels sprout(s)
  Leaves, Halibut with Black Olives, Chili and, 235
  Pan-Roasted Turnips, Beets and, with Warm Farro, 61–62
bulgur
  Lamb and, Tartare (Kibbeh Naye), 30–31
  Salad, Minty, 306–8, 307
  Tabouli with Many Grains, 46–47
butters
  Anchovy, 293–94
  Aromatic Herb, 199–200
  "Snail," 209

cabbage
  and Chickpea Soup, 121–22
  red, in Winter Root Salad with English Farmhouse Cheddar, 84, 85
  Red, Long Pasta with Bacon, Walnuts, Rosemary and, 150–52, 151
Cacciucco alla Livornese (Mediterranean shellfish stew), 206, 206–8
Cake, Lemon Olive Oil, 348, 349
Calf's Liver with Brown Butter, Sage, and Wilted Dandelion Greens, 297–99, 298
cannellini beans
  Maccheroni with White Beans, Mustard Greens, and Anchovy, 156, 157
  Slow-Cooked, 42
Cantaloupe Gazpacho with Jamón Serrano, 106, 106–7
cantucci di prato, 346
caper(s), 12, 357
  Cornichon, and Parsley Vinaigrette, 74
  Onion, and Olive Sauce, 304–5
  Salsa Verde, 223
caponata, 232
  Tunisian Grilled (Mechuia), 50–51
Cardamom Coffee Crème Caramel, 339–40, 341
Carnaroli rice, 13, 183
Carpaccio, Scallop, with Lime Juice, Sea Salt, and Chives, 29

carrot(s)
  Baby, Free-Range Veal Shoulder with, and Mustard Greens, 295–96
  Roasted Vegetables, 228–29, 229
  Salad with Lemon, Sea Salt, Parsley, and Olive Oil, 25, 25–26
  Soup, Velvety (Vellutata di Carote), 111–12
  Winter Lamb Stew with Turnips, Celery Root and, 312–13
  Winter Root Salad with English Farmhouse Cheddar, 84, 85
  Winter Vegetables, 292–93, 292–94
cast-iron skillets, 34
cauliflower
  Roasted, Pasta with Olives, Capers, Bread Crumbs and, 153, 153–55
  Roasted, with Tahini Sauce, 54, 55
Cecchini, Dario, 166
celery
  Cherry Tomato, and Bottarga Salad, 79
  Potato, and Leek Soup, 129
  Shaved, and Fried Bread Salad, 274–76, 275
celery root
  Winter Lamb Stew with Turnips, Carrots and, 312–13
  Winter Root Salad with English Farmhouse Cheddar, 84, 85
Chanterelles, Duck Breast with Chestnuts, Pearl Onions and, 265–67, 266
Cheddar, English Farmhouse, Winter Root Salad with, 84, 85
cheeses, 17–18, 357
  Many, Pasta Shells with, 158
  see also specific cheeses
chestnut(s), 357
  Duck Breast with Chanterelles, Pearl Onions and, 265–67, 266
  puree, in Montebianco, 342–43
chestnut honey, 20, 357
  -and-Chili-Roasted Duck with Fennel and Farro, 268–69
  Pecorino and Pears with, 329
  and Walnut Semifreddo, 332–33
Chianina cows, 284
chicken, 241–64
  Bacon-and-Herb-Rubbed Salt-Baked, 252, 253

broth, homemade vs. store-bought, 13
Broth, Rich, 108–9
with Escarole, Apples, and Potatoes, *262*, 263–64
Hash, Braised, with Wild Mushrooms and Herbed Rice, 260–61
pasture-raised or grass-fed, 242
poaching, 256, *257*
resting after cooking, 246
Roast, with Braised Red Peppers and Onion, 258–59, *259*
Roast, with Farro Salad with Preserved Lemon, 254–55
Roast, with Oyster-Sage Stuffing, 250–51
Roast, with Sage, Garlic, and Lemon Peel, 246–47
Salad with Tarragon, Toasted Pine Nuts, and Golden Raisins, 256–57
Soup, Rich, with Greens, 126–28, *127*
Za'atar, 248–49
chicken liver(s)
buying, 297
Crostini, 67–68
Spaghetti with Rosemary, Lemon and, 166–67
chickpea(s), 358
and Cabbage Soup, 121–22
Salt Cod Stewed with Greens and, 230–31
chilies, 16, 17, 359
Spicy Lemon-Chocolate Ganache Tart, 350–51, *351*
chili varieties, 16–17
chocolate, 20
Lemon Ganache Tart, Spicy, 350–51, *351*
Shaved Dark, Jasmine Tea Panna Cotta with, 338
Cider-Braised Leeks, 322–23
cipollini in agrodolce, 48
cipollini onions, 293
Roasted Vegetables, 228–29, *229*
citrus (fruits), 7, 8–9
Pea Sprout Salad, *216–17*, 218–19
zesting, 8–9, 348
see also specific fruits
clams, in *Cacciucco alla Livornese* (Mediterranean shellfish stew), *206*, 206–8
cod, 202, 203

Broiled, with Red Wine Sauce and Roasted Vegetables, 228–29, *229*
Cacciucco alla Livornese (Mediterranean shellfish stew), *206*, 206–8
Salt, Stewed with Chickpeas and Greens, 230–31
Seared, with Green Olive, Lemon, and Parsley Relish, 226–27
Coffee Cardamom Crème Caramel, 339–40, *341*
Concord grapes
Braised Lamb Shoulder with Green Tomatoes and, 310–11
Semolina Bread Pudding with, 344–45
cookies: Tuscan Biscotti with Lemon, Pine Nuts, and Thyme, 346–47, *347*
cordials, 354–56
Fragolino, 354, *355*
Fresh Bay Leaf *Rosolio*, 356
corn
Roasted, and Brioche Pudding, 58–59
Sweet, Pasta with, 148
Sweet, *Sformato*, 56–57
corncobs, getting corn flavor from, 56
cornichon(s)
Caper, and Parsley Vinaigrette, 74
Salsa Verde, 223
cranberry beans, in Bluefish and Summer Vegetables, 238–39
Crème Caramel, Coffee Cardamom, 339–40, *341*
Crisp Bitter Greens with Anchovy Vinaigrette, 76
Crostini, Chicken Liver, 67–68
cucumber(s)
and Avocado Salad, 281
Beet, and Arugula Salad with Yogurt Dressing, 91
Minty Bulgur Salad, 306–8, *307*
cucuzza squash, 144
custards
Coffee Cardamom Crème Caramel, 339–40, *341*
Sweet Corn *Sformato*, 56–57

dandelion greens
Barley and, 270–71
Wilted, 297–99, *298*
Dario's (Panzano, Chianti), 286

deep-frying foods, in extra-virgin olive oil, 303
defatting broth, 109
desserts, *see* sweets
Dill and Greek Yogurt Sauce, 214–15
"Dirty" Squid with Watercress, *96*, 96–97
dressings
Anchovy, Hot, 77–78
Garlic-Lemon, 88
Yogurt, 91
see also vinaigrettes
duck, 241, 242, 265–69
Breast with Chanterelles, Chestnuts, and Pearl Onions, 265–67, *266*
Honey-and-Chili-Roasted, with Fennel and Farro, 268–69
melting fat from, 265, 268

eel, 202
eggplant
Balls, Fried, 60
Bluefish and Summer Vegetables, 238–39
Mechuia (Tunisian Grilled Caponata), 50–51
Parmesan, Classic Tuscan, 197–98
eggs
Baked Spinach and, 39
hard-boiling, 34
endive, in Crisp Bitter Greens with Anchovy Vinaigrette, 76
escarole
Chicken with Apples, Potatoes and, *262*, 263–64
Salad, Warm, with Hot Anchovy Dressing, 77–78

farro, 14, 358
Fennel and, 268–69
Flank Steak Salad with Arugula, Fresh Horseradish and, 98–99
and Kale Soup, 130–31, *131*
Salad with Preserved Lemon, 254–55
Tomato Salad with, Tuscan-Style (*Panzanella di Farro*), 86, *87*
Warm, Pan-Roasted Brussels Sprouts, Turnips, and Beets with, 61–62
Fattouche (Lebanese Salad with Pita), 88
Fava Bean, Raw, Salad with Pecorino, 80–81, *81*

fennel
and Farro, 268–69
Shaved, Salad, 65–66
see also wild fennel pollen
Feta, Red and Yellow Tomatoes
with Fresh Coriander Seeds
and, 28
fish, 201–40, 358
Bluefish and Summer
Vegetables, 238–39
buying, 201–2
Cacciucco alla Livornese
(Mediterranean shellfish
stew), *206,* 206–8
Cod, Broiled, with Red
Wine Sauce and Roasted
Vegetables, 228–29, *229*
Cod, Seared, with Green Olive,
Lemon, and Parsley Relish,
226–27
cooking time for, 203
flavor families of, 202–3
Hake with Salsa Verde, 223
Halibut with Brussels Sprout
Leaves, Black Olives, and
Chili, 235
Lemon Sole, Spaghetti with
Almonds, Capers, Parsley
and, 160–61, *161*
Mackerel, Grilled, with
Kohlrabi Slaw, 240
Mako Shark Skewers, Grilled,
with Shaved Radish and
Parsley Salad, *224,* 225
Monkfish with Olives, Potatoes,
and Sun-Dried Tomatoes,
232–34, *233*
Salmon, Cold Poached, with
Greek Yogurt and Dill Sauce,
214–15
Salmon with Parsnip Puree and
Citrus–Pea Sprout Salad,
216–17, 218–19
Salmon with Sugar Snap Peas
and Bacon, 213
Salt Cod Stewed with Chickpeas
and Greens, 230–31
Sardines, Grilled, with
Accompaniments, 64–66
Scallop Carpaccio with Lime
Juice, Sea Salt, and Chives, 29
Scallops, Roasted, with
"Snail Butter" and Mâche,
209–11, *210*
Shrimp, Maine, Panfried in
Olive Oil, 63
Shrimp, Maine, Risotto,
184–86, *185*

Shrimp, North African Spiced,
212
Skate with Blood Orange, Red
Onion, and Bottarga Salad,
236–37
Squid, "Dirty," with Watercress,
96, 96–97
sustainability issues and, 202
Tuna, Grilled, with Tomatoes,
Grilled Red Onion, and
Arugula, 220, *221*
Tuna, Seared, in *Porchettata,* 222
see also anchovy(ies); bottarga
Flank Steak Salad with Farro,
Arugula, and Fresh
Horseradish, 98–99
Flavors of Tuscany
(N. H. Jenkins), 206
flounder, 202
fluke, 202
food mills, 140
Fragolino, 354, *355*
Fra'Mani, 12, 359
French (flavors)
Carrot Salad with Lemon, Sea
Salt, Parsley, and Olive Oil,
25, 25–26
Coffee Cardamom Crème
Caramel, 339–40, *341*
Herb Vinaigrette, Fresh, 73
Lamb Stew, Winter, with
Turnips, Carrots, and Celery
Root, 312–13
Lemon-Chocolate Ganache Tart,
Spicy, 350–51, *351*
Plum Galette, 352
Pork Loin, Braised, with
Prunes, 321
Scallops, Roasted, with "Snail
Butter" and Mâche,
209–11, *210*
Walnut Vinaigrette, 75
frisée, in Crisp Bitter Greens with
Anchovy Vinaigrette, 76
fruit(s)
Apple, Turnip, and Jerusalem
Artichoke Soup, 113
Apples, Chicken with Escarole,
Potatoes and, *262,* 263–64
Blood Orange, Red Onion, and
Bottarga Salad, 236–37
Cantaloupe Gazpacho with
Jamón Serrano, *106,* 106–7
Cider-Braised Leeks, 322–23
citrus, cooking with, 7, 8–9
citrus, zesting, 8–9, 348
Citrus–Pea Sprout Salad,
216–17, 218–19

Concord Grapes, Braised
Lamb Shoulder with Green
Tomatoes and, 310–11
Concord Grapes, Semolina
Bread Pudding with, 344–45
Grapefruit, Smoked Trout Salad
with Spicy Arugula and, 94, *95*
Orange and Mint Leaf Salad
with Roasted Beets, 92, *93*
Orange Juice, Red Onions
Cooked in, 48, *49*
Orange Panna Cotta with
Orange Marmalade, *336,* 337
Peach Cordial, 354
Peaches, Baked Pork Chops
with, 314–15
Pear, Basil, and Pecorino
Toscano Salad, 82, *83*
Pears and Pecorino with
Chestnut Honey, 329
Plum Galette, 352
Plum (or Blackberry) Sorbetto,
330, *331*
Prunes, Braised Pork Loin
with, 321
strawberries, in *Fragolino,* 354, *355*
Strawberries with Prosecco, 327
Strawberry Risotto, 190–91
Summer, with Lemon, Sugar,
and Mint, 328
see also lemon(s)

Galette, Plum, 352
game
marinade for, 286, 288
Rabbit Ragù, Braised,
174–75, *175*
Wild Boar Ragù, Tuscan,
176–77
Ganache, Spicy Lemon-Chocolate,
Tart, 350–51, *351*
garlic
chopping herbs, olives and, into
paste, 309
Green, Soup, 110
Lemon Dressing, 88
"Snail Butter," 209
softening flavor of, 121
gazpacho
Almond, White, 104, *105*
Cantaloupe, with Jamón
Serrano, *106,* 106–7
Gelato, Lemon, 334
Gnocchi, Potato, 194–96, *195*
grains, 13–14, 358
Tabouli with Many Grains,
46–47
see also barley; farro; rice

Grana Padana, 17–18

Grapefruit, Smoked Trout Salad with Spicy Arugula and, 94, *95*

grapes, *see* Concord grapes

Greek (flavors)

    Beet, Arugula, and Cucumber Salad with Yogurt Dressing, 91

    Salmon, Cold Poached, with Greek Yogurt and Dill Sauce, 214–15

green beans

    Fresh Summer Beans Simmered in Tomato Sauce, 43

    with Shaved Onion, Fried Almonds, and Parmigiano-Reggiano, *89,* 89–90

Green Garlic Soup, 110

greens

    Cooking, Wilted, 37–38

    Crisp Bitter, with Anchovy Vinaigrette, 76

    Dandelion, Barley and, 270–71

    Dandelion, Wilted, 297–99, *298*

    Escarole, Chicken with Apples, Potatoes and, *262,* 263–64

    Escarole Salad, Warm, with Hot Anchovy Dressing, *77*–78

    Kale and Farro Soup, 130–31, *131*

    Mustard, 295–96

    Mustard, Maccheroni with White Beans, Anchovy and, 156, *157*

    purslane, in *Panzanella di Farro* (Tuscan-Style Tomato Salad with Farro), 86, *87*

    Ribollita (Tuscan-Style Vegetable and Bread Soup), 118–20

    Rich Chicken Soup with, 126–28, *127*

    salad, washing, 69

    Salt Cod Stewed with Chickpeas and, 230–31

    Spinach and Eggs, Baked, 39

    see also arugula

grilled

    Bistecca Chianina, 282–83, 284–85

    Caponata, Tunisian (*Mechuia*), 50–51

    Lamb Brochettes with Shaved Onion Salad, 300–301

    Mackerel with Kohlrabi Slaw, 240

    Mako Shark Skewers with Shaved Radish and Parsley Salad, *224,* 225

Sardines with Accompaniments, 64–66

Skirt Steak with Cucumber and Avocado Salad, 281

Tuna with Tomatoes, Grilled Red Onion, and Arugula, 220, *221*

guanciale, 12, 359

guinea hen(s), 241, 242, 358

    Breasts, Oven-Roasted, with Barley and Dandelion Greens, 270–71

    Ragù, Braised, 172–73

haddock, 202

hake, 202

    with Salsa Verde, 223

halibut, 202, 203

    with Brussels Sprout Leaves, Black Olives, and Chili, 235

ham, *see* jamón serrano

harissa, 16–17

    Tunisian Raw Turnip Salad, 27

Hash, Braised Chicken, with Wild Mushrooms and Herbed Rice, 260–61

herb(ed)(s), 15

    Butter, Aromatic, 199–200

    chopping garlic, olives and, into paste, 309

    Fresh, Vinaigrette, 73

    Rice, 260–61

    spoon-basting hot oil or butter with, 226

    in sweets, 324

honey, *see* chestnut honey

Il Buco (New York City), 64, 79, 358, 359

Innocenti, Alberta, 207

inzimino, 230

Italian (flavors)

    battuto technique, 100

    Bay Leaf *Rosolio,* 356

    Beans, Fresh Summer, Simmered in Tomato Sauce, 43

    Biscotti with Lemon, Pine Nuts, and Thyme, Tuscan, 346–47, *347*

    Bistecca Chianina, 282–83, 284–85

    Brussels Sprouts, Turnips, and Beets, Pan-Roasted, with Warm Farro, 61–62

    Cacciucco alla Livornese (Mediterranean shellfish stew), *206,* 206–8

    Cannellini Beans, Slow-Cooked, 42

Cantaloupe Gazpacho with Jamón Serrano, *106,* 106–7

Celery, Cherry Tomato, and Bottarga Salad, 79

Chestnut Honey and Walnut Semifreddo, 332–33

Chicken, Roast, with Braised Red Peppers and Onion, 258–59, *259*

Chicken Liver Crostini, 67–68

Chicken Salad with Tarragon, Toasted Pine Nuts, and Golden Raisins, 256–57

Chicken Soup, Rich, with Greens, 126–28, *127*

Corn, Sweet, *Sformato,* 56–57

Cornichon, Caper, and Parsley Vinaigrette, 74

Eggplant Balls, Fried, 60

Eggplant Parmesan, Classic Tuscan, 197–98

Escarole Salad, Warm, with Hot Anchovy Dressing, *77*–78

Farro and Kale Soup, 130–31, *131*

Fava Bean, Raw, Salad with Pecorino, 80–81, *81*

Fragolino, 354, *355*

Green Beans with Shaved Onion, Fried Almonds, and Parmigiano-Reggiano, *89,* 89–90

Green Garlic Soup, 110

Greens, Crisp Bitter, with Anchovy Vinaigrette, 76

Greens, Wilted Cooking, 37–38

Guinea Hen Ragù, Braised, 172–73

Hake with Salsa Verde, 223

Lamb Shoulder, Braised, with Green Tomatoes and Concord Grapes, 310–11

Lemon Gelato, 334

Lemon Olive Oil Cake, 348, *349*

Lentil Soup, 123

Meat Ragù, Classic Central Italian, 168–69

Monkfish with Olives, Potatoes, and Sun-Dried Tomatoes, 232–34, *233*

Montebianco, 342–43

Orange and Mint Leaf Salad with Roasted Beets, 92, *93*

Oxtail, Braised, 289

Panzanella di Farro (Tuscan-Style Tomato Salad with Farro), 86, *87*

Parmesan Broth with Pea Shoots, 117

Italian (flavors) *(cont.)*
  Pear, Basil, and Pecorino
    Toscano Salad, 82, *83*
  Pecorino and Pears with
    Chestnut Honey, 329
  Plum Sorbetto, 330, *331*
  Polenta with Aromatic Herb
    Butter, 199–200
  Pork Ragù, Southern Italian,
    170–71
  Pork Shoulder, Slow-Roasted,
    318–20, *319*
  Potato Gnocchi, 194–96, *195*
  Potato Salad, Tiny-, Teverina,
    40–41, *41*
  Pumpkin, Sweet, and Rice Bean
    Soup with Crème Fraîche and
    Crispy Seeds, *114*, 114–16
  Rabbit, Braised, with Lemon
    and Rosemary, 272–73
  Rabbit, Roasted, with Shaved
    Celery and Fried Bread
    Salad, 274–76, *275*
  Rabbit Ragù, Braised,
    174–75, *175*
  Red Onions Cooked in Orange
    Juice, 48, *49*
  Red Peppers, Roasted, with
    Garlic and Celery Leaves, *52*,
    52–53
  Ribollita (Tuscan-Style Vegetable
    and Bread Soup), 118–20
  Ricotta-Stuffed Squash
    Blossoms in Fresh Summer
    Tomato Sauce, 44–45
  Salt Cod Stewed with Chickpeas
    and Greens, 230–31
  Scallop Carpaccio with Lime
    Juice, Sea Salt, and Chives, 29
  Semolina Bread Pudding with
    Concord Grapes, 344–45
  Short Ribs, Peppery Braised,
    286–88, *287*
  Skate with Blood Orange, Red
    Onion, and Bottarga Salad,
    236–37
  sources for, 357–60
  Spinach and Eggs, Baked, 39
  Strawberries with Prosecco, 327
  Summer Fruit with Lemon,
    Sugar, and Mint, 328
  Tuna, Seared, in *Porchetta*, 222
  Veal Saltimbocca, 290, *291*
  Vellutata di Carote (Velvety
    Carrot Soup), 111–12
  White Bean Soup with Ramps,
    124–25
  Wild Boar Ragù, Tuscan, 176–77

  Winter Root Salad with English
    Farmhouse Cheddar, *84*, 85
  see also panna cotta; pasta;
    risotto

jamón serrano, 12–13
  Cantaloupe Gazpacho with, *106*,
    106–7
  Jasmine Tea Panna Cotta with
    Shaved Dark Chocolate, 338
  Jerusalem Artichoke, Turnip, and
    Apple Soup, 113

Kale and Farro Soup, 130–31, *131*
Kibbeh Naye (Lamb and Bulgur
    Tartare), 30–31
Kohlrabi Slaw, 240

La Chiusa (near Siena,
    Tuscany), 138
lamb, 277–78, 300–313
  Brochettes, Grilled, with Shaved
    Onion Salad, 300–301
  and Bulgur Tartare (*Kibbeh
    Naye*), 30–31
  Chops, Crisp Fried, with Lemon
    and Rosemary, *302, 303*
  Chops, Pan-Roasted, with
    Capers, Olives, Onions, and
    Smashed Potatoes, 304–5
  Ground, Spaghettini with
    Yogurt, Mint and, 164–65
  Leg of, Roasted, with Black
    Olives, 309
  Rack of, Roasted, with Minty
    Bulgur Salad, 306–8, *307*
  Shoulder, Braised, with Green
    Tomatoes and Concord
    Grapes, 310–11
  Stew, Winter, with Turnips,
    Carrots, and Celery Root,
    312–13
La Quercia, 12, 359
Lasagna, Homemade, 178–82
Lebanese (flavors)
  Coffee Cardamom Crème
    Caramel, 339–40, *341*
  Fattouche (Salad with Pita), 88
  Kibbeh Naye (Lamb and Bulgur
    Tartare), 30–31
  Lamb, Roasted Rack of, with
    Minty Bulgur Salad,
    306–8, *307*
  Tabouli with Many Grains,
    46–47
leek(s)
  Cider-Braised, 322–23
  Potato, and Celery Soup, 129

Short Pasta with Prosciutto
    and, 149
  wild, *see* ramp(s)
legumes, 13, 14, 358
  see also bean(s); chickpea(s);
    lentil(s)
lemon(s), 7, 8, 9
  Biscotti with Pine Nuts, Thyme
    and, Tuscan, 346–47, *347*
  Chocolate Ganache Tart, Spicy,
    350–51, *351*
  Garlic Dressing, 88
  Gelato, 334
  Green Olive, and Parsley Relish,
    226–27
  limoncello, 354
  Olive Oil Cake, 348, *349*
  preserved, 359
  Preserved, Farro Salad with,
    254–55
  zest, in Salsa Verde, 223
Lemon Sole, Spaghetti with
    Almonds, Capers, Parsley
    and, 160–61, *161*
lentil(s), 13, 358
  as accompaniment, 316–17
  Soup, 123
limes, 8, 9
limoncello, 354
liver(s)
  buying, 297
  Calf's, with Brown Butter,
    Sage, and Wilted Dandelion
    Greens, 297–99, *298*
  Chicken, Crostini, 67–68
  Chicken, Spaghetti with
    Rosemary, Lemon and,
    166–67

Maccheroni with White Beans,
    Mustard Greens, and
    Anchovy, 156, *157*
mackerel, 202
  Grilled, with Kohlrabi Slaw, 240
  and Summer Vegetables, 238–39
Mako Shark Skewers, Grilled,
    with Shaved Radish and
    Parsley Salad, *224*, 225
Malabar peppercorns, 14
marinades, 7
  for red meats, 286, 288
  for venison, 322–23
  for wild boar, 176–77
meat ragùs, *see* ragùs
meats, 277–323
  buying, 277–78
  cuts and cooking techniques for,
    278

marinade for, 286, 288
organic and grass-fed, 277
seasoning after vs. before
cooking, 284
see also specific meats
Mechuia (Tunisian Grilled
Caponata), 50–51
Meringues, for Montebianco,
342–43
mezze, 21, 22, 27, 30, 53, 55, 91
see also small plates
Middle Eastern (flavors)
Cauliflower, Roasted, with
Tahini Sauce, *54*, 55
Chicken, Roast, with Farro
Salad with Preserved Lemon,
254–55
Lamb Brochettes, Grilled, with
Shaved Onion Salad, 300–301
Mako Shark Skewers, Grilled,
with Shaved Radish and
Parsley Salad, *224*, 225
Red and Yellow Tomatoes with
Feta and Fresh Coriander
Seeds, 28
Za'atar Chicken, 248–49
see also Lebanese (flavors)
millet, in Tabouli with Many
Grains, 46–47
minestra maritata, 126
mint (leaf)
Bulgur Salad with, 306–8, *307*
and Orange Salad with Roasted
Beets, 92, *93*
Penne with Zucchini and,
144–45
Short Pasta with Mushrooms
and, 146–47
Spaghettini with Ground Lamb,
Yogurt and, 164–65
Monkfish with Olives, Potatoes,
and Sun-Dried Tomatoes,
232–34, *233*
Montebianco, 342–43
Morels, Skillet-Cooked Pork
Chops with, and Lentils,
316–17
Moroccan (flavors)
Chicken, Roast, with Farro
Salad with Preserved Lemon,
254–55
Duck, Honey-and-Chili-
Roasted, with Fennel and
Farro, 268–69
Salad, 66
Moulins Mahjoub, Les,
12, 17, 357, 359
mullet bottarga, 11

mushrooms
Chanterelles, Duck Breast with
Chestnuts, Pearl Onions and,
265–67, *266*
Morels, Skillet-Cooked Pork
Chops with, and Lentils,
316–17
Short Pasta with Mint and,
146–47
Wild, Braised Chicken Hash
with, and Herbed Rice,
260–61
mussels, in *Cacciucco alla Livornese*
(Mediterranean shellfish
stew), *206*, 206–8
mustard greens
as accompaniment, 295–96
Maccheroni with White Beans,
Anchovy and, 156, *157*
mustards, 7
for vinaigrette, 70

navarin d'agneau, 312
Niman Ranch, 12
North African (flavors)
Lamb Brochettes, Grilled,
with Shaved Onion Salad,
300–301
Shrimp, Spiced, 212
see also Moroccan (flavors);
Tunisian (flavors)
nuts, 19
buying and storing, 150
see also almond(s); walnut(s)

octopus
Cacciucco alla Livornese
(Mediterranean shellfish
stew), *206*, 206–8
tenderizing, 207
oils
for vinaigrette, 70
see also olive oil (extra-virgin)
olive(s), 10–11
Black, Halibut with Brussels
Sprout Leaves, Chili and, 235
Black, Roasted Leg of Lamb
with, 309
chopping herbs, garlic and, into
paste, 309
Green, Lemon, and Parsley
Relish, 226–27
Onion, and Caper Sauce, 304–5
Pasta with Roasted Cauliflower,
Capers, Bread Crumbs and,
153, 153–55
Potatoes, and Sun-Dried
Tomatoes, 232–34, *233*

olive oil (extra-virgin), 5–7, 358
for cooking, 6, 7
deep-frying in, 303
for finishing dishes, 6–7
Lemon Cake, 348, *349*
storing, 7
in sweets, 324
tossing just-cooked vegetables
with, 90
onion(s)
Braised Red Peppers and,
258–59, *259*
cipollini, 293
cipollini, in Roasted Vegetables,
228–29, *229*
Mechuia (Tunisian Grilled
Caponata), 50–51
mellowing and sweetening, 225
Olive, and Caper Sauce, 304–5
Pearl, Duck Breast with
Chanterelles, Chestnuts and,
265–67, *266*
Pearl, Pickled, 65
Red, Blood Orange, and
Bottarga Salad, 236–37
Red, Cooked in Orange Juice,
48, *49*
Red, Grilled, with Tomatoes,
and Arugula, 220, *221*
Shaved, Green Beans with
Fried Almonds, Parmigiano-
Reggiano and, *89*, 89–90
Shaved, Salad, 300–301
Winter Vegetables, *292–93*,
292–94
orange(s)
Juice, Red Onions Cooked in,
48, *49*
and Mint Leaf Salad with
Roasted Beets, 92, *93*
Panna Cotta with Orange
Marmalade, *336*, 337
see also blood orange(s)
oregano, dried wild, 15
Oxtail, Braised, 289
Oyster-Sage Stuffing, Roast
Chicken with, 250–51

pancetta, 12, 359
panna cotta, 335
Jasmine Tea, with Shaved Dark
Chocolate, 338
Orange, with Orange
Marmalade, *336*, 337
with Pomegranate Molasses, 335
Panzanella di Farro (Tuscan-Style
Tomato Salad with Farro),
86, *87*

Parmigiano-Reggiano, 17–18
    Eggplant Parmesan, Classic
        Tuscan, 197–98
    Fried Eggplant Balls, 60
    Green Beans with Shaved
        Onion, Fried Almonds and,
        89, 89–90
    Parmesan Broth with Pea
        Shoots, 117
    Pasta Carbonara, 159
    Roasted Corn and Brioche
        Pudding, 58–59
parsley
    Cornichon, and Caper
        Vinaigrette, 74
    Green Olive, and Lemon Relish,
        226–27
    Salsa Verde, 223
    and Shaved Radish Salad, *224*,
        225
    "Snail Butter," 209
Parsnip Puree, *216–17*, 218–19
pasta, 14, 132–82, 358–59
    al dente, 134
    with Bottarga, 162–63
    Carbonara, 159
    with Cauliflower, Olives,
        Capers, and Bread Crumbs,
        153, 153–55
    cooking, 133–34
    with Corn, 148
    Dough, Fresh, 180
    dried *(pasta secca)*, 132–33, 134
    "fresh" *(pasta fresca)*, 133
    Guinea Hen Ragù for, Braised,
        172–73
    Lasagna, Homemade, 178–82
    Long, with Bacon, Red
        Cabbage, Walnuts, and
        Rosemary, 150–52, *151*
    Maccheroni with White
        Beans, Mustard Greens, and
        Anchovy, 156, *157*
    Meat Ragù for, Classic Central
        Italian, 168–69
    Penne with Zucchini and Mint,
        144–45
    Pork Ragù for, Southern Italian,
        170–71
    Potato Gnocchi, 194–96, *195*
    Rabbit Ragù for, Braised,
        174–75, *175*
    saucing, 134–35
    Shells with Many Cheeses, 158
    Short, with Leeks and
        Prosciutto, 149
    Short, with Mushrooms and
        Mint, 146–47

Spaghettini with Burst Cherry
    Tomatoes, 142, *143*
Spaghettini with Ground Lamb,
    Yogurt, and Mint, 164–65
Spaghetti with Chicken Livers,
    Rosemary, and Lemon,
    166–67
Spaghetti with Lemon Sole,
    Almonds, Capers, and
    Parsley, 160–61, *161*
Tomato Sauce for, Fresh
    Summer, 138–39
Tomato Sauce for, Slow-Cooked,
    140–41
Wild Boar Ragù for, Tuscan,
    176–77
pasta fazool, 156
pea(s)
    Sugar Snap, Salmon with Bacon
        and, 213
    Sweet, and Squash Blossom
        Risotto, 187–89, *188*
peach(es)
    Baked Pork Chops with, 314–15
    Cordial, 354
    Summer Fruit with Lemon,
        Sugar, and Mint, 328
pear(s)
    Basil, and Pecorino Toscano
        Salad, 82, *83*
    Pecorino and, with Chestnut
        Honey, 329
Pea Shoots, Parmesan Broth
    with, 117
Pea Sprout–Citrus Salad,
    216–17, 218–19
pecorino, 18
    and Pears with Chestnut
        Honey, 329
    Raw Fava Bean Salad with,
        80–81, *81*
    Romano, 18
    Romano, in Pasta
        Carbonara, 159
    Toscano, 18
    Toscano, Pear, and Basil Salad,
        82, *83*
penne
    Short Pasta with Leeks and
        Prosciutto, 149
    Short Pasta with Mushrooms
        and Mint, 146–47
    with Zucchini and Mint, 144–45
peperonata, 258
peposo di Brunelleschi, 286
peppercorns, black, 14
    Peppery Braised Short Ribs,
        286–88, *287*

peppers
    chili, *see* chilies
    Mechuia (Tunisian Grilled
        Caponata), 50–51
    Red, Braised Onions and,
        258–59, *259*
    roasted, peeling, 50
    Roasted Red, with Garlic and
        Celery Leaves, *52*, 52–53
pequin chilies, dried, 16
pici, 133
Pickled Pearl Onions, 65
piment d'Espelette, 16, 17
Pine Nuts, Biscotti with
    Lemon, Thyme and, Tuscan,
    346–47, *347*
Pita, Lebanese Salad with
    (Fattouche), 88
plum(s)
    Galette, 352
    Sorbetto, 330, *331*
    Summer Fruit with Lemon,
        Sugar, and Mint, 328
polenta
    with Aromatic Herb Butter,
        199–200
    ragùs for, *see* ragùs
pomegranate molasses, 20
    Panna Cotta with, 335
Porchettata, Seared Tuna in, 222
pork, 277–78, 314–21
    Chops, Baked, with Peaches,
        314–15
    chops, ensuring even cooking
        of, 314
    Chops, Skillet-Cooked, with
        Morels and Lentils, 316–17
    cured, products, 12–13
    Loin, Braised, with Prunes, 321
    Meat Ragù, Classic Central
        Italian, 168–69
    Ragù, Southern Italian, 170–71
    Shoulder, Slow-Roasted,
        318–20, *319*
    see also guanciale, jamón serrano,
        pancetta, prosciutto
potato(es)
    Celery, and Leek Soup, 129
    Chicken with Escarole, Apples
        and, *262*, 263–64
    fresh-dug, 40
    Gnocchi, 194–96, *195*
    Olives, and Sun-Dried
        Tomatoes, 232–34, *233*
    Roasted Vegetables, 228–29, *229*
    Smashed, 304–5
    Tiny-, Salad, Teverina, 40–41, *41*
Principato di Lucedio, 13

prosciutto, 12, 13, 359
 Short Pasta with Leeks and, 149
 Veal Saltimbocca, 290, *291*
Prosecco, Strawberries with, 327
Prunes, Braised Pork Loin with, 321
puddings
 Roasted Corn and Brioche, 58–59
 Semolina Bread, with Concord Grapes, 344–45
 see also Crème Caramel, Coffee Cardamom; panna cotta
Pumpkin, Sweet, and Rice Bean Soup with Crème Fraîche and Crispy Seeds, *114*, 114–16
puntarelle alla romana, 76
Puree, Parsnip, *216–17*, 218–19
purslane, in *Panzanella di Farro* (Tuscan-Style Tomato Salad with Farro), 86, *87*

Queso Iberico, Asparagus with Olive Oil and, 36
quinoa, in Tabouli with Many Grains, 46–47

rabbit, 241, 242, 272–76
 Braised, with Lemon and Rosemary, 272–73
 Ragù, Braised, 174–75, *175*
 Roasted, with Shaved Celery and Fried Bread Salad, 274–76, *275*
radish(es)
 Shaved, and Parsley Salad, *224*, 225
 Winter Root Salad with English Farmhouse Cheddar, *84*, 85
ragùs, 169
 Guinea Hen, Braised, 172–73
 Meat, Classic Central Italian, 168–69
 Pork, Southern Italian, 170–71
 Rabbit, Braised, 174–75, *175*
 Wild Boar, Tuscan, 176–77
ramp(s)
 and Bacon Risotto, 192–93
 White Bean Soup with, 124–25
raspberries, in Summer Fruit with Lemon, Sugar, and Mint, 328
red cabbage
 Long Pasta with Bacon, Walnuts, Rosemary and, 150–52, *151*
 Winter Root Salad with English Farmhouse Cheddar, *84*, 85
Red Wine Sauce, 228–29

Relish, Green Olive, Lemon, and Parsley, 226–27
Ribollita (Tuscan-Style Vegetable and Bread Soup), 118–20
rice
 Herbed, 260–61
 superfino, 13
 see also risotto
rice bean(s), 115, 358
 and Sweet Pumpkin Soup with Crème Fraîche and Crispy Seeds, *114*, 114–16
Ricotta-Stuffed Squash Blossoms in Fresh Summer Tomato Sauce, 44–45
risi e bisi, 187
risotto, 135, 183–93
 Bacon and Ramp, 192–93
 broth for, 183
 cooking, 183
 al dente, 183
 rices for, 13, 183
 Shrimp, Maine, 184–86, *185*
 soupy vs. drier style, 183
 Strawberry, 190–91
 Sweet Pea and Squash Blossom, 187–89, *188*
roasts
 basting with wine, 318
 Lamb, Leg of, with Black Olives, 309
 Lamb, Rack of, with Minty Bulgur Salad, 306–8, *307*
 Pork Shoulder, Slow-Roasted, 318–20, *319*
 Veal Shoulder, Free-Range, with Baby Carrots and Mustard Greens, 295–96
 Venison with Cider-Braised Leeks, 322–23
romano beans, in Fresh Summer Beans Simmered in Tomato Sauce, 43
root vegetable salads, 26, 70
 Carrot, with Lemon, Sea Salt, Parsley, and Olive Oil, *25*, 25–26
 Turnip, Raw, Tunisian, 27
 Winter, with English Farmhouse Cheddar, *84*, 85
Rosolio, Fresh Bay Leaf, 356

sage
 Oyster Stuffing, Roast Chicken with, 250–51
 Veal Saltimbocca, 290, *291*
salad greens, washing, 69

salads, 69–99
 additions for, 70
 Beet, Arugula, and Cucumber, with Yogurt Dressing, 91
 Blood Orange, Red Onion, and Bottarga, 236–37
 Bulgur, Minty, 306–8, *307*
 Carrot, with Lemon, Sea Salt, Parsley, and Olive Oil, *25*, 25–26
 Celery, Cherry Tomato, and Bottarga, 79
 Celery, Shaved, and Fried Bread, 274–76, *275*
 Chicken, with Tarragon, Toasted Pine Nuts, and Golden Raisins, 256–57
 Citrus–Pea Sprout, *216–17*, 218–19
 Crisp Bitter Greens with Anchovy Vinaigrette, 76
 Cucumber and Avocado, 281
 Escarole, Warm, with Hot Anchovy Dressing, *77–78*
 Farro, with Preserved Lemon, 254–55
 Fattouche (Lebanese Salad with Pita), 88
 Fava Bean, Raw, with Pecorino, 80–81, *81*
 Fennel, Shaved, 65–66
 Flank Steak, with Farro, Arugula, and Fresh Horseradish, 98–99
 green, simple, 69
 Green Beans with Shaved Onion, Fried Almonds, and Parmigiano-Reggiano, *89*, 89–90
 Kohlrabi Slaw, 240
 Moroccan, 66
 Onion, Shaved, 300–301
 Orange and Mint Leaf, with Roasted Beets, 92, *93*
 Panzanella di Farro (Tuscan-Style Tomato Salad with Farro), 86, *87*
 Pear, Basil, and Pecorino Toscano, 82, *83*
 Potato, Tiny-, Teverina, 40–41, *41*
 Radish, Shaved, and Parsley, *224*, 225
 Red and Yellow Tomatoes with Feta and Fresh Coriander Seeds, 28
 Smoked Trout, with Spicy Arugula and Grapefruit, 94, *95*
 Squid, "Dirty," with Watercress, *96*, 96–97

salads (cont.)
    Tabouli with Many Grains,
      46–47
    Tomatoes, Grilled Red Onion,
      and Arugula, 220, *221*
    Turnip, Raw, Tunisian, 27
    Winter Root, with English
      Farmhouse Cheddar, *84*, 85
    see also dressings; vinaigrettes
salami, 12, 359
salmon
    Cold Poached, with Greek
      Yogurt and Dill Sauce,
      214–15
    with Parsnip Puree and Citrus–
      Pea Sprout Salad, *216–17*,
      218–19
    with Sugar Snap Peas and
      Bacon, 213
Salsa Verde, 223
salt, 9–10, 359
    -Baked Bacon-and-Herb-
      Rubbed Chicken, *252*, 253
    in sweets, 324
Salt Cod Stewed with Chickpeas
    and Greens, 230–31
salty flavor agents, 9–13
    anchovies, 11
    bottarga, 11
    capers, 12
    cured pork products, 12–13
    olives, 10–11
Salumi Artisan Cured Meats
    (Seattle), 12, 359
San Marzano canned
    tomatoes, 19
sardines, 202
    Grilled, with Accompaniments,
      64–66
sauces
    Besciamel, 181–82
    Greek Yogurt and Dill, 214–15
    Onion, Olive, and Caper, 304–5
    Red Wine, 228–29
    see also ragùs; tomato sauce
scallop(s)
    Carpaccio with Lime Juice, Sea
      Salt, and Chives, 29
    "dry" vs. "wet," 29
    Roasted, with "Snail Butter" and
      Mâche, 209–11, *210*
schiacciata con l'uva, 344
seafood, *see* fish
Semifreddo, Chestnut Honey and
    Walnut, 332–33
Semolina Bread Pudding with
    Concord Grapes, 344–45
serrano ham, 12–13

Cantaloupe Gazpacho with,
    106, 106–7
Sformato, Sweet Corn, 56–57
shallots
    mellowing and sweetening, 225
    slicing thinly, 94
shellfish, *see* fish
sherry vinegar, 7, 8, 360
Short Ribs, Peppery Braised,
    286–88, *287*
shrimp
    Broth, 186
    Cacciucco alla Livornese
      (Mediterranean shellfish
      stew), *206*, 206–8
    Maine, Panfried in Olive Oil, 63
    Maine, Risotto, 184–86, *185*
    North African Spiced, 212
side dishes
    Barley and Dandelion Greens,
      270–71
    Blood Orange, Red Onion, and
      Bottarga Salad, 236–37
    Celery, Shaved, and Fried Bread
      Salad, 274–76, *275*
    Chanterelles, Chestnuts, and
      Pearl Onions, 265–67, *266*
    Citrus–Pea Sprout Salad,
      216–17, 218–19
    Cucumber and Avocado
      Salad, 281
    Dandelion Greens, Wilted,
      297–99, *298*
    Farro Salad with Preserved
      Lemon, 254–55
    Fennel, Shaved, Salad, 65–66
    Fennel and Farro, 268–69
    Green Olive, Lemon, and
      Parsley Relish, 226–27
    Herbed Rice, 260–61
    Kohlrabi Slaw, 240
    Leeks, Cider-Braised, 322–23
    Lentils, 316–17
    Minty Bulgur Salad, 306–8, *307*
    Moroccan Salad, 66
    Mustard Greens, 295–96
    Olives, Potatoes, and Sun-Dried
      Tomatoes, 232–34, *233*
    Onion, Shaved, Salad, 300–301
    Parsnip Puree, *216–17*, 218–19
    Pearl Onions, Pickled, 65
    Polenta with Aromatic Herb
      Butter, 199–200
    Potatoes, Smashed, 304–5
    Radish, Shaved, and Parsley
      Salad, *224*, 225
    Red Peppers and Onions,
      Braised, 258–59, *259*

    Tomatoes, Grilled Red Onion,
      and Arugula, 220, *221*
    Vegetables, Roasted, 228–29, *229*
    Winter Vegetables, *292–93*,
      292–94
    see also small plates
Skate with Blood Orange, Red
    Onion, and Bottarga Salad,
    236–37
skewers
    Lamb Brochettes, Grilled, with
      Shaved Onion Salad, 300–301
    Mako Shark, Grilled, with
      Shaved Radish and Parsley
      Salad, *224*, 225
skillets, cast-iron, 34
Skirt Steak, Grilled, with
    Cucumber and Avocado
    Salad, 281
Slaw, Kohlrabi, 240
small plates, 21–68
    Asparagus, Pan-Roasted, with
      Bacon, *32–33*, 34–35
    Asparagus with Olive Oil and
      Queso Iberico, 36
    Beans, Fresh Summer,
      Simmered in Tomato Sauce, 43
    Brussels Sprouts, Turnips, and
      Beets, Pan-Roasted, with
      Warm Farro, 61–62
    Cannellini Beans,
      Slow-Cooked, 42
    Carrot Salad with Lemon, Sea
      Salt, Parsley, and Olive Oil,
      25, 25–26
    Cauliflower, Roasted, with
      Tahini Sauce, *54*, 55
    Chicken Liver Crostini, 67–68
    Corn, Roasted, and Brioche
      Pudding, 58–59
    Corn, Sweet, *Sformato*, 56–57
    Eggplant Balls, Fried, 60
    Fennel, Shaved, Salad, 65–66
    Greens, Cooking, Wilted, 37–38
    Kibbeh Naye (Lamb and Bulgur
      Tartare), 30–31
    Lamb Brochettes, Grilled, with
      Shaved Onion Salad, 300–301
    Mechuia (Tunisian Grilled
      Caponata), 50–51
    Moroccan Salad, 66
    Orange and Mint Leaf Salad
      with Roasted Beets, 92, *93*
    Potato Salad, Tiny-, Teverina,
      40–41, *41*
    Red and Yellow Tomatoes with
      Feta and Fresh Coriander
      Seeds, 28

Red Onions Cooked in Orange Juice, 48, *49*

Red Peppers, Roasted, with Garlic and Celery Leaves, *52*, 52–53

Ricotta-Stuffed Squash Blossoms in Fresh Summer Tomato Sauce, 44–45

Sardines, Grilled, with Accompaniments, 64–66

Scallop Carpaccio with Lime Juice, Sea Salt, and Chives, 29

Shrimp, Maine, Panfried in Olive Oil, 63

Spinach and Eggs, Baked, 39

Tabouli with Many Grains, 46–47

Turnip Salad, Raw, Tunisian, 27

Smoked Trout Salad with Spicy Arugula and Grapefruit, 94, *95*

"Snail Butter," 209

snapper, 202

sole, 202

Lemon, Spaghetti with Almonds, Capers, Parsley and, 160–61, *161*

Sorbetto, Plum, 330, *331*

soups, 100–131

Almond Gazpacho, White, 104, *105*

for breakfast, 100

broths for, 101

Cabbage and Chickpea, 121–22

Cantaloupe Gazpacho with Jamón Serrano, *106*, 106–7

Chicken, Rich, with Greens, 126–28, *127*

Farro and Kale, 130–31, *131*

Green Garlic, 110

layering flavors in, 100–101

Lentil, 123

Parmesan Broth with Pea Shoots, 117

Potato, Celery, and Leek, 129

Pumpkin, Sweet, and Rice Bean, with Crème Fraîche and Crispy Seeds, *114*, 114–16

Ribollita (Tuscan-Style Vegetable and Bread Soup), 118–20

Rich Chicken Broth for, 108–9

Turnip, Apple, and Jerusalem Artichoke, 113

Vellutata di Carote (Velvety Carrot Soup), 111–12

White Bean, with Ramps, 124–25

spaghetti

with Chicken Livers, Rosemary, and Lemon, 166–67

with Lemon Sole, Almonds, Capers, and Parsley, 160–61, *161*

Long Pasta with Bacon, Red Cabbage, Walnuts, and Rosemary, 150–52, *151*

Pasta Carbonara, 159

Pasta with Bottarga, 162–63

spaghettini

with Burst Cherry Tomatoes, 142, *143*

with Ground Lamb, Yogurt, and Mint, 164–65

Spanish (flavors)

Almond Gazpacho, White, 104, *105*

Asparagus with Olive Oil and Queso Iberico, 36

Cantaloupe Gazpacho with Jamón Serrano, *106*, 106–7

sources for, 358, 359

Squid, "Dirty," with Watercress, *96*, 96–97

Spiced Shrimp, North African, 212

spices, 14, 15, 359

whole, toasting and grinding, 212

Spinach and Eggs, Baked, 39

spoon-basting with herbs and hot oil or butter, 226

squab, 241

squash blossom(s)

Penne with Zucchini and Mint, 144–45

Ricotta-Stuffed, in Fresh Summer Tomato Sauce, 44–45

separating base from petals of, 144

and Sweet Pea Risotto, 187–89, *188*

squid

braising then searing, 97

Cacciucco alla Livornese (Mediterranean shellfish stew), *206*, 206–8

"Dirty," with Watercress, *96*, 96–97

stews

Lamb, Winter, with Turnips, Carrots, and Celery Root, 312–13

Salt Cod with Chickpeas and Greens, 230–31

Shellfish, Mediterranean (*Cacciucco alla Livornese*), *206*, 206–8

stocks

corn, 56

see also broths

strawberry(ies)

Fragolino, 354, *355*

with Prosecco, 327

Risotto, 190–91

striped bass, 202, 203

Stuffing, Oyster-Sage, Roast Chicken with, 250–51

sugar, 20

Sugar Snap Peas, Salmon with Bacon and, 213

sumac, 15, 88

Summer Fruit with Lemon, Sugar, and Mint, 328

sweet ingredients, 20

sweets, 324–53

Biscotti with Lemon, Pine Nuts, and Thyme, Tuscan, 346–47, *347*

Chestnut Honey and Walnut Semifreddo, 332–33

Coffee Cardamom Crème Caramel, 339–40, *341*

Jasmine Tea Panna Cotta with Shaved Dark Chocolate, 338

Lemon-Chocolate Ganache Tart, Spicy, 350–51, *351*

Lemon Gelato, 334

Lemon Olive Oil Cake, 348, *349*

Montebianco, 342–43

Orange Panna Cotta with Orange Marmalade, *336*, 337

Panna Cotta with Pomegranate Molasses, 335

Pecorino and Pears with Chestnut Honey, 329

Plum Galette, 352

Plum Sorbetto, 330, *331*

salt and other savory ingredients in, 324

Semolina Bread Pudding with Concord Grapes, 344–45

Strawberries with Prosecco, 327

Summer Fruit with Lemon, Sugar, and Mint, 328

Tart Dough, Favorite, 353

Swiss chard, in Salt Cod Stewed with Chickpeas and Greens, 230–31

Tabouli with Many Grains, 46–47

Tahini Sauce, Roasted Cauliflower with, *54*, 55

tart(s)

Dough, Favorite, 353

Plum Galette, 352

tart(s) *(cont.)*
    Spicy Lemon-Chocolate
        Ganache, 350–51, *351*
Tellicherry peppercorns, 14
Thyme, Biscotti with Lemon, Pine
    Nuts and, Tuscan, 346–47, *347*
tomato(es)
    Celery, and Bottarga Salad, 79
    Cherry, Burst, Spaghettini with,
        142, *143*
    Green, Braised Lamb Shoulder
        with Concord Grapes and,
        310–11
    Grilled Red Onion, and
        Arugula, 220, *221*
    Mechuia (Tunisian Grilled
        Caponata), 50–51
    Moroccan Salad, 66
    Red and Yellow, with
        Feta and Fresh Coriander
        Seeds, 28
    Salad with Farro, Tuscan-Style
        (*Panzanella di Farro*), 86, *87*
    San Marzano canned, 19
    sun-dried, loose-packed vs.
        packed in oil, 232
    Sun-Dried, Olives, Potatoes
        and, 232–34, *233*
tomato paste, 19
tomato sauce, 138
    Fresh Summer, 138–39
    Fresh Summer, Ricotta-Stuffed
        Squash Blossoms in, 44–45
    Fresh Summer Beans Simmered
        in, 43
    Slow-Cooked, 140–41
Treasures of the Italian Table
    (Anderson), 183
Trout, Smoked, Salad with Spicy
    Arugula and Grapefruit,
    94, *95*
tuna, 202
    bottarga, 11
    Grilled, with Tomatoes, Grilled
        Red Onion, and Arugula,
        220, *221*
    Seared, in *Porchetta*, 222
Tunisian (flavors)
    Caponata, Grilled (*Mechuia*),
        50–51
    Turnip Salad, Raw, 27
Turkish (flavors)
    Beet, Arugula, and Cucumber
        Salad with Yogurt
        Dressing, 91

Spaghettini with Ground Lamb,
    Yogurt, and Mint, 164–65
turnip(s)
    Apple, and Jerusalem Artichoke
        Soup, 113
    Pan-Roasted Brussels Sprouts,
        Beets and, with Warm Farro,
        61–62
    Raw, Salad, Tunisian, 27
    Winter Lamb Stew with Carrots,
        Celery Root and, 312–13
    Winter Vegetables, *292–93*,
        292–94
Tuscan, *see* Italian (flavors)

veal, 277–78, 290–96
    Chops, Roasted, with Winter
        Vegetables and Anchovy
        Butter, *292–93*, 292–94
    Meat Ragù, Classic Central
        Italian, 168–69
    Saltimbocca, 290, *291*
    Shoulder, Free-Range, with
        Baby Carrots and Mustard
        Greens, 295–96
vegetable(s)
    and Bread Soup, Tuscan-Style
        (*Ribollita*), 118–20
    Roasted, 228–29, *229*
    Winter, *292–93*, 292–94
    see also specific vegetables
Vellutata di Carote (Velvety Carrot
    Soup), 111–12
venison, 277–78
    Roasted, with Cider-Braised
        Leeks, 322–23
Vialone Nano rice, 183
vinaigrettes, 7, 70
    Anchovy, 76
    Cornichon, Caper, and Parsley,
        74
    Herb, Fresh, 73
    Walnut, 75
    see also dressings
vinegars, 7–8, 360
    for vinaigrette, 70
Vin Santo vinegar, 8, 360
vodka
    Fragolino, 354, *355*
    Fresh Bay Leaf *Rosolio*, 356
Volpaia vinegars, 8, 360

walnut(s)
    and Chestnut Honey
        Semifreddo, 332–33

Long Pasta with Bacon, Red
    Cabbage, Rosemary and,
    150–52, *151*
Vinaigrette, 75
Watercress, "Dirty" Squid with,
    96, 96–97
White Almond Gazpacho,
    104, *105*
white bean(s)
    Maccheroni with Mustard
        Greens, Anchovy and,
        156, *157*
    Ribollita (Tuscan-Style Vegetable
        and Bread Soup), 118–20
    Slow-Cooked Cannellini
        Beans, 42
    Soup with Ramps, 124–25
Wild Boar Ragù, Tuscan, 176–77
wild fennel pollen, 15, 359
    Seared Tuna in *Porchetta*, 222
Wilted Cooking Greens, 37–38
wine
    as acid, 7
    basting with, 318
    for cooking, 19
    for drinking, 20
    Prosecco, Strawberries with, 327
    Red, Sauce, 228–29
wine vinegars, 7–8, 360
Winter Lamb Stew with Turnips,
    Carrots, and Celery Root,
    312–13
Winter Root Salad with English
    Farmhouse Cheddar, *84*, 85
Winter Vegetables, *292–93*,
    292–94

yard-long beans, in Fresh Summer
    Beans Simmered in Tomato
    Sauce, 43
yogurt
    Dressing, 91
    Greek, and Dill Sauce, 214–15
    Spaghettini with Ground Lamb,
        Mint and, 164–65

za'atar, 15
    Chicken, 248–49
zesting citrus fruits, 8–9
    capturing flavorful oil in, 348
zucchini
    Mechuia (Tunisian Grilled
        Caponata), 50–51
    Penne with Mint and, 144–45